The

Writer's
Legal Guide

The
Writer's
Legal Guide

SECOND EDITION

Tad Crawford
Tony Lyons

ALLWORTH PRESS • NEW YORK

The Writer's Legal Guide was fully revised in 1996 and reissued as a "revised edition." In 1998, when an update was added in the front of the book and a few matters wer updated in the text, "revised edition" was changed to "second edition."

Published by Allworth Press
an imprint of Allworth Communications, Inc.
10 East 23rd Street, New York, NY 10010

Cover design: Douglas Design Associates, New York, New York

Book design: Sharp Des!gns, Inc., Lansing, Michigan

ISBN: 1-58115-004-0

Library of Congress Catalog Card Number: 98-72758

Printed in Canada

For Elsie B. Meyer and Elsie K. Mills,
whose standards and generosity to a
young writer were, I now understand,
gifts that last a lifetime.
—*T.C.*

For Helena Hjalmarsson,
a great writer, a great human being,
and my best friend.
—*T.L.*

Contents

Scope of the Agency
Agent's Commissions and Expenses
Payments and Accountings

Acknowledgments

The authors would like to express their appreciation for the many professionals who gave generously of their time and expertise in reviewing portions of this second edition of *The Writer's Legal Guide:* Paul Basista, Executive Director, Graphic Artists Guild; James R. Cohen, Esquire, of Kleinberg, Kaplan, Wolff & Cohen; John Johnson, Esquire, of Heslin & Rothenberg; Ralph E. Lerner, Esquire, of Sidley & Austin; Charles Lyons, Ph.D, of Mud Pony Productions/The Walt Disney Company; Jennifer Lyons, M.A., of Writer's House; Nick Lyons, Ph.D, of The Lyons Press, Publishers; Laura Mankin; Philip Mattera, National Book Grievance Officer, National Writers Union; Daniel Y. Mayer, Esquire, Executive Director, Volunteer Lawyers for the Arts (NYC); Kay Murray, Esquire, Director of Legal Services, Ed McCoyd, Esquire, Staff Attorney, and Carol Williams, Esquire, Staff Attorney, of the Authors Guild; Michael D. Remer, Esquire, of Cowan, Gold, DeBaets, Abrahams & Gross; Kirk T. Schroder, Esquire, of LeClair Ryan; Eric Schwartz, Esquire, of Proskauer Rose Goetz & Mendelsohn.

In addition, this book would not have been possible without those who offered constructive criticism in the development of the First Edition: Arthur F. Abelman, Esquire; Alan Berlin, Esquire; Jeffrey Cooper, Esquire; Professor Jack Crawford, Jr.; Darcie Denkert, Esquire; Donald C. Farber, Esquire; Eileen Farley; James L. Garrity, Esquire; Paul Jacobs, Esquire; Professor John Kernochan; Elsie K. Mills; Jean V. Naggar; Professor Joseph M. Perillo; Nelson Richardson; Carolyn Trager; and Carl Zanger, Esquire.

Update

$\mathcal{T}$he law is constantly changing. *The Writer's Legal Guide* was completely revised in 1996. Fortunately, it is being reprinted in October 1998, which allows the changes that have taken place since 1996 to be covered. The text itself has been updated where the changes to the law are minor, but the more substantive changes are covered in this update, which follows the page numbers and headings of the book. In the text, asterisks (*) mark the passages affected by these changes, so the reader may refer back to the current information when necessary.

Chapter 2. Copyright: Gaining and Keeping Protection

Pages 17–18. Although the copyright legislation dealing with transmission of digital works seemed assured of passage as the book went to press in 1996, that legislation did not in fact pass. Similar legislation was finally enacted in October of 1998 and will be discussed in this update with respect to page 82.

Term of Copyright: Pages 24–25. Legislation to extend the term of copyright has been enacted. It extends the term of copyright to the writer's life plus seventy years. For works created anonymously or under a pseudonym, the term will be ninety-five years from first publication or one hundred twenty years from creation. For joint works, the term will be the life of the surviving writer plus seventy years. Renewal terms will be extended from forty-seven to sixty-seven years (bringing the total term for pre-1978 works to ninety-five years). Works created but neither published nor copyrighted before 1978 will have a term ending on December 31, 2047.

Termination: Pages 27–28. The twenty-year extension of the copyright term will affect the right of termination. If the right of termination has not been exercised, then it may be exercised with respect to the twenty-year extension during the five-year period commencing at the end of seventy-five years from when the copyright was secured.

Publication with Copyright Notice: Page 31. The pending legislation did not pass, but a modified version was enacted into law in October of 1998. It is discussed in the update entry for page 82.

Defective Notice: Page 34. The writer's life plus seventy years is the new copyright term.

Chapter 3. Copyright: Registration and Deposit

Page 37. In fact, the Copyright Office has not yet adopted easier group registration rules for photographs.

Choosing the Copyright Form/Filling Out the Copyright Forms: Pages 38, 44–45. The Copyright Office has also made available Short Form TX, an even simpler application form that can be used if the writer is the sole creator and copyright owner of the work, the work is not made for hire, and the work is completely new (i.e., contains neither public domain works nor previously registered works).

Chapter 4. Copyright: Works for Hire and Joint Works

Who Is an Employee for Work for Hire?: Pages 48–49. Historically, the work-for-hire status of a relationship has been governed by seemingly capricious judicial interpretations and complex statutory definitions, making the work-for-hire concept developed in *Community for*

Creative Non-Violence v. Reid (490 U.S. 730) the focal point in determining the nature of the employment relationship. The *"Reid* factors" are rooted in agency law, making the crucial determination regarding the nature of the relationship whether the work was prepared by an employee or independent contractor. The Court in *Reid* delineated a set of criteria in an attempt to standardize the judicial distinction between employee and independent contractor. However, reliance on the *Reid* factors has yielded generally inconsistent results; outcomes tend to be determined by those factors enumerated in *Reid* the particular court has chosen to weigh more heavily. The trend in the circuit courts has been to adopt an individually modified version of these factors, with some circuits adding factors, and others paring the list down significantly. The Sixth Circuit in *Hi-Tech Video Production, Inc. v. Capital Cities* (58 F.3d 1093) placed great emphasis on the parties' perceptions of the relationship, while the Second Circuit developed a weighted five-factor derivation of the original *Reid* test in *Carter et al. v. Helmsley-Spear* (861 F. Supp. 303, 71 F.3d 77, *cert. denied*, 517 U.S. 1208). As stressed in the text, a written contract should be entered into to clarify that the writer is transferring limited rights only.

Specially Commissioned or Ordered Works: Page 50. In *Lulirama Ltd., Inc. v. Axcess Broadcast Services, Inc.* (CCH Copyright Reporter Par.27716), the court concluded that even though the written contract for advertising jingles stated the work was "for hire," such jingles did not fall into a category of specially commissioned works eligible to be work for hire and, therefore, could not be.

Joint Works: Page 53. An interesting case involving the rights of a dramaturge, a person who assists in the compilation of materials for a dramatic production, was brought by Lynn Thomson, who had worked with the late playwright Jonathan Larson in creating the Broadway play *Rent.* Claiming to be a co-author entitled to royalties, she sued for monetary compensation for the six months she spent in helping to develop *Rent* at the theater workshop. Although the court found that Thompson had significantly contributed to the creation of *Rent*, case law directed the court to look not at the amount of her contribution, but rather the intention of the parties during the play's creation. Finding that there was no evidence that Larson intended to share authorship with anyone and that there was no mutual agreement to this effect, a decision was rendered in Larson's favor.

The federal district court decision was affirmed on appeal to the circuit court. In rejecting Thomson's joint-work claim, the circuit court recognized that Thomson had "made at lease some non-de minimis copyrightable contribution," and that Thomson's contributions to the *Rent* libretto were "certainly not zero." An interesting issue was raised in terms of copyright ownership between parties working together on something that may or may not be construed as a joint work. Thomson claimed that if she was not deemed co-author of the work, she should retain copyright interest in her contributions to the work. Although this issue was not decided in this case, the confusion over intent, copyright ownership, and entitlement to royalty payments underscores the need for a written agreement (*Thomson v. Larson* 147 F.3d 195). Ultimately, the parties settled and Thomson did receive some payment from the estate, due to the implication in the circuit court's decision that Thomson might have retained copyright in segments that she had contributed to *Rent*.

Chapter 5. Copyright: Infringement, Fair Use, and Permissions

Who Is Liable for Infringement: Page 61. The effectiveness of the Copyright Remedy Clarification Act has been drawn into question by two recent court decisions. Traditionally, the courts have utilized a two-step inquiry to determine whether or not Congress has abrogated the immunity of states from being sued in federal court: first, whether or not Congress has clearly expressed its intent to abrogate that immunity; and, second, whether in purporting to abrogate the immunity, Congress has overstepped its Constitutional authority under the Fourteenth Amendment's enforcement provision.

The Fifth Circuit federal appeals court recently upheld prior cases in finding that the provisions of the copyright law and Lanham Act, which require states to submit to suit in federal court for violations of those statutes, exceed Congress' Constitutional powers (*Chaves v. Arte Publico Press* 139 F.3d 504). The *Chaves* Court determined that state entities are subject to federal laws when they undertake activities that are regulated by the federal government, but states cannot be required to waive their sovereign immunity as a condition to participating in such federally regulated activities.

However, a split in the circuits occurred when an even more recent decision was handed down by the Federal Circuit, which is a court reserved solely for appeals of patent cases (*College Savings Bank v. Florida Prepaid Postsecondary Education Expense Board*, 148 F.3d 1343). The Federal Circuit Court held that: (1) Congress had clearly expressed its intent to abrogate the immunity of states under the Eleventh Amendment in patent infringement actions, and (2) abrogation of immunity was within Congress' authority under the Fourteenth Amendment.

A split such as this can only be definitively answered by a decision by the United States Supreme Court. The assistant attorney general of the state of Florida indicated that there is a "strong probability" that the state will appeal the *College Savings Bank* decision to the United States Supreme Court.

Permissions: Page 69. The writer should consider whether electronic rights must be obtained as well as traditional print rights. If so, the permission form should explicitly reflect this. For example, the use of the word "book" might be modified to "work" and the extent of usage expanded to "in my work and in future revisions and editions thereof, including nonexclusive electronic rights and nonexclusive world rights in all languages." While the permission form should not be made overly complex, the writer might define "electronic rights" as follows: "Electronic rights are defined as rights in the digitized form of works that can be encoded, stored, and retrieved from such media as computer disks, CD-ROMs, computer databases, and network servers."

Chapter 6. Copyright: Past and Present

Protecting Electronic Rights: Page 82 (*). The legislation proposed in 1995 actually failed to pass, because opposition developed from a coalition of groups representing libraries, educational institutions, and high technology. Of particular concern to these groups was the possibility that the bill might narrow the fair use defense. Closely related to the fair use issue was the objection to making illegal the use of anti-encryption devices, since breaking through such devices allows a person browsing the Internet, for example, to gain access to information in digital form. Fair use is only of value if there can be access to the information that might be used. In October, 1998, the Digital Millennium Copyright Act was enacted after compromises that alleviated these concerns. In handling the illegality of using anti-encryption devices, the Act provides, "Nothing in this section shall affect rights, remedies, limitations, or defenses to copyright infringement, including fair use, under this title." In addition, an exemption states, "A nonprofit library, archives, or educational institution which gains access to a commercially exploited copyrighted work solely in order to make a good faith determination of whether to acquire a copy of that work for the sole purpose of engaging in conduct permitted under this title shall not be in violation. . . ." There are several restrictions on this exemption, such as the fact that the exemption is only available "with respect to a work when an identical copy of that work is not reasonably available in another form." In the larger picture, the prohibition of anti-encryption devices has been postponed for two years so the Secretary of Commerce can review the impact of digital technologies on the copyright system. The prohibition will automatically take effect after two years, subject to certain exceptions for activities such as testing computer security, research on encryption, certain software development, protection of privacy, and the monitoring of children's Internet usage. The important point, however, is that digital information is now unambiguously protected by the copyright law.

Page 82 (**). In August of 1997, the court interpreted copyright law as applied to electronic publication in the case of *Tasini v. New York Times* (972 F. Supp. 804). The plaintiffs, all freelance writers, claimed that the defendants, all large publishing companies, had infringed their copyrights by placing the contents of their periodicals on electronic databases and CD-ROMs without first securing the permission of the plaintiffs whose contributions were included in those periodicals. The plaintiffs contended that it was understood by all concerned that they were selling only first North American serial rights and reserving secondary rights such as syndication, translations, and anthologies for separate sale. In deciding in favor of the defendants, the court found the articles originally appearing in the magazine to be substantially similar to the online and disc versions, so as to be construed as permissible "revisions" under the Copyright Act. The court urged Congress to clarify the "unclear" copyright statute with regard to the electronic media industry. (See Dina Marie Pascarelli, Note, *Electronic Rights: After Tasini Who Owns What, When? Tasini v. New York Times*, 8 DePaul-LCAJ.Art & Ent. L. 45.) The case was then denied rehearing at the circuit level, and has created a great deal of confusion in this area. The writer should seek written contracts that expressly reserve all rights not expressly transferred, including electronic rights, to the writer.

Chapter 12. Magazines and Syndication

Licensing to Magazines: Page 166. The text points out how bad it is for both the writer and the magazine if there is no written contract between them covering the key points. *Tasini v. New York Times*, discussed in the update entry for page 82, is a confirmation of this warning with respect to the failure to deal with electronic rights.

Chapter 16. Collaboration Agreements

Copyright and Authorship: Page 210. The new copyright term for a joint work is the life of the last surviving co-author, plus seventy years. The caution about an editor asserting joint authorship in a work is borne out by the *Rent* case discussed in this update with respect to page 53. In that case, a dramaturge asserted joint authorship. Such joint authorship might also be asserted by an illustrator. A written collaboration agreement will clarify ownership and greatly lessen the risk of litigation.

Chapter 19. Taxes: Income and Expenses

Types of Income: Page 231. The long-term capital gains tax rates have been lowered, so that the highest rate is now 20 percent. The holding period for long-term capital gains was increased to eighteen months and then reduced to twelve months again.

Writing Supplies and Other Deductions: Page 234. For the self-employed, the percentage of health insurance premiums that is deductible will steadily increase from 40 percent in 1997, to 45 percent in 1998 and 1999, to 50 percent in 2000 and 2001, to 60 percent in 2002, to 80 percent in 2003 through 2005, to 90 percent in 2006, and to 100 percent in 2007 and thereafter.

Work Space: Page 235. The legislation to change the impact of the *Soliman* case did pass. For tax years that start after 1998, a principal place of business will include a place of business used by the writer for administrative or management activities if there is no other fixed location where the writer performs such activities.

Retirement Plans: Page 250. The legislation was enacted that permits a $2,000 IRA contribution and deduction for a nonworking spouse, subject to certain qualifications and limitations. Also, new forms of nondeductible IRAs have been created. While contributions are nondeductible, any growth in value of a Roth IRA or an education IRA will escape taxation because distributions are not taxed. While these new IRAs apply to all taxpayers and are beyond the scope of this book to cover in detail, they are worth considering when the writer is planning for retirement or education (such as education of the writer's children).

Child and Disabled Dependent Care: Page 251. The proposed tax credit was enacted. It is $400 per child for 1998 and increases to $500 per child for 1999 and thereafter. It is reduced or eliminated if adjusted gross income exceeds certain limits.

Net Operating Losses: Page 252. For tax years commencing after August 5, 1997, net operating losses may be carried back two years and carried forward twenty years.

American Writers Living Abroad: Page 252. The $72,000 exclusion will increase to $74,000 for 1999, $76,000 for 2000, $78,000 for 2001, and $80,000 for 2002 and thereafter.

Forms of Doing Business: Page 255. The corporate tax rates continue as follows: 34 percent from $335,000 to $10,000,000; 35 percent from $10,000,000 to $15,000,000; 38 percent from $15,000,000 to $18,333,333; and 35 percent over $18,333,333.

Chapter 22. The Writer's Estate

Unified Estate and Gift Tax: Page 274. The pending legislation to increase the unified gift and estate tax credit did in fact pass. The effective exemption is increased from $600,000 to $625,000 for 1998, $650,000 for 1999, $675,000 for 2000 and 2001, $700,000 for 2002 and 2003, $850,000 for 2004, $950,000 for 2005, and $1,000,000 for 2006 and thereafter.

1 The Business of Writing

Writing and business often seem unlikely bedfellows and action in the legal sphere may therefore appear to be an anomaly for the writer involved in the creative process. As a result, many writers just sign the "standard" publishing contract without so much as reading it once through.

This is especially true with the writer who has never been published. Flattered, elated, the writer can become psychologically incapable of conducting a tough negotiation—perhaps from fear that the deal will fall through. The writer often cannot envision success and therefore does not see the point in creating problems. Writers should always think positively; one can never tell when an unlikely book will capture the attention of the world. While some authors speak of carving their work from the soul's underside, or writing to forge the "uncreated conscience" of the race, most writers reading this book will be writing to earn part or all of a livelihood. And, in fact, the laws that protect the writer's rights have always been closely connected to commerce.

Domestic copyright protection, for example, is the result of an implacable economic tension between the right of creators to benefit from the products of individual imagination and the societal need to build on the creativity of the past. It is no secret that Shakespeare borrowed liberally from Plutarch's *Lives* or that Melville appropriated from various seafaring memoirs. Would these writers have been subject to litigation under the current copyright laws? For two reasons, the answer to this question must be no. First, because the work they borrowed would certainly have been in the public domain. Second, because the progress that results from allowing writers to ride "on the shoulders of giants" at times outweighs the desirability of having an individual profit from his or her work. In a similar way, the needs of the day and the balance of economic interests have controlled international protection of copyright throughout the nineteenth and twentieth century. Today, increasingly, that balance favors protection of the writer. The United States Supreme Court has stated explicitly that the copyright laws are based on an economic philosophy: that "sacrificial days" devoted to creativity ultimately benefit the general public and must be encouraged by commensurate personal profit.

Each writer, however pure his or her motivation to write, must be capable of resolving business and legal issues. In this respect, a greater familiarity with law and other sources of support should prevent the writer from feeling intimidated, helpless, or victimized. While no handbook can solve the unique problems of each writer, the writer's increased awareness of the general legal issues involved will certainly aid in avoiding costly risks and gaining important benefits.

This second edition of *The Writer's Legal Guide* has a broad scope and uses the term writer to include creators of non-fiction books, journalists, novelists, poets, playwrights, screenwriters, and all others who put pen to paper for profit, conviction, or pleasure. Writers of every type need and will benefit from the business and legal information offered in this book. While the legal issues that concern many writers often parallel those that concern publishing firms, the central difference is in the perspective taken. This book is about protecting the rights of authors, not those of publishers.

More than a decade has passed since the first edition of *The Writer's Legal Guide*. In the interim, new technology—from computers, to multimedia CD-ROMs, to the World Wide Web and the Internet—has changed the way in which information, including the information contained in written works, can be processed and disseminated to the public. Among many other important topics, the text will explain how the current copyright laws and other existing protections can be used to protect the author's increasingly valuable electronic rights.

The Writer's Legal Guide seeks to introduce authors to the legal issues that arise in the commerce of writing as well as in the protection of an author's individual rights. It deals with each of the sequences of issues that begin as soon as the writer contemplates creating a written work, including copyright, contracts of all types, taxes, estate planning, public support for writers, and more.

Writers Groups

Membership in a writers organization will increase the writer's awareness of legal and business risks. Such groups provide a valuable support network. There are too many of these groups across the country to mention each by name, but those with a special interest in authors' rights, including legal and business issues, are listed below.

The Authors Guild
330 West 42nd Street
New York, NY 10036
(212) 563-5904

The Dramatists Guild
234 West 44th Street
New York, NY 10036
(212) 398-9366

The National Writers Union
873 Broadway, Suite 203
New York, NY 10003
(212) 254-0279

The American Society of Journalists
and Authors (ASJA)
1501 Broadway

New York, NY 10036
(212) 997-0947

P.E.N.
568 Broadway
New York, NY 10012
(212) 334-1660

Writers Guild of America—East
555 West 57th Street
New York, NY 10019
(212) 767-7800

Writers Guild of America—West
8955 Beverly Boulevard
Los Angeles, CA 90048
(310) 550-1000

Many of these groups offer newsletters and other up-to-date information services. A few provide legal services, while others lobby for legislation favorable to writers. Health, life, and even automobile insurance are frequently offered at group rates.

Joining a writers' group can be an important step for a writer in terms of protecting rights and increasing professional prestige.

Lawyers for the Arts

The search for a lawyer is often time-consuming and disheartening. Not only are fees high, but most general practitioners are not knowledgeable about the issues encountered by writers. Standard techniques for finding a lawyer include asking a friend who consulted a lawyer for a similar problem, calling a local bar association's referral service, or going to a legal clinic. All of these approaches have merits, but today the writer may be able to locate a knowledgeable lawyer with far greater precision.

In recent years, the amount of literature and the number of educational programs that deal with legal issues pertaining to writers have increased substantially. Law schools offer publishing law courses and are integrating issues affecting writers into their intellectual property courses. Bar associations are paying greater attention to the subject as well. The Selected Bibliography lists some of the books that are now available for lawyers interested in helping writers. Although few lawyers would define themselves as narrowly as a "writer's lawyer," the increasing interest in this area is an encouraging sign.

Equally encouraging are the lawyers across the country volunteering to help needy artists of all kinds. If the writer cannot afford legal assistance, one of these groups should be considered. Even if they are unable to provide free legal advice on a specific subject, some of these groups maintain referral rosters of knowledgeable attorneys.

CALIFORNIA
California Lawyers for the Arts/Fort
   Mason Center
Building C, Room 255
San Francisco, CA 94123
(415) 775-7200
   or
1549 11th Street, Suite 200
Santa Monica, CA 90401
(310) 395-8893

ILLINOIS
Lawyers for the Creative Arts
213 West Institute Place, Suite 411
Chicago, IL 60610
(312) 944-2787

NEW YORK
Volunteer Lawyers for the Arts
1 East 53rd Street
New York, NY 10022
(212) 319-2787

Value of *The Writer's Legal Guide*

The Writer's Legal Guide encourages a writer to think in a new way—like a lawyer. It is not that the writer who uses this handbook will become a legal expert with respect to copyright or the other legal areas discussed. *The Writer's Legal Guide* is not meant to serve as an alternative to seeking legal advice on specific issues. There is no substitute for consultation with a lawyer who can carefully evaluate each writer's unique legal problems. Nevertheless, a close reading and understanding of the text will alert the writer to pitfalls that are likely to trap the unwary. It will open doors to those who seek to better their business practices, increase their incomes, and protect their work. Knowing when it is advisable to consult with a lawyer (or in some cases an agent, accountant, or other professional) can itself be a great asset.

The writer who learns to conduct business affairs with clarity is likely to have more money (by protecting rights and negotiating effectively), more time (by avoiding stressful and time-wasting legal problems), better luck (because "chance favors the prepared mind"), and more strength (which will come from knowing more and therefore worrying less). For those writers who seek greater self-reliance, confidence, and peace of mind, *The Writer's Legal Guide* will be an invaluable companion.

2 Copyright: Gaining and Keeping Protection

*T*he Constitution of the United States provides that "Congress shall have the power . . . promote the Progress of Science and useful Arts, by securing for limited Times to Authors and Inventors the exclusive Right to their respective Writings and Discoveries . . ." (Article 1, Section 8, Clause 8). Historically, laws protecting literary property had evolved under English common law and statutes. In 1790, Congress responded to its constitutional prerogative by enacting the first federal copyright law. This series of laws, in their current incarnation, can be used to protect virtually every kind of original work in written or other form (electronic symbols, magnetic tape, photos, film, videotape, canvas, etc.). As we go to press, legislation has been introduced in both the House and Senate to amend the copyright law so that it functions more effectively with respect to the transmission of works in digitized form (for example, over the Internet). This legislation, based on the "White Paper of The Working Group on Intellectual Property Rights of the Information Infrastructure Task Force" (chaired by the

Commissioner of Patents and Trademarks), seems assured of passage* and will be discussed at appropriate points in the treatment of copyright.

The Value of Copyright

Copyright is the source of all the reproduction, distribution, and other rights that a writer sells in his or her work. The value of copyright protection can be shown by comparing two instances of literary piracy, one involving the early plays of Eugene O'Neill and the other involving the early short stories of J. D. Salinger. Eugene O'Neill, during 1913, 1914, and 1915, copyrighted a number of his plays by registering them with the Copyright Office in Washington, D.C. He did not value these works highly, nor did he wish to see them published. However, in the 1940s he failed to renew his copyrights for additional twenty-eight-year terms after the original twenty-eight-year terms had expired. The result of this omission was that the plays went into the public domain, available to all who might wish to copy, perform, or publish them. New Fathoms Press, Ltd. published them as the *Lost Plays of Eugene O'Neill*.

J. D. Salinger similarly wished to let his early short stories, which had appeared between 1940 and 1948 in such magazines as *The Saturday Evening Post*, *Colliers*, and *Esquire*, remain in obscurity. However, in 1974 a pirated collection of these stories appeared under the title *The Complete Uncollected Short Stories of J. D. Salinger, Vols. 1 and 2*. In San Francisco, Chicago, New York, and elsewhere, different men using the alias John Greenberg sold between twenty-five and thirty thousand copies of the book. Salinger, perturbed by this invasion of his privacy, broke a twenty-year public silence to denounce the pirated collection. But Salinger's situation differed from O'Neill's, because Salinger had valid copyrights on these short stories. He sued the bookstores that had sold the book, obtained an injunction to prevent them from making further sales, and demanded damages of two hundred and fifty thousand dollars. Furthermore, federal prosecutors commenced an investigation, because a violation of the copyright laws can sometimes be punished by criminal penalties. *The Complete Uncollected Short Stories of J. D. Salinger, Vols. 1 and 2* slipped back into the obscurity that their author desired, his objections to unauthorized publication sustained because of the protection provided by the copyright laws.

The "New" Copyright Law

This and the following chapters will explain how a writer can obtain and benefit from the protections available under the copyright laws of the United States of America. The rules of copyright that applied to the

O'Neill and Salinger works have undergone substantial changes. On January 1, 1978, an entirely new copyright law, known as The Copyright Act of 1976, replaced the law that had been in effect since 1909. While the changes in the 1976 Act (and several additional changes since 1976) generally favored the creator, each writer must still be aware of the often intricate provisions of the law which maximize the benefits of copyright protection. Furthermore, the 1976 Act is an evolving creature, pressured and stretched by the development of new technologies as well as by economically sensitive political maneuverings. While the copyright law has sometimes proven remarkably adaptable as technological changes have ushered in dramatic revisions in the creation, storage, and delivery of literary works, some commentators have argued that it will be unable to meet future technological challenges.

Nicholas Negroponte, in his book *Being Digital*, reflects the view of many cyberspace gurus when he argues that: "Copyright law is totally out of date. It is a Gutenberg artifact. Since it is a reactive process, it will probably have to break down completely before it is corrected." Reasoning that the ease of copying will destroy copyright is a bit facile, however, in view of the many technologies (such as computer programs, sound recordings, films, and television) that copyright has already survived to protect. In fact, the United States is a net exporter of intellectual property and the creation of such property is important for our gross national product. In order to maintain an incentive for creativity, the copyright law will only be made more vital as it is adjusted to technological innovation.

One helpful, and free, aid that every writer should obtain is a Copyright Information Kit, which can be requested from the Copyright Office, Library of Congress, Washington, D.C. 20559. The Copyright Information Kit includes the Copyright Office's regulations, the copyright application forms, and circulars explaining both the copyright law and the operation of the Copyright Office. Free publications that help give an overview include Circular 1, "Copyright Basics," and Circular 2, "Publications on Copyright." For writers wishing to purchase a copy of the complete copyright law, it can be ordered as Circular 92, or stock #030-002-00182-9, for $4.75 from the Superintendent of Documents, Government Printing Office at (202) 512-1800. A hotline number, (202) 707-9100, has been established by the Copyright Office to expedite requests for registration forms. The public information number for the Copyright Office is (202) 707-3000. The Copyright Office also has a site on the World Wide Web from which frequently requested copyright circulars, proposed regulations, final regulations, and announcements can be viewed and downloaded. The address is: http://lcweb.loc.gov/copyright.

Effective Date

The majority of provisions in the current copyright law became effective January 1, 1978. While younger writers will most likely have created all of their work after 1978, it is important to keep in mind that copyright transactions prior to January 1, 1978, are governed by the 1909 law. For example, if the copyright on a work has gone into the public domain (which means that it can be copied freely by anyone) under the 1909 law, the current law would not revive this lost copyright, even if the copyright would not have gone into the public domain had the current law been in effect when the work was created. However, the 1976 law does govern the treatment of valid copyrights that had not fallen into the public domain prior to January 1, 1978.

Single Copyright System

Before 1978, copyright existed in two quite distinct forms: common-law copyright and statutory copyright. Common-law copyright derived from precedent in the courts, while statutory copyright derived from federal legislation. Common-law copyright protected works as soon as created without any copyright notice; statutory copyright protected works only when registered with the Copyright Office or published with copyright notice. Common-law copyright lasted forever unless the work was published or registered; statutory copyright lasted for a twenty-eight-year term which could be renewed for an additional twenty-eight years.

The new law almost entirely eliminated common-law copyright, a reform that substantially simplified the copyright system. All works are now protected by statutory copyright as soon as they are "first fixed in a tangible medium of expression, now known or later developed, from which they can be perceived, reproduced or otherwise communicated, either directly or with the aid of a machine or device." Under the requirement of fixation, an extemporaneous speech would not normally be subject to copyright protection, but a speech keyboarded onto a computer screen and saved as a file would be protected.

This immediate statutory copyright protection, regardless of registration or publication with copyright notice, was an important change in the law and made our law consistent with the copyright laws found in most other countries. Today, it is not necessary to comply with any formalities in order to obtain statutory copyright. Protection attaches as soon as the writer creates ("fixes") a work.

Nevertheless, as explained in chapter 3, the formalities of registration and deposit are neither difficult nor expensive to comply with and do offer distinct legal and commercial advantages.

What Is Copyrightable?

The writer can only copyright his or her original work. But the test for originality is generally easy to pass. Originality simply means that the work originated with the writer, that the writer created the work and did not copy it from some other copyrighted work. The writer's expression need not be brilliant or even unique. It is enough that the work show some minor level of creativity, some minimal artistic qualities.

However, it is the copying and not specifically the similarity to another work that constitutes copyright infringement. If two writers, by some unlikely turn of fate, happened independently to create identical works, both would be copyrightable. As Judge Learned Hand wrote, "Borrowed the work must indeed not be, for a plagiarist is not himself pro tanto an 'author'; but if by some magic a man who had never known it were to compose anew Keats's 'Ode on a Grecian Urn,' he would be an 'author,' and, if he copyrighted it, others might not copy that poem, though they might of course copy Keats's" (*Sheldon v. Metro-Goldwyn Pictures Corporation*, 81 F.2d 49, 55). A poem by Keats can be copied because it has long since entered the public domain. Two writers choosing the same general subject matter, such as an historical event or well-known person, could, of course, each copyright the resulting work.

Ideas, facts, concepts, principles, discoveries, titles, names, slogans, short phrases, blank forms, general topics, common plots or themes, stock characters, and processes or procedures are generally not copyrightable, although some may be protected under other legal theories discussed in chapter 7. Nevertheless, the creative expression of any of these categories, the writer's special realization of the subject, is copyrightable. Thus, the original description (expression) of an idea is copyrightable, as is the way facts are selected and arranged, and common themes and stock characters can be fleshed out to create copyrightable works. But the underlying ideas, facts and themes remain forever in the public domain, available to anyone.

The increasing importance of sequels, spinoffs, and the like has raised the issue of whether a specific character can be copyrightable apart from the story containing that character.

While it is clear that stock characters or literary types, such as a "riotous knight" or a "a vain and foppish steward," are not copyrightable, there are instances in which a character is copyrightable. The test of copyrightability for characters is not an easy one. As one court put it: "the less developed the characters, the less they can be copyrighted: that is the penalty an author must bear for marking them too indistinctly" (*Nichols v. Universal Pictures Corp.*, 45 F.2d 119). Subsequently, another court, in a case involving Sam Spade of *Maltese Falcon* fame, enunciated a different test in noting that a character in a piece of writing would be independently copyrightable if that character actually "constitut[ed] the story being told" (*Warner Brothers, Inc. v. Columbia Broadcasting System*, 216 F.2d 945). While it appears that in particular circumstances a unique character can have some protection per se, cases involving copyright infringement of characters will generally turn on detailed determinations of fact as well as a consideration of the equities involved.

Compilations of individually uncopyrightable elements can sometimes be copyrightable. A factual compilation is a work formed by the collection and assembling of preexisting materials or data that are selected, coordinated, and arranged in such a way that the resulting work is in some sense original. Examples range from the yellow pages of the phone book to annotated listings of the best restaurants in New York. Whether the copyright in such a compilation has been infringed depends on the nature of the collected material, the manner in which it is presented, and the nature of the appropriation.

Copyright protection does not extend to the discovery of what is objectively true (i.e., the facts themselves), but it does protect the way objective facts are described. In *Feist Publications, Inc. v. Rural Telephone Service Company, Inc.* (111 S. Ct. 1282), for example, the United States Supreme Court held that a white pages telephone directory was not a copyrightable compilation because its selection, arrangement, and coordination failed to meet constitutional standards of originality. Basically, it was a straight alphabetical listing of all the names and addresses in a particular area code.

While the result in *Feist* is clearly consistent with general copyright principles, it overturned a long-standing copyright anomaly known as "the sweat of the brow doctrine." Under that doctrine, courts had "handed out proprietary interests in facts and declared that authors are absolutely precluded from saving time and effort by relying upon the facts contained in prior works." The Supreme Court, noting that not all copying amounts to copyright infringement, concluded that in this case even an exact copy, which included names that were added specifically to detect copying (called "franking"), did not infringe the copyright of the compiler. After *Feist*, writers can take the bare facts from prior works, although they should verify those facts and be sure to select, coordinate, and arrange those facts independently. The copyright law no longer protects raw data regardless of the time and effort involved in finding it.

The fact that part of a work infringes someone else's copyright, or takes public domain material, will not prevent the writer from securing protection for the rest of the work. For example, if a writer writes a group of articles to appear in a book but also includes someone else's copyrighted piece, without obtaining permission, the original contributions of the writer, whatever they were, would still be copyrightable.

Derivative works, which are distinguishable variations of existing works, can be copyrighted in appropriate circumstances. The writer of the original work has the exclusive rights to make a derivative work based on the original or to authorize someone else to make such a derivative work. A writer who owns a copyright can add new elements to the previously copyrighted work and copyright those new elements. Also, if a work is in the public domain (which means that the work is no longer protected by copyright and may be freely copied by anyone) any writer can create a copyrightable work by adding original elements to such a work. For example, a writer could create a copyrightable work by adding new elements to Keats's "Ode on a Grecian Urn." But if the writer copyrighted the new poem, he or she would only be able to prevent copying of the new elements; others could take freely from the original poem. Such derivative works as abridgments, adaptations, and translations all require original effort and are copyrightable in their own right. But if the derivative work is based on copyrighted material, the consent of the copyright owner must be obtained. If such consent is not obtained, the maker of the derivative work might be liable for copyright infringement.

Computer programs are copyrightable. So are multimedia works, which combine two or more media. For a discussion of all kinds of electronic and new media rights, see chapter 14.

The Copyright Office may refuse to register a work on the grounds that it is not copyrightable, but this exercise of the Copyright Register's discretion can be reviewed by the courts. It is the courts, not the Copyright Office, that act as the final arbiters of what is and is not copyrightable.

Who Can Benefit from Copyright?

If works are unpublished, the law protects them without regard for the writer's nationality or place of residence. If works are published, the law will protect them if one or more of the writers is (1) a national or permanent resident of the United States; (2) a stateless person; or (3) a national or a permanent resident of a nation covered by a copyright treaty with the United States or by a presidential proclamation.

The United States is a party to the Universal Copyright Convention (dating back to 1955), so publication in any nation that is a party to that Convention will also gain protection in the United States. The copyright notice for the Universal Copyright Convention must include the symbol ©, the writer's full name, and the year of first publication. Thus, the short form notice © JA (discussed under copyright notice later in this chapter) should be avoided when protection is desired under the Universal Copyright Convention. For the older Buenos Aires Convention, covering many Western Hemisphere countries, the phrase "All rights reserved" should be added to the notice.

The United States joined an international copyright convention known as the Berne Union on March 1, 1989. As a result, it is no longer necessary for United States writers to publish simultaneously in a Berne Union country to gain protection under the Berne Convention. In fact, because the Berne Convention forbids member countries from imposing copyright formalities as a condition of copyright protection for the works of foreign writers, a number of changes have been made in the United States copyright law. These changes will be described in relation to the appropriate sections of the text. Copyright Office Circular 93, "Highlights of U.S. Adherence to the Berne Convention," and Circular 93a, "The United States Joins the Berne Union," offer an excellent overview.

Details of the international copyright relations of the United States can be obtained from the Copyright Office in Circular 38a, "International Copyright Relations of the United States." Circular 38a, covering copyright relations as of March 11, 1996, shows that sixty-nine countries belonged to both the Universal Copyright Convention and the Berne Convention. An additional twenty-six countries belonged to the Berne Convention but not to the Universal Copyright Convention, while yet another nineteen countries belonged to the Universal Copyright Convention but not the Berne Convention. Writers automatically obtain protection under both conventions when they publish a work in the United States.

Term of Copyright

The term of copyright under the 1978 law is the writer's life plus fifty years (although legislation has been proposed, and may pass in 1996, to extend this term to life plus seventy years).* The 1909 copyright law had an original twenty-eight-year term and a renewal term of twenty-eight additional years, so the life-plus-fifty term is longer in almost every case. For works created anonymously, under a pseudonym, or as a work for hire, the term shall be either seventy-five years from first publication of the work or a hundred years from its creation, whichever period is shorter. The Copyright Office maintains records as to when a writer dies, but a presumption exists that a copyright has expired if seventy-five years have passed and the records disclose no information indicating the copyright term might still be in effect. If the name of a writer who has created a work anonymously or under a pseudonym is recorded with the Copyright Office, the copyright term then runs for the writer's life plus fifty years.

The term of copyright for a jointly created work is the life of the last surviving writer plus fifty years. A joint work is defined as a work created by two or more writers with the intention that their contributions be merged into inseparable or interdependent parts of a unitary whole.

Copyrights in their renewal term (under the 1909 law) that would have expired on or after September 19, 1962, were extended due to the deliberations over the revision of the copyright law. They fall under the general rule that the terms of statutory copyrights in existence on January 1, 1978, are extended to seventy-five years (twenty-eight years in the first term, forty-seven years in the renewal term).

However, any copyrights obtained prior to 1978 that were still in their first twenty-eight year term would have had to be renewed on Form RE in order to benefit from the extension to a total term of seventy-five years. A 1992 amendment waived this renewal requirement, so that all works copyrighted between January 1, 1964, and December 31, 1977, automatically have their term extended by forty-seven years. However, there are important legal benefits to filing Form RE and paying the twenty-dollar fee for renewal, including that the renewal certificate is considered proof that the copyright is valid and the facts stated in the certificate are true. As shown on Form RE, it may be possible to make a group renewal for a number of copyrights expiring in the same year. Circular 15, "Renewal of Copyright," offers additional information about copyright renewal.

Circular 15t, "Extension of Copyright Terms," discusses the extended terms of copyrights in existence on January 1, 1978, whether the copyright was in its first twenty-eight year term or in its renewal term.

Since common-law copyright has basically been eliminated, all works protected by common-law copyright as of January 1, 1978, were given a statutory copyright term of the writer's life plus fifty years. In no event, however, will such a copyright previously protected under the common law expire prior to December 31, 2002, and, if the work is published, the copyright will extend at least until December 31, 2027.

The 1978 law provides that all copyright terms will run through December 31 of the year in which they are scheduled to expire. This greatly simplified determining a copyright's term and, when necessary, renewing a copyright.

Exclusive Rights

The owner of a copyright has the exclusive rights to do, or authorize another to do, any of the following: reproduce the work, sell and distribute the work, prepare derivative works, perform the work publicly, and display the work publicly. A derivative work adapts or transforms an earlier work, such as making a film from a novel, or adding new chapters to a non-fiction book so that the new work would be a substantial variation from the original work. The right to sell and distribute the work will not, of course, prevent someone who has purchased a lawfully made copy from reselling it.

The right to display the work does not prevent the owner of a copy of the work from displaying it directly or with the aid of a projector to people present at the place of display, such as exhibiting a beautifully designed novel at a lecture on book design. For an audiovisual work, including a motion picture, a display is defined as showing its images nonsequentially. The owner of a copy could do this publicly. Performing an audiovisual work, which is showing its images sequentially, would be allowed only if the owner of the copy did it in private. To perform the work publicly, either in a public place or to an audience including a substantial number of people beyond the family or one's normal circle of friends, requires permission of the copyright owner.

Copyright is traditionally defined as a bundle of rights. Each of the exclusive rights belonging to the copyright owner can be subdivided. For example, the reproduction rights sold might be "first North American serial rights" instead of "all rights." All rights would be the entire copyright. First North American serial rights is a subdivided part of the exclusive right to authorize reproduction of the work. It is still an exclusive right, because it gives a magazine the right to be first to publish the work in a given geographical area. It is important to understand how to subdivide rights, because this is how the writer limits what rights are transferred to another party and retains the greatest possible amount of rights for future use.

There are some limited exceptions to the exclusive rights of the copyright owner. The most important exception is fair use, which sometimes allows use of a copyrighted work without obtaining permission of the copyright owner. Fair use is discussed in chapter 5. As a general rule, however, anyone using a work in violation of the copyright owner's exclusive rights is an infringer who must pay damages and can be restrained from continuing the infringement.

Transfers and Licenses

All copyrights and subdivided parts of copyrights must be transferred in writing, except for nonexclusive licenses. This requirement of a written transfer is an important protection for the writer.

An exclusive license gives someone a right that no one else can exercise. For example, a writer might give a publisher the right to publish and distribute a paperback edition of his or her novel until the work goes out of print. This would be giving an exclusive license to the publisher. The exclusivity could be increased or decreased based on duration of the license, geographic extent of the license, and any other factors that the writer believes are useful and can be obtained in the negotiation with the publisher.

On the other hand, nonexclusive licenses, which can be granted verbally, allow two parties to do the same thing, at the same time, in the same place. For example, a writer could give two magazines "simultaneous rights" to publish an article. Something similar to this occurs when newspapers are granted syndication rights. The effect is a kind of simultaneous license under which many newspapers can run the story or article as long as they pay a licensing fee to the syndicator (which may be the original publisher, a syndication agency, or even an unusually enterprising author). The syndicator in turn pays a set fee to the writer for each time the work is "picked up."

Since nonexclusive licenses can be transferred verbally, they require increased vigilance on the part of the writer to ensure that an implied and/or unwanted agreement is not made. For example, the writer should be wary of verbal statements or unsigned writings (such as a memorandum on a publisher's letterhead) that suggest the publisher has a right to use the work. Carefully worded licenses, assignments, and transfers should spell out what rights are "transferred" and should "reserve" to the writer all other rights, including the now important electronic and other new media rights.

Copies of documents recording transfers of copyrights or exclusive licenses should be filed with the Copyright Office by the person receiving the transfer to protect that person's ownership rights. This filing should be done within one month if the transfer took place in the United States and within two months if the transfer took place outside of the United States. Nonexclusive licenses can also be recorded with the Copyright Office. The Copyright Office has a recommended "cover sheet" that can be obtained from the Office to accompany, and speed up the handling, of any recorded document, such as an assignment.

A form for the assignment of all right, title, and interest in a copyright is included here. In general, it should not be used to sell rights, since limited rights transfers are far better for the author. However, this form can be used when the writer is reacquiring rights in a copyright—for example, if a right granted reverts back to the writer by contract.

Termination

Another significant provision of the 1978 law is the writer's right to terminate transfers of either exclusive or nonexclusive rights. If, after January 1, 1978, a writer grants exclusive or nonexclusive rights in a copyright, he or she has the right to terminate this grant during a five-year period starting at the end of thirty-five years after the execution of the grant or, if the grant includes the right of publication, during a five-year period beginning at the end of thirty-five years from the date of publication or forty years from the date of execution of the grant, whichever term ends earlier.*

Similarly, if before January 1, 1978, the writer or the writer's surviving family members made a grant of the renewal right in one of the

---

COPYRIGHT ASSIGNMENT FORM

For valuable consideration, the receipt of which is hereby acknowledged, (name of party assigning the copyright), whose offices are located at (address), does hereby transfer and assign to (name of party receiving the copyright), whose offices are located at (address), his or her heirs, executors, administrators, and assigns, all its right, title, and interest, throughout the world and in perpetuity, in the copyrights and all related rights in the works described as follows: (describe work, including registration number, if work has been registered) _____

_____

_____

_____ ,

including any statutory copyright and all rights under copyright therein including but not limited to the right to secure renewals and extensions of such copyright throughout the world, for the full term of said copyright or statutory copyright and any renewal or extension of same that is or may be granted throughout the world.

In Witness Whereof, (name of party assigning the copyright) has executed this instrument by the signature of its duly authorized corporate officer on the _____ day of _____ ,19____ .

ABC Corporation

By: _____
AUTHORIZED SIGNATURE

_____
NAME PRINTED OR TYPED

_____
TITLE

---

writer's copyrights, that grant can be terminated during a five-year period starting fifty-six years after the copyright was first obtained. However, the writer has no right of termination in transfers by will or in works for hire.

The mechanics of termination involve giving notice two to ten years prior to the termination date and complying with regulations the Copyright Office can provide, but the important point is to remember that such a right exists. The purpose of the right of termination is to provide creators the opportunity to share in an unexpected appreciation in the value of what was transferred years before the work's value was known.

Selling to Magazines and Other Collective Works

Magazines, newspapers, anthologies, encyclopedias—anything in which a number of separate contributions are combined—are defined as "collective works." The law specifically provides that the copyright in each contribution is separate from the copyright in the entire collective work. The copyright in a contribution belongs to the contributor who can give the owner of the copyright in the entire work whatever rights the contributor wishes in return for compensation.

However, especially where magazines are concerned, it is not uncommon for a contribution to be published without any express agreement ever being made as to what rights are being transferred to the magazine. The current law deals with this situation by providing that, in a case where there is no express agreement, the owner of copyright in the collective work gets the following rights: (1) the nonexclusive right to use the work in the issue of the collective work for which it was contributed; (2) the right to use the contribution in a revision of that collective work; and (3) the right to use the contribution in any later collective work in the same series.

For example, a work is contributed to a magazine without any agreement with respect to what rights are being transferred. The magazine can now use that work in one issue and again in later issues, but it cannot publish that work in a different magazine. Magazines are not usually revised, but anthologies and encyclopedias are. In that case the work could be used in the original issue of the anthology or encyclopedia and any later revisions, but it couldn't be used for a new anthology or a different encyclopedia.

Of course, in the absence of a written agreement, only nonexclusive rights are transferred to the magazine or other collective work, so the work could be contributed elsewhere at the same time, although this might be construed by the purchaser as a moral breach and spoil any opportunity for future dealings.

The best solution is simply to have a written agreement signed by the writer or his or her authorized agent transferring limited rights. For example, the limited rights might be defined as "first North America rights" in the contribution to the collective work. This transfers exclusive first-time rights in North America, but it has the advantage of restricting the magazine or other collective work from making subsequent uses of the contribution without payment. It also makes the sale governed by terms agreed to and understood by both parties, instead of by a law that may not satisfactorily achieve the end result desired by either party. The need for a signed written transfer can be satisfied by a simple letter stating:

> "This is to confirm that in return for your agreement to pay me $_____, I am transferring to you first North American rights in my work titled _____ described as follows:_____ for publication in your magazine titled:_____. All other rights, including but not limited to electronic rights, are reserved by me."

If the magazine wants to use the contribution in another way, such as in an on-line edition, an additional fee and appropriate usage limitations can be negotiated. (For further information, see the update entry for page 82.)

Entering Contests

The writer may want to enter contests sponsored by publications or professional organizations. Many contests pose no problem, but any application form should be closely scrutinized with respect to reproduction and other rights of the copyright owner. Does winning, or even entering, the contest require that the writer transfer the copyright, or some segment thereof, to the sponsor? If so, depending on the circumstances of the writer, it may be unwise to enter the contest.

If the contest requires that exclusive rights be transferred to the sponsor in the event that the writer wins, then the writer must evaluate whether this transfer of rights is reasonable. The sponsor should only seek limited rights, such as the right to publish the submission in a book of contest winners. If the sponsor seeks more than this, the writer should demand fair compensation for the additional rights that appear unnecessary to fulfill the purpose of the contest.

In addition, if the sponsor seeks free articles or works of fiction to use for commercial purposes, such as promoting or advertising its products, then the writer should be especially wary of entering. Not only does this situation appear very similar to working on speculation, which should be anathema to all writers, but it would require a prize that would be a fair fee for the winner.

Contest applications must be read carefully and contests entered only after thoroughly weighing whether the impact of the contest on ownership of the copyright is fair and ethical.

Ownership of the Physical Work

Copyright is completely separate from ownership of a physical manuscript (or a computer disk containing the manuscript in a file). A writer can sell the physical work verbally, but the copyright or any exclusive license must always be transferred in writing and the writer or the writer's authorized agent must sign that transfer.

Publication with Copyright Notice

Due to United States adherence to the Berne Copyright Convention, as of March 1, 1989, the United States copyright law no longer requires copyright notice to be placed on published works. In fact, however, most copyright proprietors will continue to use copyright notice. The notice warns potential infringers of the copyright. Use of the copyright notice prevents an infringer from being allowed to ask the court for mitigation of damages on the grounds that the infringement was innocent. Also, the Universal Copyright Convention still requires copyright notice and, as pointed out, has a number of member countries which are not signatories of the Berne Convention.

In some cases, the time when publication occurs can be confusing. Publication in the current law basically means public distribution. This occurs when one or more copies of a work are distributed to people who are not restricted from disclosing the work's content to others. Distribution can take place by sale, rental, lease, lending, or other transfer of copies to the public. Also, offering copies to a group of people for the purpose of review, further distribution, public performance, or public display is a publication. In circulating copies of a work to publishers or other potential purchasers, it would be wise to indicate on the copies that the contents are not to be disclosed to the public without the writer's consent. Even if this is not done, however, it should be implicit that such public disclosure is not to be allowed.

Pending legislation defines a transmission as a publication (though many copyright lawyers are satisfied that current distribution rights include electronic transmissions). If passed, this legislation would bring the on-line world unequivocally within the purview of the copyright law.*

Form of Copyright Notice

The form of the copyright notice is as follows: Copyright or Copr. or ©, the writer's name or an abbreviation by which that name can be recognized or an alternative designation by which the writer is known, and the year of publication (or the year of creation, if the work is unpublished and the writer chooses to place notice on it). Valid notice could, therefore, be © JA 1995, if the writer's initials were JA. In general, the Copyright Office takes the position that a writer's initials are insufficient unless the writer is well known by his or her initials. If the writer is not well known by his or her initials, the Copyright Office will treat the notice as lacking any name. If a work consists preponderantly of one or more works created by the United States Government, a statement indicating this must be included with the copyright notice. If this is not done, the work will be treated as if notice had been completely omitted.

Circular 3, "Copyright Notice" discusses both the form and placement of copyright notice.

Placement of Copyright Notice

The copyright notice should be placed so as to give reasonable notice to an ordinary user of the work of the copyright. The Copyright Office regulations are very liberal as to where notice can be placed; in fact, any reasonable placement of notice will be valid. Of course, it would be wise to follow the guidelines given in the regulations and reproduced below.

In the case of work published in book form, a notice reproduced on the copies in any of the following positions is acceptable:

1. The title page, if any;
2. The page immediately following the title page, if any;
3. Either side of the front cover, if any; or if there is no front cover, either side of the front leaf of the copies;
4. Either side of the back cover, if any; or, if there is no back cover, either side of the back leaf of the copies;
5. The first page of the main body of the work;
6. The last page of the main body of the work;
7. Any page between the front page and the first page of the main body of the work, if: (i) There are no more than ten pages between the front page and the first page of the main body of the work; and (ii) the notice is reproduced prominently and is set apart from other matter on the page where it appears;
8. Any page between the last page of the main body of the work and back page, if: (i) There are no more than ten pages between the last page of the main body of the work and the back page; and (ii) the notice is reproduced prominently and is set apart from the other matter on the page where it appears;
9. In the case of a work published as an issue of a periodical or serial, in addition to any of the locations listed in paragraphs (d)(1) through (8) of this section, a notice is acceptable if it is located: (i) As a part of, or adjacent to, the masthead; (ii) on the page containing the masthead if the notice is reproduced prominently and is set apart from the other matter appearing on the page; or (iii) adjacent to a prominent heading, appearing at or near the front of the issue, containing the title of the periodical or serial and any combination of the volume and issue number and date of the issue.

For a contribution to a collective work, such as a magazine or anthology, the regulations state that copyright notice can be placed in any of the following ways:

1. If a contribution is on a single page, the copyright notice may be placed under the title of the contribution, next to the contribution or anywhere on the same page as long as it's clear that the copyright notice is to go with the contribution;
2. If the contribution takes up more than one page in the collective work, the copyright notice may be placed under the title at or near the beginning of the contribution, on the first page of the body of the contribution, immediately following the end of the contribution, or on any of the pages containing the contribution as long as the contribution is less than twenty pages and it's clear the notice applies to the contribution;
3. As an alternative to numbers (1) or (2), the copyright notice may be placed on the page bearing the notice for the collective work as a whole or on a clearly identified and readily accessible table of contents or listing of acknowledgments appearing either at the front or back of the collective work as a whole. For (3), there must be a separate listing of the contribution by its title or, if it has no title, by an identifying description.

For motion pictures and other audiovisual works the copyright notice is acceptable if it is embodied in the copies by a photomechanical or electronic process so that it appears whenever the work is performed in its entirety and is located in any of the following positions:

1. With or near the title;
2. With the cast, credits, or similar information;
3. At or immediately following the beginning of the work; or,
4. At or immediately preceding the end of the work.

Since a series of related slides intended to be shown together is considered an audiovisual work, the notice would have to be visible when the work is performed in one of the positions just listed. There would be no requirement, however, that notice appear on the mounting of the slides as in the case of a slide that is not part of a related series. Also, a motion picture or other audiovisual work distributed to the public for private use (such as a video recording cassette) may have the notice on the container in which the work is permanently housed if that would be preferred to one of the four placements listed above.

Defective Notice

Since copyright notice is permissive after March 1, 1989, works published without notice are fully protected and the provisions on defective notice are not relevant. However, the changes in the copyright law are not retroactive, so works published without copyright notice prior to March 1, 1989, may have gone into the public domain. There are two categories of pre-March 1, 1989 works that must be discussed: those works published between January 1, 1978 and March 1, 1989, and those works published before January 1, 1978.

Between January 1, 1978 and March 1, 1989, a copyright was not necessarily lost if the copyright notice was incorrect or omitted when authorized publication took place either in the United States or abroad. For example, if the wrong name appeared in the copyright notice, the copyright was still valid. This meant that if an writer contributed to a magazine or other collective work but there was no copyright notice in the writer's name with the contribution, the copyright was still protected by the copyright notice in the front of the magazine even though the notice was in the publisher's name. Notice in the publisher's name did not, however, protect advertisements that appeared without separate notice (unless the publisher was also the advertiser). If an earlier date than the actual date of publication appeared in a copyright notice, the term of copyright was simply computed from the earlier date, but the copyright remained valid. Computing the copyright from the earlier date would not make any difference, since the term of the copyright is measured by the writer's life plus fifty years (not a fixed time period which could be shortened by computing the term from the earlier date).*

If the name or date was simply omitted from the notice, or if the date was more than one year later than the year in which publication actually occurred, the validity of the copyright was governed by the same provisions that applied to the complete omission of copyright notice. In such a case, the copyright was valid and did not go into the public domain if any one of the following three tests was met: (1) the notice was omitted from only a relatively small number of copies distributed to the public; (2) the notice was omitted from more than a relatively small number of copies, but registration was made within five years of publication and a reasonable effort was made to add notice to copies distributed in the United States that did not have notice (such a reasonable effort at least required notifying all distributors of the omission and instructing them to add the proper notice; foreign distributors did not have to be notified); or (3) the notice had been left off the copies against the writer's written instructions that such notice appear on the work.

However, an innocent infringer who gave proof of having been misled by the type of incorrect or omitted notice discussed in the preceding paragraph would not have been liable for damages for infringing acts committed prior to receiving actual notice of the registration. Also, the court in its discretion might have allowed the infringement to continue and required the infringer to pay a reasonable licensing fee.

Prior to 1978, a defective notice usually caused the loss of copyright protection because statutory copyright for published works was obtained by publication with copyright notice. If, for example, a year later than the year of first publication was placed in the notice, copyright protection was lost. There were exceptions, however. For example, the use of a year prior to that of first publication merely reduced the copyright term but did not invalidate the copyright. Also, if copyright notice was omitted from a relatively small number of copies, the copyright continued to be valid, but an innocent infringer would not have been liable for the infringement.

3 Copyright: Registration and Deposit

$\mathcal{A}$ll works may be registered with the Copyright Office, whether or not they have been published. Before 1978 some people would place manuscripts in a self-addressed envelope and send the envelope to themselves by registered mail. This was called "poor man's copyright" and was, quite frankly, of little value even before 1978. Today, it should never be done.

The Copyright Office is the official repository for copyright applications and all the useful and beneficial information (now on the Internet) contained therein. All works, whether published or unpublished, can be registered. The cost of registration is not great, and groups of works can be registered for one fee in many cases. The Office continues to liberalize its group registration rules. For example, new rules, effective in early 1996, will make it significantly easier to register groups of photographs.* There are substantial evidentiary and other benefits to registering a work with the Copyright Office.

Perhaps the only situation in which a self-help procedure would have some value would be in the case of an uncopyrightable work, which the Copyright Office refuses to register. Even in such a case, however, it would be better to have a notary, or other neutral third party, witness and keep documentation for the work, since any interested party holding the self-addressed envelope used in poor man's copyright is likely to be accused of tampering with evidence.

Choosing the Copyright Form

Form TX is the appropriate form to use for all non-dramatic literary works. A copy of Form TX appears on pages 44–45. This is a simple two-page form with step-by-step directions explaining how to fill it out.* Along with the appropriate form, the filing fee of twenty dollars and copies of the work being registered must be sent to the Copyright Office. The application form, copies of the work, and the fee should be mailed in one package, unless the writer doesn't have to include the fee because he or she maintains a deposit account with the Copyright Office. Periodicals or serial issues would be registered on Form SE. Works meant to be performed, such as songs, scripts, or plays, would be registered on Form PA.

Advantages of Registration

Registration is not necessary to gain copyright protection; under the current law that protection exists the moment a work is created. But registration does have the following important advantages: (1) the certificate of registration, if issued either before or within five years of first publication, is presumptive proof of the validity of the copyright and the facts stated on the copyright application; (2) registration must be made before an infringement commences in order for the copyright holder to be eligible to receive attorney's fees and "statutory" damages (a special kind of damages that a writer can elect to receive if actual damages are hard to prove), except that a published work registered within three months of publication would still qualify; (3) registration is necessary in order to bring a suit for infringement of copyright (unless the infringed work is protected under the Berne Convention and its country of origin is not the United States); and (4) with respect to works published from January 1, 1978 to March 1, 1989, registration cuts off certain defenses that an innocent infringer might be able to assert due to a defective copyright notice. It also protects against potential mitigation of damages.

While legislation was proposed a few years ago that would have eliminated the need for registration as a prerequisite to bringing an infringement lawsuit and as a requirement for eligibility to receive attorney's fees and statutory damages, this legislation was never enacted into law.

As mentioned, works originating in a Berne Union country other than the United States do not have to be registered prior to commencing a lawsuit for infringement. Because of the other advantages of registration, the copyright owners of such foreign works should still be inclined toward registration.

The effective date of registration is the day on which an acceptable application, deposit, and fee have all reached the Copyright Office.

To correct a mistake or amplify information contained in a completed registration, Form CA for supplementary registration is used. Form CA may only be submitted after a registration number has been obtained for the work.

Group Registration

A group registration of unpublished works can be made under a single title for a twenty-dollar registration fee. Registering an unpublished collection can sharply reduce the cost of registering each work in the collection (and no copyright notice need be placed on unpublished work). To qualify for such a group deposit, the following conditions have to be met: (1) the deposit materials are assembled in an orderly form; (2) the collection bears a single title identifying the work as a whole, such as "Collected Writing of Jane Writer, January, 1995"; (3) the person claiming copyright in each work forming part of the collection is also the person claiming copyright in the entire collection; and (4) all the works in the collection are by the same person or, if by different persons, at least one of them has contributed copyrightable material to each work in the collection.

There is no limit on the number of works which can be included in a collection. Also, the law specifically states that a work registered when unpublished need not be registered again when published. Of course, if new material is added to the work or it is transposed into a new medium, creating a substantial variation from the registered work, it would be desirable to register the work again to protect the changed version. In the event of litigation, it is important that the work deposited with the Copyright Office show all of the aspects protected by the copyright. Also, for any deposit with the Copyright Office, the deposit materials should not be likely to fade or alter with time.

But what if work has already been published in a number of magazines? The law specifically provides for group registration of contributions to periodicals and newspapers made by an writer during a twelve-month period, as long as each contribution has the same copyright claimant (and, if published before March 1, 1989, also had copyright notice in the name of the copyright claimant). In such a case, Form GR/CP is used as an addition to the basic application on Form TX. A copy of Form GR/CP appears on page 46.

The writer will want to register contributions, even if the periodical or newspaper is also registered by the owner of its copyright. The registration of the collective work by its owner will not confer the benefits of registration on each individual writer, since his or her copyright in the contribution is separate from the copyright in the collective work (although at least one case has held that the registration of a collective work did register a contribution contained therein). Also, if the writer is going to use Form GR/CP with Form TX, it would be wise to file every three months in order to be certain of qualifying for attorney's fees and statutory damages in the event of an infringement, as explained in the section on registration.

Deposit

With the registration form and fee, one complete copy of an unpublished work or two copies of a published work should be sent to the Copyright Office. If editions of differing quality have been published, the Copyright Office regulations provide guidelines to determine which edition is to be considered "the best edition." These guidelines are examined in Circular 7b, "'Best Edition' of Published Copyrighted Works for the Collections of the Library of Congress." For works first published outside of the United States, only one complete copy of the work need be deposited. If a work is published simultaneously in the United States and abroad, it is treated as if first published in the United States.

For registrations under the provision allowing group registrations for contributions to periodicals and newspapers, the deposit materials can be one copy of any of the following: (1) one complete copy of each periodical or section of a newspaper in which the work appeared; (2) the entire page containing the contribution; (3) the contribution clipped from the collective work; or (4) one photocopy of the contribution.

For a multimedia kit first published in the United States, the required deposit is one complete copy of the best edition. Circular 55, "Copyright Registration for Multimedia Works," discusses the variety of deposit requirements, as well as the appropriate applications forms, for the different combinations of works that may compose a multimedia kit.

The deposit for works fixed in CD-ROM format is one complete copy, which includes a copy of the disk, a copy of any accompanying operating software and instructional manual, and, if the work is in print as well as on the disk, a printed version of the work. All of these components should be provided, whether or not individually copyrightable.

Alternate Deposit

In certain situations, such as in the publication of limited editions or fine printings, it is possible to make an alternate deposit in place of a valuable copy of the actual work. Such deposit can save a great deal of money. A special request must be made to the Copyright Office for permission to submit identifying material rather than copies of the work. The Copyright Office will rule on requests for "special relief" on a case by case basis so a clear, written request is advisable.

Regardless of whether a work is published or unpublished, generally only one set of alternate deposit materials need be sent in. Combining this with the group deposit provisions, all the benefits of registration may be gained without great cost.

Deposit for the Library of Congress

In addition to depositing copies for copyright registration, copies also have to be deposited with the Library of Congress for works published in the United States on or after March 1, 1989 (or if the work was published with a copyright notice in the United States from January 1, 1978 to March 1, 1989). For a published work, the requirement of deposit for the Library of Congress can be satisfied simply by making the correct deposit for registration and sending in the application form and fee with the deposit within three months of publication. For works that have previously been registered as unpublished, within three months of publication two copies of the best edition of the work should be deposited for the Library of Congress.

However, many works will be exempt from deposit, including lectures, speeches, and addresses when published individually and not as a collection; contributions to collective works; greeting cards, picture postcards, and stationery; prints, labels, advertising catalogs, and other advertising matter published in connection with renting, leasing, lending, licensing, or selling merchandise, works of authorship, or services; and any works published only on jewelry, dolls, toys, plaques, floor coverings, wallpaper, textiles, and other fabrics, packaging, or other useful articles.

The requirement of deposit for the Library of Congress does not in any way affect the copyright protection already in effect. If, for example, a writer registered a work when unpublished and didn't bother to send in the required copies upon publication, the Register of Copyrights could request copies from the writer or his or her publisher to add to the collections of the Library of Congress. Only if the writer failed to comply with such a request within three months would he or she become liable for fines and other penalties. However, the copyright would remain valid.

Filling Out the Copyright Forms

The application forms have directions that are not difficult to follow. However, to simplify the process even further, here are some of the types of answers a writer would be most likely to give to the questions asked in the copyright forms. The assumption is that an individual author, working under his or her own name, created a work and now wants to register it.

1. Unpublished non-dramatic literary work. Use Form TX. SPACE 1: Fill in the title of the work and the nature of the work, such as fiction, non-fiction, poetry, textbook, advertising copy, or computer program. SPACE 2: Give the writer's name and indicate that the work is not a work for hire. Give the date of the writer's birth, indicate the appropriate country of his or her citizenship or permanent residence, and indicate that the work is neither anonymous nor written under a pseudonym. Where it says "Nature of Authorship," briefly explain the writer's particular contribution (such as "entire text"). SPACE 3: For an unpublished work give the year the work was finished; leave blank the date and nation of first publication. SPACE 4: The writer's name and address should be shown for the copyright claimant. A claimant is either the writer or an owner of *all* rights (who obtained rights from the writer); it is *not* a licensee or an owner of some but not all exclusive rights. SPACE 5: Answer *no*, as the writer will not have previously registered the work. A *yes* answer would be appropriate if the writer were adding new material to work that had been previously registered, in which case the appropriate box should be checked. SPACE 6: If the writer has added new material to a previously registered work, explain what material the writer added to the old work to make a derivative work (i.e., "new text" or "revisions"). The writer's registration would then protect the new elements of the derivative work. SPACE 7: Fill in the information about a deposit account if the writer has one. Also, give the writer's name and address for correspondence purposes. SPACE 8: Check the box for author, sign your name, and then print or type it. SPACE 9: Enter the writer's name and address so that the certificate of registration will be mailed to the writer.
2. Group registration for unpublished non-dramatic literary works. Use Form TX, filling it out exactly as for an unpublished non-dramatic literary work, except for the changes shown here. SPACE 1: The collection must have its own title, and it is that title which is used here. SPACE 3: The year in which creation of the work was completed is the year in which the most recently completed work contained in the collection was completed.
3. Published non-dramatic literary works. Use Form TX, filling it

out exactly as for an unpublished non-dramatic literary work, except for the changes shown here. SPACE 3: In addition to giving the date of creation, give the date and nation of first publication of the work.

4. Group registration of published contributions to periodicals. Use Form TX if the contributions are non-dramatic literary works, along with the adjunct Form GR/CP. To qualify, the contributions must meet the criteria listed on page 39. Form TX is filled out exactly as for a published non-dramatic literary work, except for the changes shown here. SPACE 1: In the space for the title, write "See Form GR/CP, attached" and leave the other parts of Space 1 blank. SPACE 3: Give the year of creation of the last work completed and leave blank the date and nation of first publication.

   Then fill out Form GR/CP. SPACE A: Mark Form TX as the basic application and give the writer's name as both writer and copyright claimant. SPACE B: For each box, fill in the requested information about the title of the contribution, the title of and other information about the periodical, and the date and nation of first publication. Mail Form GR/CP with Form TX, the deposit copies, and the filing fee.

5. Unpublished works of the performing arts, which include works prepared to be performed for an audience that is physically present at the performance and also works delivered indirectly to an audience by means of a device or process. Use Form PA. This is filled out in essentially the same way as for an unpublished non-dramatic work.

6. Published works of the performing arts. Use Form PA. This is filled out essentially the same way as for a published non-dramatic literary work.

FORM TX
For a Literary Work
UNITED STATES COPYRIGHT OFFICE

REGISTRATION NUMBER

_____

TX _____ TXU _____

EFFECTIVE DATE OF REGISTRATION

_____

Month _____ Day _____ Year _____

DO NOT WRITE ABOVE THIS LINE. IF YOU NEED MORE SPACE, USE A SEPARATE CONTINUATION SHEET.

1

TITLE OF THIS WORK ▼

_____

PREVIOUS OR ALTERNATIVE TITLES ▼

_____

PUBLICATION AS A CONTRIBUTION If this work was published as a contribution to a periodical, serial, or collection, give information about the collective work in which the contribution appeared. **Title of Collective Work ▼**

_____

If published in a periodical or serial give: **Volume ▼** **Number ▼** **Issue Date ▼** **On Pages ▼**

2 a

NAME OF AUTHOR ▼

DATES OF BIRTH AND DEATH
Year Born ▼   Year Died ▼

Was this contribution to the work a "work made for hire"?
☐ Yes
☐ No

AUTHOR'S NATIONALITY OR DOMICILE
Name of Country
OR { Citizen of ▶_____
Domiciled in ▶_____

WAS THIS AUTHOR'S CONTRIBUTION TO THE WORK
Anonymous?   ☐ Yes ☐ No
Pseudonymous? ☐ Yes ☐ No

If the answer to either of these questions is "Yes," see detailed instructions.

NATURE OF AUTHORSHIP Briefly describe nature of material created by this author in which copyright is claimed. ▼

NOTE

Under the law, the "author" of a "work made for hire" is generally the employer, not the employee (see instructions). For any part of this work that was "made for hire" check "Yes" in the space provided, give the employer (or other person for whom the work was prepared) as "Author" of that part, and leave the space for dates of birth and death blank.

b

NAME OF AUTHOR ▼

DATES OF BIRTH AND DEATH
Year Born ▼   Year Died ▼

Was this contribution to the work a "work made for hire"?
☐ Yes
☐ No

AUTHOR'S NATIONALITY OR DOMICILE
Name of Country
OR { Citizen of ▶_____
Domiciled in ▶_____

WAS THIS AUTHOR'S CONTRIBUTION TO THE WORK
Anonymous?   ☐ Yes ☐ No
Pseudonymous? ☐ Yes ☐ No

If the answer to either of these questions is "Yes," see detailed instructions.

NATURE OF AUTHORSHIP Briefly describe nature of material created by this author in which copyright is claimed. ▼

c

NAME OF AUTHOR ▼

DATES OF BIRTH AND DEATH
Year Born ▼   Year Died ▼

Was this contribution to the work a "work made for hire"?
☐ Yes
☐ No

AUTHOR'S NATIONALITY OR DOMICILE
Name of Country
OR { Citizen of ▶_____
Domiciled in ▶_____

WAS THIS AUTHOR'S CONTRIBUTION TO THE WORK
Anonymous?   ☐ Yes ☐ No
Pseudonymous? ☐ Yes ☐ No

If the answer to either of these questions is "Yes," see detailed instructions.

NATURE OF AUTHORSHIP Briefly describe nature of material created by this author in which copyright is claimed. ▼

3 a

YEAR IN WHICH CREATION OF THIS WORK WAS COMPLETED This information must be given ◀Year in all cases.

b

DATE AND NATION OF FIRST PUBLICATION OF THIS PARTICULAR WORK
Complete this information ONLY if this work has been published.
Month ▶ _____ Day ▶ _____ Year ▶ _____ ◀ Nation

4

See instructions before completing this space.

COPYRIGHT CLAIMANT(S) Name and address must be given even if the claimant is the same as the author given in space 2. ▼

TRANSFER If the claimant(s) named here in space 4 is (are) different from the author(s) named in space 2, give a brief statement of how the claimant(s) obtained ownership of the copyright. ▼

DO NOT WRITE HERE OFFICE USE ONLY

APPLICATION RECEIVED

ONE DEPOSIT RECEIVED

TWO DEPOSITS RECEIVED

FUNDS RECEIVED

MORE ON BACK ▶ • Complete all applicable spaces (numbers 5-11) on the reverse side of this page.
• See detailed instructions. • Sign the form at line 10.

DO NOT WRITE HERE
Page 1 of _____ pages

EXAMINED BY	FORM TX
CHECKED BY	
☐ CORRESPONDENCE ☐ Yes	FOR COPYRIGHT OFFICE USE ONLY

DO NOT WRITE ABOVE THIS LINE. IF YOU NEED MORE SPACE, USE A SEPARATE CONTINUATION SHEET.

PREVIOUS REGISTRATION Has registration for this work, or for an earlier version of this work, already been made in the Copyright Office?
☐ Yes ☐ No If your answer is "Yes," why is another registration being sought? (Check appropriate box) ▼
a. ☐ This is the first published edition of a work previously registered in unpublished form.
b. ☐ This is the first application submitted by this author as copyright claimant.
c. ☐ This is a changed version of the work, as shown by space 6 on this application.
If your answer is "Yes," give: **Previous Registration Number** ▼   **Year of Registration** ▼

5

DERIVATIVE WORK OR COMPILATION Complete both space 6a and 6b for a derivative work; complete only 6b for a compilation.
a. Preexisting Material Identify any preexisting work or works that this work is based on or incorporates. ▼

b. Material Added to This Work Give a brief, general statement of the material that has been added to this work and in which copyright is claimed. ▼

6

See instructions before completing this space.

—space deleted—

7

REPRODUCTION FOR USE OF BLIND OR PHYSICALLY HANDICAPPED INDIVIDUALS A signature on this form at space 10 and a check in one of the boxes here in space 8 constitutes a non-exclusive grant of permission to the Library of Congress to reproduce and distribute solely for the blind and physically handicapped and under the conditions and limitations prescribed by the regulations of the Copyright Office: (1) copies of the work identified in space 1 of this application in Braille (or similar tactile symbols); or (2) phonorecords embodying a fixation of a reading of that work; or (3) both.

a ☐ Copies and Phonorecords   b ☐ Copies Only   c ☐ Phonorecords Only

8

See instructions.

DEPOSIT ACCOUNT If the registration fee is to be charged to a Deposit Account established in the Copyright Office, give name and number of Account.
Name ▼   **Account Number** ▼

CORRESPONDENCE Give name and address to which correspondence about this application should be sent.   Name/Address/Apt/City/State/ZIP ▼

9

Area Code and Telephone Number ▶

Be sure to give your daytime phone ◀ number

CERTIFICATION* I, the undersigned, hereby certify that I am the
Check only one ▶
{
☐ author
☐ other copyright claimant
☐ owner of exclusive right(s)
☐ authorized agent of _____
}
of the work identified in this application and that the statements made by me in this application are correct to the best of my knowledge.
Name of author or other copyright claimant, or owner of exclusive right(s) ▲

Typed or printed name and date ▼ If this application gives a date of publication in space 3, do not sign and submit it before that date.
_____   Date ▶ _____

☞ Handwritten signature (X) ▼

10

MAIL CERTIFI-CATE TO

Certificate will be mailed in window envelope

Name ▼

Number/Street/Apt ▼

City/State/ZIP ▼

YOU MUST:
• Complete all necessary spaces
• Sign your application in space 10
SEND ALL 3 ELEMENTS IN THE SAME PACKAGE:
1. Application form
2. Nonrefundable $20 filing fee in check or money order payable to *Register of Copyrights*
3. Deposit material
MAIL TO:
Register of Copyrights
Library of Congress
Washington, D.C. 20559-6000

11

*17 U.S.C. § 506(e): Any person who knowingly makes a false representation of a material fact in the application for copyright registration provided for by section 409, or in any written statement filed in connection with the application, shall be fined not more than $2,500.

May 1995—300,000   ♻ PRINTED ON RECYCLED PAPER   ☆U.S. GOVERNMENT PRINTING OFFICE: 1995-387-237/47

ADJUNCT APPLICATION
for Copyright Registration for a Group of Contributions to Periodicals

 **FORM GR/CP**

UNITED STATES COPYRIGHT OFFICE

- Use this adjunct form only if you are making a single registration for a group of contributions to periodicals, and you are also filing a basic application on Form TX, Form PA, or Form VA. Follow the instructions, attached.

- Number each line in Part B consecutively. Use additional Forms GR/CP if you need more space.

- Submit this adjunct form with the basic application form. Clip (do not tape or staple) and fold all sheets together before submitting them.

REGISTRATION NUMBER		
TX	PA	VA

EFFECTIVE DATE OF REGISTRATION

. . . .
(Month)   (Day)   (Year)

FORM GR/CP RECEIVED

Page _____ of _____ pages

DO NOT WRITE ABOVE THIS LINE. FOR COPYRIGHT OFFICE USE ONLY

(A)

Identification of Application

IDENTIFICATION OF BASIC APPLICATION:
● This application for copyright registration for a group of contributions to periodicals is submitted as an adjunct to an application filed on: (Check which)

☐ Form TX   ☐ Form PA   ☐ Form VA

IDENTIFICATION OF AUTHOR AND CLAIMANT: (Give the name of the author and the name of the copyright claimant in all of the contributions listed in Part B of this form. The names should be the same as the names given in spaces 2 and 4 of the basic application.)

Name of Author: . . . .

Name of Copyright Claimant: . . . .

(B)

Registration for Group of Contributions

COPYRIGHT REGISTRATION FOR A GROUP OF CONTRIBUTIONS TO PERIODICALS: (To make a single registration for a group of works by the same individual author, all first published as contributions to periodicals within a 12-month period (see instructions), give full information about each contribution. If more space in needed, use additional Forms GR/CP.)

☐
Title of Contribution: . . . .
Title of Periodical: . . . . Vol. . . . . . No. . . . . Issue Date . . . . Pages . . . . . .
Date of First Publication: . . . . Nation of First Publication . . . .
(Month) (Day) (Year)   (Country)

☐
Title of Contribution: . . . .
Title of Periodical: . . . . Vol. . . . . . No. . . . . Issue Date . . . . Pages . . . . . .
Date of First Publication: . . . . Nation of First Publication . . . .
(Month) (Day) (Year)   (Country)

☐
Title of Contribution: . . . .
Title of Periodical: . . . . Vol. . . . . . No. . . . . Issue Date . . . . Pages . . . . . .
Date of First Publication: . . . . Nation of First Publication . . . .
(Month) (Day) (Year)   (Country)

☐
Title of Contribution: . . . .
Title of Periodical: . . . . Vol. . . . . . No. . . . . Issue Date . . . . Pages . . . . . .
Date of First Publication: . . . . Nation of First Publication . . . .
(Month) (Day) (Year)   (Country)

☐
Title of Contribution: . . . .
Title of Periodical: . . . . Vol. . . . . . No. . . . . Issue Date . . . . Pages . . . . . .
Date of First Publication: . . . . Nation of First Publication . . . .
(Month) (Day) (Year)   (Country)

☐
Title of Contribution: . . . .
Title of Periodical: . . . . Vol. . . . . . No. . . . . Issue Date . . . . Pages . . . . . .
Date of First Publication: . . . . Nation of First Publication . . . .
(Month) (Day) (Year)   (Country)

☐
Title of Contribution: . . . .
Title of Periodical: . . . . Vol. . . . . . No. . . . . Issue Date . . . . Pages . . . . . .
Date of First Publication: . . . . Nation of First Publication . . . .
(Month) (Day) (Year)   (Country)

4 Copyright: Works for Hire and Joint Works

$\mathcal{T}$he copyright law gives the copyright to the writer of the work. However, both works for hire and joint works present potential pitfalls by raising questions as to who is the author.

Under Section 101 of the Copyright Act of 1976, a work made for hire can come into being under two clauses: (1) an employee creating copyrightable work in the course of his or her employment, or (2) certain specially ordered or commissioned works, if both parties sign a contract agreeing it is work for hire. When a writer does work for hire, the employer or other commissioning party owns the copyright in the work as if they, in fact, created the work. This means that the writer does not even have the ability to get the rights back by termination after thirty-five years, because there was no transfer initially. Also, if a writer were to copy all or part of a work that he or she had done as work for hire, the writer would be an infringer.

Because of the detrimental "work for hire" consequences under the Copyright Act, writers should be extremely careful about the work they do on assignment.

The Copyright Office offers information about work for hire in Circular 9, "Works-Made-for-Hire Under the 1976 Copyright Act."

A joint work is a work prepared by two or more writers with the intention, at the time the work is created, that their contributions be merged into inseparable or interdependent parts of a unitary whole. If, for example, an editor commissioning an article were to contend that he or she were a joint author with a writer, the writer would risk loss of control over the work. Each co-author of a joint work is free to license it, although royalties are shared by both co-authors. Co-authors own equal shares in a work (in the absence of a contract), regardless of who did the majority of the work.

This chapter discusses works for hire, joint works, community property, and a reform proposal.

Who Is an Employee for Work for Hire?

If an employee creates copyrightable work in the course of his or her employment, the employer will be treated as the creator of the work, the writer, and the owner of the copyright. But what makes a person fit the definition of an employee? Someone who is paid a salary for working from 9:00 A.M. to 5:00 P.M., Monday through Friday, under the control, direction, and supervision of an employer and at that employer's office is certainly an employee. This type of employee will have state and federal tax payments withheld from the weekly paycheck and receive any benefits to which employees are entitled.

What if the writer is a freelancer who receives an assignment and executes it in his or her home office? This writer is unlikely to be viewed as an employee, although court cases have considered a variety of additional factors in determining who is an employee for copyright purposes.

In the 1980s, a writer working under the direction and supervision of an employer, creating a work at the "instance and expense" of an employer or where the employer was the motivating factor for the work, might lose copyright in his or her creations. Many courts had adopted the now discredited rationale that, when the commissioning party exercises sufficient control and direction, the writer becomes an employee for purposes of copyright. A split between federal appellate courts over the issue of work for hire finally led to the 1989 Supreme Court decision in *Community for Creative Non-Violence v. Reid* (490 U.S. 730).* This was an unusual case and with a unique cast of characters. James Earl Reid, a Baltimore sculptor, was commissioned to create a sculpture for the Community for Creative Non-Violence (referred to as "CCNV"), a Washington, D.C., group that helps the homeless. The idea was conceived by the late Mitch Snyder, the founder of CCNV, who wanted a modern Nativity scene with the Holy Family replaced by two adults and an infant who are homeless. Titled *Third World America*, the tableau was set on a steam grate with a legend reading "And Still There Is No Room At The Inn."

Reid executed the sculpture without a fee, receiving payment only for his expenses. CCNV built the pedestal in the form of the steam grate and gave ideas as the work progressed (such as insisting that the family have their belongings in a shopping cart rather than bags or suitcases). After the work was finished, a dispute arose over ownership of the copyright when CCNV wanted to take the sculpture on tour. No written contract had been signed between the parties.

In an important victory for all creators, the Court decided that whether someone is an employee must be decided under the law of agency. Under the law of agency one factor is "the hiring party's right to control the manner and means by which the product is accomplished." However, the Court went on to state:

> Among the other factors relevant to this inquiry are the skill required; the source of the instrumentalities and tools; the location of the work; the education of the relationship between the parties; whether the hiring party has the right to assign additional projects to the hired party; the extent of the hired party's discretion over when and how long to work; the method of payment; the hired party's role in hiring and paying assistants; whether the work is part of the regular business of the hiring party; whether the hiring party is in business; the provision of employee benefits; and the tax treatment of the hired party.

Based on these factors, it is unlikely that a freelance writer working on an assignment for a magazine, newspaper, or publisher will be found to be an employee in the absence of a contract as discussed in the next section.

Specially Commissioned or Ordered Works

For freelance writers to create a work for hire under current law, an assignment would have to fall under clause 2 of the work for hire definition. With respect to specially commissioned or ordered works, the parties must agree in writing that the work is work for hire, both parties must sign the contract, and the work must fall into one of the following nine categories:
- a contribution to a collective work, such as a magazine, newspaper, encyclopedia, or anthology;
- a contribution used as part of a motion picture or other audiovisual work;
- a translation;

- a compilation, which is a work formed by collecting and assembling preexisting materials or data;
- an instructional text;
- a test;
- answer material for a test;
- an atlas;
- and a supplementary work, defined as a work used to supplement a work by another author for such purposes as illustrating, explaining, or assisting generally in the use of the writer's work. Examples of supplementary works are forewords, afterwards, pictorial illustrations, maps, charts, tables, editorial notes, appendixes, and indexes.

In a later case, an advertising company that created a flyer for another company was deemed an independent contractor because the drafting was accomplished in the advertising company's own offices with its own tools and materials. Hired for a limited amount of time, the company made its own scheduling decisions, exercised discretion when dealing with its own employees, paid its own taxes, withheld payroll taxes from its employees, and could only have been assigned an additional job by entering into a new contract (*M.G.B. Homes, Inc. v. Ameron Homes, Inc.*, 903 F.2d 1486).

Another case simplified the CCNV test by eliminating several of the factors. It spelled out a five-factor inquiry: (1) the hiring party's right to control the manner and means of creation; (2) the skill required; (3) provision of employee benefits; (4) tax treatment of the hired party; and (5) whether the hiring party has the right to assign additional projects to the hired party (*Aymes v. Bonelli*, 980 F.2d 857).

The crucial point is that unless the writer agrees in writing that a work is for hire, then the work is not made for hire unless the writer is treated as an employee under clause 1. Since it is not clear whether other language can be used in place of the phrase "work for hire," writers should also refuse to sign anything with language in it that sounds similar to "work for hire" or an employment-type relationship.

Also, if a writer does a specially ordered or commissioned work that is outside of the categories shown above, it cannot be a work for hire (unless the writer is treated as an employee).* If work is created independently and submitted in final form to a potential buyer, the work-for-hire problem should not arise. But, even here, caution dictates that, in order to avoid confusion, the writer not sign anything indicating that the work is to be for hire.

Of course, in some cases a writer may be perfectly willing to work under an agreement specifying that work in one of the enumerated categories will be work for hire. In that case, it is important that the writer be aware that he or she is not the author of the work—the party commissioning or ordering the work is. They will own the copyright completely, so that it cannot be terminated after thirty-five years. This complete ownership is, therefore, even more than the transfer of "all rights" in a copyright. With this in mind, the writer should consider carefully what to charge for such work. The greater the right of usage the other party gets, the more they should pay for it.

The courts are divided as to whether the requisite writing must precede the creation of the work or can memorialize, after the fact, the intentions of the parties (compare *Schiller & Schmidt, Inc. v. Nordisco Corporation et al.*, 969 F.2d 410, *aff'd in part, vacated in part, and remanded* by the Seventh Circuit in Nos. 91-2195 and 91-2781, with *Playboy Enterprises, Inc. v. Dumas*, 831 F. Supp. 295, *aff'd in part, rev'd in part, vacated in part, and remanded* by the Second Circuit in Nos. 94-7500L and 94-7452XAP). The writer should be careful not to accept a check with an endorsement specifying that the payment is for a work for hire. In fact, the writer should clarify all contractual arrangements before starting work and should insist that any endorsement on a check be in conformity with those understandings.

Joint Works

After the work for hire decision favoring creators in *CCNV*, and the restrictions it placed upon the right of a commissioning party to claim that a work was done as a work for hire, commissioning parties may assert joint authorship with the writer. This would mean that they would jointly own the copyright. Each party would be able to license nonexclusive usage of the work without asking the permission of the other. Any money received from this licensing would have to be equally shared (regardless of whether the creative contribution was equal). However, to sell any exclusive license, all joint authors must sign a written authorization.

Why wouldn't a commissioning party obtain a written transfer explicitly setting forth the rights of copyright needed to exploit the work? Certainly this should be done. However, the decision in *CCNV* has presented a chaos factor for corporate counsels. From 1984 through 1989, many companies relied on their right to supervise a commissioned work as creating work for hire. After *CCNV*, however, it is clear that this reliance was misplaced. Without a written contract, companies may have already infringed a commissioned work by additional usage or, if this is not the case, may wish to make additional usage but feel uncertain whether this is permissible. If the commissioned works were joint works, the company would not be an infringer if it used the work, but would have to account to the other joint author and share any profits earned from the usage.

Whether or not a work is a joint work will turn on whether the writers intended their contributions to be merged into inseparable or interdependent parts of a unitary whole at the time the work was created. Since writers often fail to take the precaution of a written agreement, the intention of the parties working together on a project may be difficult to ascertain. Similarly, the words "inseparable" or "interdependent" will often prove difficult to define.

Before these issues can be resolved, each party must contribute copyrightable subject matter. Each party must be an author. Ideas are not copyrightable; only the original expression of an idea qualifies. The idea to do a statue of a modern Nativity scene showing two adults and a child as homeless people huddled on a steam grate is not copyrightable. Reid sculpted everything but the steam grate which was supplied by CCNV (with some input from Reid). The steam grate was built by a cabinet maker and the steam was supplied by using special effects equipment from Hollywood.

There is no doubt that Reid contributed sufficient expression to make his sculpture copyrightable. But did CCNV? If the steam grate is not copyrightable, then CCNV could not claim joint authorship. Even if the steam grate is copyrightable, the issues of intention and merger into an interdependent work would still have to be addressed. While observing that the record lacked sufficient facts to decide this issue, the Court of Appeals stated that the case:

> ... might qualify as a textbook example of a jointly-authored work in which the joint authors co-own the copyright. ... CCNV's contribution to the steam grate pedestal added to its initial conceptualization and ongoing direction of the realization of "Third World America"; and the various indicia of the parties' intent, from the outset, to merge their contributions into a unitary whole, and not to construct and separately preserve discrete parts as independent works.

The United States Supreme Court sent this issue back to the federal district court for further factual findings. In a judgment to which both parties consented, the court ordered that Reid be recognized as the sole author of *Third World America*. However, CCNV was made the sole owner of the original copy of the works and all copyrights in that original. Reid was given the copyright with respect to three-dimensional reproductions, while both CCNV and Reid were given the right to make and sell two-dimensional reproductions without sharing any revenues earned with the other party. Other restrictions on the manner of portrayal of the sculpture in reproductions, authorship credit, use of the steam grate, and use of the inscription, "And Still There Is No Room At The Inn," were also part of the compromise.

The settlement avoided a showdown on the issue of what constitutes a joint work. It also offered an artful illustration of how a copyright can be subdivided between parties with differing or competing interests. With this settlement, *CCNV* is no longer an active case but rather a landmark in copyright history (although one further round of litigation was necessary for Reid to gain temporary possession of the sculpture so he could make the master mold necessary for him to benefit from his three-dimensional reproduction rights). What is difficult to accept, however, is that so little creativity might qualify CCNV as a joint author. Certainly, the artistry of the sculpture is far greater than any artistry present in the pedestal. If Reid and CCNV had been found to be joint authors, each would have had the right to license usage of the work and be entitled to 50 percent of any income, despite the disparity of their artistic contributions.

A number of joint work cases have recently come before the courts, but there is one that is consistently cited and followed. In that case, the defendant performed independent, historical research in order to write a play but then hired the plaintiff to help out for a fee. They discussed the play and the scenes together, but the plaintiff actually wrote the majority of the script. Later, the defendant wrote her own script on the same subject and the plaintiff claimed that the subsequent script infringed the copyright of the first.

When the defendant claimed to be a joint author of the first script, the lower court, and the Second Circuit on appeal, held that the defendant could not be a joint author because she had contributed only general ideas and research, neither of which are copyrightable. While several scholars, such as Professor David Nimmer, have contended that independent copyrightability of contribution need not be present, the so-called Childress Rule is steadily gaining momentum (*Childress v. Taylor*, 945 F.2d 500). Courts have held that although the contribution must be copyrightable, it need not be qualitatively or quantitatively equal.

Joint works in the realm of computer programs were dealt with in a recent case. The court concluded that a user interface for a spreadsheet program had not become a joint work. It noted that: "Even though this issue is not completely settled in the case law, our circuit holds that joint authorship requires each author to make an independently copyrightable contribution." So the defendant's contribution of ideas for the interface did not make him a co-owner or make the interface a joint work, since ideas are not copyrightable (*Ashton-Tate Corporation v. Ross and Bravo*, 916 F.2d 516).

Writers who wish to avoid the pitfalls of works for hire or joint works can do so by finalizing contracts before work is commenced.*

Community Property

Community property laws have been adopted by nine states— Arizona, California, Idaho, Louisiana, Nevada, New Mexico, Texas, Washington, and Wisconsin. While there are variations from state to state, community property laws make both spouses the owners of property acquired during the marriage (with some exceptions, such as gifts or bequests). The question naturally arises as to whether copyrights created during a marriage are community property in these states.

A California case raised this issue for the first time, when a husband argued that books he wrote during the marriage were not community property. The court wrote:

> Our analysis begins with the general proposition that all property acquired during marriage is community property. Thus, there seems little doubt that any artistic work created during the marriage constitutes community property. . . . Since the copyrights derived from the literary efforts, time and skill of husband during the marriage, such copyrights and related tangible benefits must be considered community property (*In re Worth*, 241 Cal. App.3d 768).

The court rejected the argument that the federal copyright law, which vests copyright in the author (rather than in the author and the author's spouse), would preempt the state community property law. While *In re Worth* can hardly be definitive, and other state or federal courts may take a different view, it certainly seems that copyrights are likely to be considered community property. This case leaves unresolved such matters as who has the right to renew a copyright or terminate a grant of rights once a copyright is designated community property. These and other complex issues are explored in "Copyright Ownership by the Marital Community: Evaluating Worth," by David Nimmer (36 UCLA Law Review 383).

A Proposal for Reform

Throughout the 1980s, the Copyright Justice Coalition sought to reform the copyright law with respect to works for hire and joint works. As this book goes to press, no bill is currently pending to amend the law and protect writers and other creators. After expending so much effort, creators' groups have accepted, for the moment, the reality that reform will be immensely difficult to achieve. This is true despite hearings before a Senate subcommittee in 1982 and 1989 that documented widespread abuses with respect to work for hire.

In the hope that these reform efforts will be revived, this chapter concludes with a brief discussion of what must be included in any bill to reform the law. These proposals are drawn from the best versions of the bills that Tad Crawford authored on behalf of the Graphic Artists Guild and the American Society of Media Photographers, before the inevitable negotiation and compromise in the legislative process diluted the effectiveness of the proposed safeguards.

With respect to clause 1, an "employee" should be defined as a "formal salaried employee." This would be even more restrictive than the agency test adopted by the Supreme Court in *Community for Creative Non-Violence v. Reid*, since employees would have to receive a salary and employee benefits.

With respect to clause 2, certain categories should be deleted from those types of assignments that can be done as work for hire by a freelancer. The categories deleted should include all those in which visual creators are most likely to work: (1) contributions to collective works; (2) parts of audiovisual works (but not parts of motion pictures); (3) instructional texts; and (4) supplementary works.

If no more were done than to remove these categories from those which can be work for hire, undoubtedly "all rights" contracts would immediately become standard for publishers in place of work for hire. Safeguards need to be provided against the indiscriminate use of all rights transfers in the categories being removed from work for hire. This saves the writer from being cut off from the future stream of residual income that each work potentially represents.

Existing law has a presumption as to what rights are acquired in a contribution to a collective work if no explicit agreement has been reached between the parties. This presumption could be extended to cover parts of audiovisual works (excluding motion pictures), instructional texts, and supplementary works. Under the presumption, a publisher licenses writing in these categories only for use in a particular larger work, such as a book, any revision of that larger work, and any work in the same series as the original larger work, unless an explicit agreement has been reached between the parties as to a different transfer of rights.

With respect to works commissioned from freelancers, any written work-for-hire contract should have to be obtained before the commencement of work and such a written contract should be required for each assignment.

The situation regarding joint works should be clarified by requiring that each writer make an original, copyrightable contribution and that the parties agree in writing if they intend a work to be a joint work.

Finally, particularly to assist visual artists, such a bill should also provide that the sale of a right of copyright does not transfer ownership of any original art unless such originals are transferred in writing. Several states, including New York and California, have enacted such legislation regarding ownership of originals when reproduction rights are sold.

Of course, these reform proposals have not been enacted, so discussing them here may simply extend the futile efforts that began in 1978. On the other hand, the legislative campaigns of the creators' organizations have helped to educate a generation of writers about the ethics of the creative business. Beyond this, who can say that future champions of reform will not be more effective in ensuring that creativity is protected and rewarded in the way that the Founding Fathers so clearly intended when they enshrined copyright in our Constitution.

5 Copyright: Infringement, Fair Use & Permissions

*I*f someone uses a work without the copyright owner's permission, that person is an infringer (subject to some exceptions, particularly that for fair use). To win an infringement suit, the writer must prove that he or she owned the copyright and that the work was copied by the infringer. Copying is often inferred from the infringer's access to a work and the substantial similarity of the work alleged to be infringing.

The Test for Infringement

The plaintiff in an infringement suit must prove that he or she owned the copyright, or at least one divisible right thereof, and that the work was copied by the infringer. If registration occurs within five years of first publication of the work, the certificate of registration serves as prima facie evidence of the validity of the copyright and the facts stated on the registration certificate. Because copyright protects against reproduction, but not against independent generation of the same or similar work, there can be no infringement unless the defendant came into contact with and in fact copied the plaintiff's work (although subconscious copying of a work can constitute infringement). Copying is therefore inferred from the defendant's access to a work and the substantial similarity of the work alleged to be infringing. The standard for judging substantial similarity is whether an ordinary observer, looking at the original work and the work allegedly copied from it, recognizes that a copying has taken place.

In some cases access is easy to prove. For example, if the plaintiff's book was on the best-seller list, widely reviewed, made into a Broadway play or a Hollywood movie, it would be difficult to argue that a defendant living in the United States at the time did not have access to the copyrighted work. Or, if the plaintiff could prove that he or she had submitted a book to a publisher, or a song to a band, that would be sufficient to show access. In practice, however, it is often difficult to prove access. As a result, courts are sometimes willing to infer access from a finding of striking similarity, where the similarities are so readily apparent that they can only be explained by copying, rather than by independent creation, or prior common source. The more common result, however, is that courts will evaluate even striking similarity in light of other available facts.

Substantial Similarity

In an early justification of the substantial similarity test, one court held that copyright protection for literary works was not limited to protecting merely the literal text of the work. Every work can be abstracted on several levels. These abstractions range from the most general statement of what the work is about to the very specific reproduction of the work. Between these series of abstractions lies the boundary between uncopyrightable ideas and their copyrightable expression. As the court noted:

> Upon any work, and especially upon a play, a great number of patterns of increasing generality will fit equally well, as more and more of the incident is left out. The last may perhaps be no more than the most general statement of what the play is about, and at times might consist of only its title; but there is a point in this series of abstractions where they are no longer protected, since otherwise the playwright could prevent the use of his "ideas," to which, apart from their expression, his property is never extended (*Nichols v. Universal Pictures Co.*, 45 F.2d 119).

Altering some parts of the original work will not avoid an infringement when application of the ordinary observer test leads to the conclusion that more than a trivial amount of the original work has been copied. As a result, altering 10, 25, or even 75 percent of a work may very well not avoid an infringement.

The ordinary observer test has undergone some refinement due to the increasing complexity of certain copyrightable works. Courts increasingly allow expert testimony on the issue of the intended audience on the theory that common sense requires that, where a narrow group and not the lay public is the intended audience, the court's inquiry into substantial similarity should focus on those with expertise in the relevant field (*Dawson v. Hinsaw Music Inc.*, 905 F.2d 731, *cert. denied*, 111 S. Ct. 511).

Damages for Infringement

The owner of a copyright, or any of the exclusive rights in a copyright, can recover his or her actual damages, plus any profits made by the infringer that accrued as a result of the infringement and are not included in the computation of actual damages. If a writer is going to have trouble proving actual damages, the court can be asked to award statutory damages (assuming the writer qualifies for statutory damages as explained in chapter 3 on registration). Statutory damages are an amount between $500 and $20,000 awarded in the court's discretion for each work infringed. These damages may be lowered, at the discretion of the court, to as little as $200 if the infringer shows the infringement was innocent, for example where there is insufficient copyright notice, or increased to not more than $100,000 if the copyright owner shows the infringement was willful.

Statutory damages will not be awarded for infringement of an unpublished work which was not registered at the time the infringement commenced. Such damages will also not be awarded for an infringement that took place after publication but before registration, except where registration is completed within three months of publication.

In addition to damages, the copyright act specifically provides for injunctions to prevent additional infringements, impounding and disposition or destruction of infringing articles (including stopping the importation of and seizing infringing copies at Customs), criminal penalties, awards for discretionary court costs, and reasonable attorney's fees (if the writer qualifies for attorney's fees as explained in chapter 3 on registration). Since attorney's fees can be substantial, sometimes wiping out awards entirely, this is major inducement to register copyrights and to register early. Injunctions, for example a court order that a publishing company can no longer distribute and sell copies of a particular book, will often be granted when the plaintiff will otherwise suffer irreparable injury. They can be granted either before the resolution of a case (a preliminary injunction) or as part of the disposition of a case (a permanent injunction) and are enforceable anywhere in the United States.

Willful copyright infringement can also result in criminal penalties, including fines of up to $100,000, imprisonment for up to one year, or both, for each act of infringement (and for certain traffickers, up to $250,000 or five years imprisonment).

Prior to March 1, 1989, one advantage of having copyright notice appear in the writer's own name with the contribution to a collective work was that such notice limited the defense of innocent infringement. Such an innocent infringer might be a person who reprinted the work because he or she obtained permission from the owner of the copyright in the collective work without knowing that the writer actually owned the rights. Copyright notice in the writer's name would cut off this defense, since such notice would warn the infringer to contact the writer for permission. Registration of the contribution, by the way, would also cut off this defense. Of course, even if the innocent infringer had a defense, the magazine or other collective work would have had to pay back to the writer whatever had been received by wrongfully selling reprint rights in the contribution. In general, copyright notice in the writer's name alerts third parties that they should go directly to the writer for reprint rights and not deal with the owner of the collective work.

The statute of limitations for a copyright infringement claim is three years from the time the claim accrued. This means that plaintiffs are barred from suing infringers who have been able to elude detection for that period of time, except that the statute is "tolled," which means extended, in certain cases. For example, this tolling occurs if the defendant fraudulently concealed the infringement or, in some jurisdictions, if the copyright owner could not, in the exercise of reasonable care and diligence, have discovered the infringement. Courts differ on the issue of how to apply the statute of limitations. Some strictly invoke the theory that the statute of limitations does not begin to run until all aspects of a continuing wrong are completed, while others separate the infringing acts for purposes of ascertaining damages, allowing relief only for acts occurring within a three-year window of the last infringement.

Who Is Liable for Infringement

Everyone knows that an important reason to incorporate, often the paramount reason, is limited liability. The corporation is liable for debts or damages from lawsuits, but the individual shareholders are not. Yet the limited liability normally provided by corporations may not prove a shield against individual liability in a copyright infringement lawsuit.

Particularly if a corporate officer participates in the infringement or uses the corporation for the purposes of carrying out infringements, courts can "pierce the corporate veil" and impose personal liability. Likewise an employee who, in exercising discretion, commits or causes the employer to commit an infringement can be liable.

Another deterrent for infringers is that this personal liability is usually, in legal terms, joint and several. This means that all of the defendants are liable for the full amount of the damages. If one defendant flees the country or goes bankrupt, the damages owed to the plaintiff will not be lessened. So four defendants who owed damages of $600,000 might each pay $150,000, but, if one of the defendants could not be found, the remaining three defendants could be made to pay $200,000 each. In one case, for example, the publisher and the printer were found jointly and severally liable for all damages when the publisher wrongfully authorized the reprint of a book for which the publisher did not own a valid copyright (*Fitzgerald Publishing Co. v. Baylor Publishing Co.*, 807 F.2d 1110).

A troubling case for artists, applied by analogy to writers, involved a state-owned university sued by a photographer for infringement. In this and other cases, the Eleventh Amendment of the Constitution was construed to give states and state-owned entities immunity from lawsuits for copyright infringement (*Richard Anderson Photography v. Radford University*, 633 F. Supp. 1154, *aff'd* 852 F.2d 114, *cert. denied* 489 U.S. 1033). In 1990, the copyright law was amended by the Copyright Remedy Clarification Act. The Act expressly provides that any state, state-owned entity, or state officer or employee is subject to lawsuits for copyright infringement. Therefore, states or state-owned entities that infringe must pay damages like any other copyright infringer.*

Fair Use

Not absolutely every unpermitted use of someone else's copyrighted work is a copyright infringement. Fair use, for example, is one of several limitations on the exclusive rights granted under the copyright law. It has been defined as an equitable rule of reason, a privilege in someone other than the owner of a copyright to use the copyrighted work in a reasonable manner without the owner's consent. Legally, fair use is a defense to an infringement. Each fair use case will be decided on its particular facts, in a sensitive balancing of interests, which is easy to state but very difficult to apply. Often the outcome turns on fairness. A key determinant is whether the use advances a significant public interest without substantially impairing the owner's economic interests or other incentives to create. The 1976 Copyright Act allows the use of a copyrighted work for "purposes such as criticism, comment, news reporting, teaching (including multiple copies for classroom use), scholarship, or research, without the consent of the copyright owner."

To determine whether a use is a fair use, courts look at four factors: (1) the purpose and character of the use, including whether or not it is for profit; (2) the nature and character of the copyrighted work; (3) the amount and substantiality of the portion used not only in relation to the copyrighted work as a whole, but also, in some cases, in relation to defendant's work (and this can be a qualitative as well as quantitative test); and (4) the effect the use will have on the market for or value of the copyrighted work. These factors are guidelines that must be considered in addition to other factors (such as whether the copy in issue is purloined); no one factor is dispositive. The importance given to any particular factor in the endless possible varieties of situations and combinations of situations is left to the discretion of the courts.

Fair use issues arise in a number of different situations. For example, a writer may be wondering whether to use someone else's historical work as a background for his or her own historical work, or whether it would be legal to quote two hundred words of a lengthy work to illustrate its style, criticize its content, or compare it to another work. Whether or not these sorts of uses amount to fair use are factual issues and must be resolved through common sense application of the four fair use factors. Satire, for example, may be a comment on another work, which legitimately uses part of the original work. Or it may cross the line by using so much of the original work that the value of the satiric piece is simply what has been copied to create the new work rather than any fair comment (in which case a copyright infringement is likely to have occurred).

Remember that the test for infringement is as follows: Will an ordinary observer, looking at the two works, believe one has been copied from the other? But, keep in mind that, in an appropriate situation, such as a review or scholarly article, a work could be copied exactly and it still wouldn't amount to an infringement. As a result, the fair use factors must be analyzed with respect to particular facts in every case to determine whether or not a writer can safely use parts of a copyright holder's work.

One interesting example of fair use given by the House Judiciary Committee involves the practice of calligraphers who reproduce excerpts from copyrighted literary works in making their artwork. The committee concluded that a calligrapher's making of a single copy for a single client would not be an infringement of the copyright in the literary work.

Archival Copying

A recent case involved fair use in the archival copying of articles from scientific and technical journals. Eighty-three publishers brought a class action suit against Texaco, Inc., for unauthorized copying. Although the researchers at Texaco numbered between four hundred and five hundred, the court, by agreement of the parties, focused on one researcher, Dr. Donald Chickering, and one journal, *The Journal of Catalysis*. Texaco had only three subscriptions to *Catalysis*, which were circulated to all the researchers, so Chickering had photocopied eight articles for easy reference. The court reviewed the four fair use factors.

1. *The Purpose and Character of the Use.* This first factor turns on an inquiry into whether the use is for profit and whether it transforms, rather than supersedes or supplants, the original work. Although a commercial purpose weighs against fair use, the court did not find the fact that Texaco was a for-profit corporation dispositive, noting that practically all research is at least partially commercially motivated. And in this case, the use itself was only indirectly commercial, although the commercial benefit to the user, Texaco, was clearly substantial. However, because cutting costs and increasing profits are so closely linked, the court found that Texaco was attempting to benefit from the copyrights held by *Catalysis* without paying the customary price. The court noted that Chickering had copied the work for the same basic purpose for which one would normally purchase the original—to have it available on his shelf for reference. The court then looked at whether the use was transformative, noting the Supreme Court's recent ruling that "the more transformative the new work, the less will be the significance of the other factors, like commercialism, that weigh against fair use." While it found that photocopying is not transformative, and could never be under the facts of this case, it noted that the benefit of a more usable format might be transformative under different circumstances, such as the spontaneous copying of specific pages during a scientific experiment, where the original would be too bulky or might be exposed to hazardous chemicals. Because there was no transformative use to overcome the essentially commercial nature of archival copying, the court found that the first factor favored *Catalysis*.

2. *The Nature of the Copyrighted Work.* This second factor favored Texaco, according to the court, because of the factual content of the articles. The copyright law only offers minimal protection to factual works because of the substantially greater public interest in their dissemination.

3. *The Amount and Substantiality of the Portion Used.* Since Texaco copied the *Catalysis* articles in their entirety, the court found that this factor weighed against fair use.

4. *The Effect on the Potential Market or Value of the Copyrighted Work.* The court found that the fourth factor, called the most important, though not dispositive, by the Supreme Court, also

weighed against fair use because the publishers had demonstrated substantial harm to the value of their copyrights.

Balancing the fair use factors, the court held in favor of the publishers and against a finding of fair use, noting that Texaco could take advantage of available licensing schemes, develop new ones, or buy a few more subscriptions (*American Geophysical Union et al. v. Texaco, Inc.*, 802 F. Supp. 1, *aff'd* 37 F.3d 881, *superceded by* 60 F.3d 913).

Parody in Advertising

Whether parody, using part of a work in order to make fun of it, is an infringement turns on whether the parody derives its value from what it took of the original work or whether its value comes from the added material that makes it a parody. If its value comes from the original work, it is likely to be an infringement. Another factor is whether the underlying work is publicly known; if it's not there cannot really be any social commentary, no comic effect that requires conjuring up the original, and therefore no parody or fair use.

A recent case found two unlikely contestants battling over the issue of parody. Eveready Battery Company had created and run an Energizer Bunny ad campaign for several years. This ad was apparently created in response to an ad by competitor Duracell in which mechanical bunnies beat drums until only the bunny with the Duracell battery continued to operate. The voice-over said that tests showed Duracell batteries outlast the batteries of competitors. Eveready's initial response was an ad in which mechanical bunnies beat on drums, but the toy Energizer Bunny enters later (dressed in sunglasses and beach thongs) and the voice-over indicates that "Energizer was never invited to their playoffs . . . because nothing outlasts the Energizer. They keep going and going and going . . ."

After the initial Energizer Bunny campaign, Eveready hired a new ad agency, Chiat/Day/Mojo, which created the commercial-within-a-commercial concept. In these nearly two dozen ads what appears to be a commercial is interrupted by the arrival of the Energizer Bunny in its characteristic sunglasses and beach thongs. The voice-over concludes by saying, "Still going. Nothing outlasts the Energizer. They keep going and going . . . [voice fades out]."

When Coors Light's Marketing Department wanted to run a series of commercials in the spring of 1991, its ad agency, Foote, Cone and Belding Communications, was given the task of creating a humorous commercial using the well-known actor Leslie Nielsen who had been featured in previous Coors Light commercials. The Coors commercial starts with a voice speaking over background music and describing the virtues of an unnamed beer. The visual shows a close-up of beer being poured into a glass. Then a drum beat accompanies Leslie Nielsen walking across the set. He is dressed in a conservative suit and also wears fake white rabbit ears, a fuzzy white tail, and rabbit feet (which look like pink slippers). Carrying a drum with the Coors Light logo, the actor beats the drum several times, then spins about half a dozen times, recovers from apparent dizziness and then says "Thank you" before exiting. As he exits, the voice-over says, "Coors Light, the official beer of the nineties, is the fastest growing light beer in America. It keeps growing and growing and growing . . . "

Under the terms of the contract with Leslie Nielsen, Coors had only six weeks in which to air this commercial (and the six weeks ended on June 28, 1991 when *Naked Gun 2½* was scheduled for release). Eveready, having heard of the Coors ad, sued Coors and an expedited hearing was granted to determine whether a preliminary injunction should be issued to prevent Coors from airing the spot. The most important factor in granting a preliminary injunction is whether the plaintiff is likely to succeed when the case is later tried on its merits.

The court observed that it was clear that Eveready owned a valid copyright and that copying had taken place. While these are requisites for winning a copyright suit, the court referred to the fair use provisions of the copyright law. If copying is a fair use, it will not be an infringement. The tests for fair use include (1) the purpose and character of the use, including whether such use is of a commercial nature. Eveready argued from this that parody in a commercial could not be protected as a fair use. The court disagreed, noting that the other factors—(2) the nature of the copyrighted work; (3) the amount and substantiality of the portion used in relation to the copyrighted work as a whole; and (4) the effect of the use upon the potential market for or value of the copyrighted work—all favored Coors.

The court concluded that the Coors spot had not borrowed too much from Eveready, but rather had used only enough to let viewers realize that the Coors ad was, in fact, a parody. So Eveready's motion for a preliminary injunction was denied and Coors was free to run the ad in the contractually specified time frame (*Eveready Battery Company, Inc. v. Adolph Coors Company*, 765 F. Supp. 440).

Unpublished Works

A landmark case on fair use of unpublished works involved the memoirs of President Gerald Ford which Ford had contracted to publish with Harper & Row. Harper & Row in turn granted *Time Magazine* the exclusive right to publish a seven-thousand-five-hundred-word excerpt from the memoirs prior to publication of the book. The licensing to a magazine of this right to publish an excerpt from a book before the book is published is referred to as first serial rights. Before *Time's* intended publication date, *The Nation* obtained a copy of the book and published an article which appropriated verbatim text from the memoirs, preempting the impact of the *Time Magazine* excerpt. *Time* withdrew the article from the intended issue and refused to pay the balance of what it owed Harper & Row. Harper & Row then sued *The Nation* for copyright infringement. *The Nation* claimed fair use. The district court found that infringement had occurred, but the Circuit Court of Appeals reversed on the basis that the appropriation amounted to fair use. The Supreme Court of the United States looked at the four fair use factors.

1. *Purpose and Character of Defendant's Use.* Although the court noted that the defendant's purpose was reporting news, which is socially beneficial, the use was still clearly for profit. The user stood to profit from exploitation of the copyrighted work without paying the customary price. Furthermore, the court found that the intended purpose of the reporting was not the dissemination of news, which would have come out soon anyway. Other cases discuss whether the work is "transformative" or "productive" in the sense that it adds to a discourse about the facts rather than merely restating them and transforms one copyrighted work into another socially useful work.

2. *Nature of the Copyrighted Work.* Fair use is more likely to be found in certain kinds of works, such as factual compilations or historical non-fiction works, than it is with others, such as science fiction or fantasies, which are pure entertainment. But the court noted that fair use has only limited applicability to unpublished works because writers have the right to decide when and whether a work will be presented to the public. Although Ford's memoirs were essentially factual, a compilation of historical events which would normally possess only "thin" copyright protection, the court noted that there are limits to the right to copy even factual works.

3. *Amount and Substantiality of Use.* The defendant took a mere three hundred words from a two-hundred-thousand-word manuscript, but the court's majority found that *The Nation* had taken "the heart of the book." Furthermore, the court noted that in examining the amount of appropriated expression, it was important to measure that portion not only in relation to the copyrighted work as a whole, but also in relation to the totality of the defendant's work. In this case, that deeper inquiry did not auger well for the defendant which had basically tied together quotes, paraphrases and factual elements to construct a two-thousand-two-hundred-fifty-word article.

4. *Effect on Potential Market or Value.* The court called this factor the most important of the four factors. Where the purpose of the

appropriation is linked to profit, the effect on the market for the work is likely to be negative. Although the critical nature of a work will often harm the potential market for the object of criticism and still be a fair use, in this case *The Nation* magazine article was not analytical or critical. It did not further the discussion of historical facts or political ideas, but rather substituted for the original, preempting its dissemination, without adding original expression to the facts contained therein.

Balancing the fair use factors, the Supreme Court held that *The Nation* had in fact infringed Harper & Row's copyright (*Harper & Row Publishers, Inc. v. Nation Enterprises*, 471 U.S. 539). Some courts have interpreted Harper & Row to stand for the proposition that appropriated content from unpublished works can never be the subject of a successful fair use defense (*Salinger v. Random House*, 811 F.2d 90, cert. denied, 108 S. Ct. 213). Still others indicate that there has never been a per se rule regarding unpublished works because fair use always involves a totality inquiry into the four factors. Where the first, third, and fourth factors favored fair use of an unpublished work, one court held against infringement (*Wright v. Warner Books, Inc.*, 953 F.2d 731). Because of the doubt and disagreement regarding fair use of unpublished works, Congress amended the copyright law in 1992 to read: "The fact that a work is unpublished shall not of itself bar a finding of fair use if such a finding is made upon consideration of all four fair use factors."

Educational Fair Use

Educators, writers, and publishers have agreed to special guidelines covering the fair use copying of books and periodicals for classroom use in nonprofit educational institutions. To give an overview, brief portions of copyrighted works may be used for a class if the teacher individually decides to do so, the copyright notice in the owner's name appears on the class materials, and this kind of use is not repeated systematically (for example, throughout a school system).

Educational use that is systematic can be punished. In *Basic Books, Inc. v. Kinko's Graphics Corporation* (758 F. Supp. 1522), Kinko's admitted that it copied excerpts from books without permission and without paying anything to the copyright owners. The excerpts were compiled into course packs for sale to college students. Rejecting Kinko's arguments, the court found no fair use and awarded damages of over $510,000 as well as attorney's fees and costs of $1,365,000. After its review of the four fair use factors, the court observed another factor: "In this case an important additional factor is the fact that the defendant has effectively created a new nationwide business allied to the publishing industry by usurping plaintiff's copyrights and profits." On the other hand, limited classroom and library copying are viewed more sympathetically because they generally involve no commercial exploitation and have socially beneficial objectives.

Permissions

Our discussion has assumed that the work the writer wishes to use is protected by copyright. Some works, however, will be in the public domain. This means that copyright was never obtained for the work or has now expired. Unfortunately, it is often difficult to learn this simply by examining the work. For works published after January 1, 1978, it is difficult to rely on the absence of notice as a basis for concluding a work is in the public domain. This is because the 1978 law had several provisions to protect copyrights even if notice was omitted from a work and, after March 1, 1989, copyright notice is no longer required. For copyrights in works published in the United States prior to 1978, the maximum term of copyright protection under our law is seventy-five years (although legislation is pending in Congress to extend this to ninety-five years). So, it is safe to assume that any work published more than seventy-five years ago in the United States is now in the public domain, as far as protection in the United States is concerned. However, if the work is protected in foreign countries, the term of protection may be based on the creator's life plus fifty years, which is likely to exceed seventy-five years. Also, new legislation, passed in 1994, restores copyright protection for virtually all foreign works that are in the public domain in the United States and less than seventy-five years old, if they lost copyright protection here because of failure to comply with the United States copyright law formalities (such as copyright notice or applying for the renewal term).

If the public domain provides little succor, what about simply obtaining permission to use the work from the creator or present copyright owner? This can be done by a brief letter setting forth the writer's project, what material the writer wants to copy, what rights the writer needs in the material, what credit line and copyright notice will be given, and what payment, if any, will be made. To make the letter binding, the words "Consented and Agreed to" should be added at the bottom with a line underneath for the signature of the person owning the copyright. If the person is signing as the representative of a magazine or other organization, the name of the organization and the title of the person signing should be indicated. The sample release form appearing here can be used as a model to be adapted to particular situations. The permitted use should be sharply delineated to protect the party selling the rights from giving up too much, to ensure that the purchaser is not buying and/or paying more than is necessary, and to enable that purchaser to prove to the world that what is needed has been lawfully acquired. The fact that re-use fees normally increase with greater usage is another reason to give an accurate description of intended usage.*

PERMISSION FORM

Dear _____:

    I am preparing a book titled _____ to be published by _____. May I please have your permission to include the following material: (specify the material and, for a published work, include the original place of publication, date, and page numbers) in my book and in future revisions and editions thereof, including nonexclusive world rights in all languages. These rights will in no way restrict republication of your material in any other form by you or others authorized by you. Should you not control these rights in their entirety, would you kindly let me know to whom else I must write? Unless you indicate otherwise, I will use the following credit line (specify credit line) and copyright notice (specify the form of the copyright notice which will protect the material the writer is asking to use): _____. I would greatly appreciate your consent to this request. For your convenience a release form is provided below and a copy of this letter is enclosed for your files.

Sincerely yours,

Jane Writer

I (We) grant permission for the use requested above.

_____   _____
SPECIFY NAME AND TITLE, IF ANY   DATE

Locating Copyright Owners

A problem with permissions arises when the copyright owner can't be located. Some work is very difficult to trace, especially if a tight deadline is involved. Copyright registrations, and all recorded assignments and licenses from January 1, 1978 to the present, can be found and searched free of charge, twenty-four hours a day, on the Internet. The World Wide Web address for Copyright Office files is: http://lcweb.loc.gov/copyright. As discussed in Circular 22, "How to Investigate the Copyright Status of a Work," the Copyright Office in Washington, D.C., will search its records for a reasonable fee. However, many works have never been registered. They may be protected by copyright, but they cannot be found by a search of the records in the Copyright Office. Even works that have been registered can be difficult to find, since titles may not aid sufficiently in locating a work. The fact that a writer cannot be located to request permission does not make copying acceptable. Such copying without permission would still be an infringement.

Infringement raises ethical questions. It is not merely that using another writer's work without permission is a copyright infringement. Infringement is a moral issue as much as it is a legal issue—it involves a sensitivity toward the advancement of human achievement through creativity.

This sensitivity is, in its deepest sense, self-protective. No writer wants his or her work copied without the opportunity to receive a fee, be credited as writer of the original work, make certain the work is not to be unacceptably altered in its new usage, or, in some cases, to forbid the use altogether. By understanding the ethical and copyright implications in these areas, writers can act in ways that uphold appropriate standards and improve the working environment for fellow professionals.

6 Copyright: Past and Present

$\mathcal{T}$he following brief history of copyright reveals some of the underlying forces that have shaped the copyright law in force today. A tension exists between the rights of the public and the rights of writers and other creators. Copyright is a monopoly and, like any monopoly, imposes limitations on the public. The writer reaps economic gains for the term of the copyright while the public is denied the fullest access to its own textual resources and culture. Justifying this monopoly by ancient concepts of property law, copyrights are called intellectual property.

Intellectual Property

The etymological derivation of property is from the Latin word *proprius*, which means private or peculiar to oneself. Intellectual comes from the Latin verb *intellegere*, which is to choose from among, hence to understand or to know. Contained within *intellegere* is the verb *legere*, which means to gather (especially fruit) and thus to collect, to choose and ultimately to assemble (the alphabetical characters) with the eyes and to read.

So the private inspiration that finds fruition in written works is rewarded by monopoly rights that last for the writer's life plus fifty years. Yet new methods to create, store, and deliver information place pressure on the system of copyright. Arguments are made for rights of public access to and use of all written works, perhaps on the model of a compulsory license in which copyright owners have no right to control usage but do receive a fee fixed either by voluntary arrangements or government fiat (albeit less than would be negotiated for by the writer). Would the public be better served by ending copyright as a monopoly and allowing the most widespread dissemination of literature, art, and other products of the mind? Is the right of the public a paramount right, greater than any right which a creator might assert?

To place this debate in perspective, we must remember that copyright is neither ancient in origin nor a right enjoyed without controversy. The Roman legal system, for example, had no copyright. If a man could own slaves (who might carry fabulous creations in their minds), why should the ownership of words be separate from the ownership of the parchment containing the words? Trained slaves took dictation to create thousands of copies of popular works for sale at low prices. The poet Martial complained that he received nothing when his works were sold. Even if works could be sold, as were the plays written by Terence, no protection existed against piracy. The profits from any sales of the copied manuscripts went to the property owner, not the author.

A Monopoly on Copying

Indeed, this collective view of creativity held sway through the Middle Ages. Religious literature predominated; individual creativity was not rewarded. The reproduction of manuscripts rested in the dominion of the Church, and it was only with the rise of the great universities in the twelfth and thirteenth centuries that lay writers began producing works on secular subjects. Extensive copying by trained scribes again became the norm, with only the publishers, or *stationarii* as they were called, gaining any profit. Even before the introduction of block printing into the west in the fifteenth century, the publishers had formed a Brotherhood of Manuscript Producers in 1357 and were soon given a charter by the Lord Mayor of London. Johannes Gutenberg's introduction of the printing press to the Western world in 1437 gave individual writers an ever greater opportunity for self-expression. The printer's movable type foreshadowed the writer's copyright protection.

William Caxton introduced these printing techniques to England in 1476, which led to an even greater demand for books. Seven years later,

Richard III lifted the restrictions against aliens, if those aliens happened to be printers. Within fifty years, however, the supply of books had far exceeded the demand and Henry VIII passed a new law providing that no person in England could legally purchase a book bound in a foreign nation (this was the forerunner to the manufacturing clause that finally expired in the United States in 1986).

At about this time, the Brotherhood of Manuscript Producers, now known as the Stationers' Company, was given a charter—that is, a monopoly—over publishing in England. No writer could publish except with a publisher belonging to the Stationers' Company. This served the dual purpose of preventing both writings seditious to the Crown and those heretical to the Church. The right of ownership was not in the writer's creation, but rather in the right to make copies of that creation. Secret presses came into existence, but the Stationer's Company sought to maintain its monopoly with the aid of repressive decrees from the notorious Star Chamber.

Due largely to the monopoly of the Stationers' Company, a recognition had come into being of a right to copy, which might also be called a common-law copyright—that is, a right supposedly existing from usages and customs of immemorial antiquity as interpreted by the courts. With this concept of property apart from the physical manuscript established, the Stationers' Company objected vehemently when their charter and powers expired in 1694 and Scotch printers began reprinting their titles. They pushed for a new law, but this law, enacted in 1710 and called the Statute of Anne, was largely drafted by two writers, Joseph Addison and Jonathan Swift. The result was a law that protected writers as well as publishers by the creation of statutory copyright (copyright protected under statute). At this point, writers had something to market, a copyright which had been created to encourage "learned men to compose and write useful books."

In the United States

The copyright laws of the United States stand on this structure built in England. The Confederation of States had no power to legislate with respect to copyright. Between 1783 and 1789 Noah Webster successfully lobbied twelve states for passage of copyright laws. Finally, the Federal Constitution provided that "The Congress shall have the power . . . To promote the Progress of Science and the useful Arts, by securing for limited Times to Authors and Inventors the exclusive Right to their respective Writings and Discoveries."

In 1790, Congress enacted our first federal copyright statute, providing copyright for an initial term of fourteen years plus a renewal term of fourteen years. It applied to the making of copies of books, maps, and charts. In 1831 the initial term of copyright was lengthened to twenty-eight years. In 1865 the law was amended to include photographs and negatives. In 1870 it was revised to cover paintings, drawings, statuaries, and models or designs of works of the fine arts.

In 1909, the copyright law was revised again. The initial term of copyright remained twenty-eight years and the renewal term was lengthened to twenty-eight years for potential protection of fifty-six years. In fact, statutory copyrights that would have expired at the end of the renewal term on or after September 19, 1962, were extended to a term of seventy-five years from the date copyright was originally obtained. Any statutory copyright obtained more than seventy-five years ago has definitely expired and the writing is in the public domain in the United States (unless Congress passes a pending twenty year "term extension"; but it will not be retroactive and therefore, if a work falls into the public domain before Congress passes the extension, the work will remain in the public domain after passage).

Radio, television, motion pictures, satellites, and other technological innovations required revision of the 1909 law. After a long gestation period, the complete revision of the law took effect on January 1, 1978. No doubt future revisions lie ahead as new tools to make, store, and deliver creative works shape the copyright needs of creators, users, and society itself. However, while technology will undoubtedly continue to test the copyright law, a number of recent amendments to that law have resulted from responses to the global economy and the desire of the United States for greater international protection of copyrights.

International Copyright Protection

Historically, copyright protection was almost exclusively limited to the nation of origin of a work, that is, the country in which the work was first published. More recently, that limited protection has been extended through international conventions and bilateral treaties. Today, most countries either offer, or are beginning to offer, at least a measure of international copyright protection.

Protection for American copyrights abroad is of increasing importance because the export of copyrightable works has become a thriving business, the fasting growing sector of the United States economy and one which may be threatened by "piracy" abroad because copyrighted works can be copied cheaply and disseminated quickly—especially via electronic means.

Although the United States has often been referred to as a "copyright island," its accession to the Berne Convention in 1989, after refusing to join for over one-hundred years, shows a sincere effort to upgrade copyright protection internationally.

The initial refusal of the United States to join Berne was the result of several factors: rivalries between American and British publishing houses; Berne's minimum standards requiring a fifty year protection floor and banning the imposition of notice, registration, recordation, or deposit formalities by any member nation; moral rights (the right to freedom from false attribution, improper editing or alternations, and mutilation, which have a long history in Europe and are largely unprecedented under United States copyright law); and national treatment (the rule that member nations must protect foreign works at least as stringently as they protect domestic works). Most importantly, international copyright protection was not a high priority because the United States was a net importer of copyrightable works.

Before Berne accession, American owners of copyrightable works could achieve Berne protection through the "back door" by simultaneously publishing a work in a Berne country (e.g., Canada), making the "country of origin" the Berne signatory and thereby affording the owner full protection in that country. One problem with this method of gaining protection was the uncertainty of the word "published" and "simultaneous" for purposes of simultaneous publication. Some countries required that, in order to be validly published, enough copies be available in the forum to satisfy the public's need for the work while others allowed a small quantity to suffice. Some countries construed the simultaneous requirement to mean publication on the same day as in the United States, while others were more lenient and allowed publication to occur within thirty days (the Berne definition). Regardless of the immediate benefits of the back door route, and its ability to circumvent the perceived costs of Berne adherence, traversing it was always difficult, usually expensive, often embarrassing, and caused justifiable resentment internationally.

United States Protection for Foreign Writers

The reluctance of the United States to adhere to the Berne Convention (which was created in 1886 and later modified a number of times), can be understood as an aspect of the reliance of the United States on the cultural wealth of Europe. From 1790 until 1891, foreign writers were utterly without rights under the United States copyright law, even if their work was under copyright protection elsewhere. The United States allowed American publishers to pirate the works of such well-known writers as Charles Dickens, Anthony Trollope, and Victor Hugo. Charles Dickens, writing in the 1840s and 1850s, was livid at the "monstrous injustice" whereby writers were denied their rightful royalties from sales consummated in the United States.

The United States pirated works out of sheer economic expediency. At that time there was no international market for American works. It was not until 1891 that, after years of controversy, Congress finally passed the Chace Act and slowly began to allow foreign writers to copyright their published works in the United States (unpublished works of foreign origin were protected "in perpetuity" under common law). Under the Chace Act, foreigners whose nations provided reciprocal protection to American nationals could obtain copyrights for their works in the United States. Nevertheless, it was difficult for foreign publishers and writers to comply with the act due to the complexity of the formal requirements necessary to secure protection.

The central problem arose from the infamous "manufacturing clause." It required all foreign books copyrighted in the United States to be printed from type set, negatives, or stone drawings made within the borders of the United States. This onerous requirement made copyright protection for foreigners illusory.

Under the Copyright Act of 1909, which governed copyright in the United States until the Copyright Act of 1976, foreign writers and publishers fared only slightly better. A foreign citizen could copyright a book in the United States as long as the writer actually lived in the United States when the book was first published and provided that all necessary formalities were adhered to. The United States copyright law was still fundamentally and irreconcilably at odds with both the specific tenets of the Berne Convention and the liberal copyright protection offered by most Western European nations.

Unwilling to join Berne, in 1952 the United States helped create the Universal Copyright Convention (UCC). In most ways, the UCC merely codified existing American law rather than offering important concessions to foreign member countries. It differed significantly in one way—it abolished the manufacturing clause with respect to UCC member nations. Under the UCC, works created by American nationals, wherever published, are afforded the same protection in any UCC member country as local works receive. Nevertheless, the United States still clung to its notice, registration, recordation, and deposit requirements while any major western country that had such provisions, and few did, abolished all such requirements. In spite of its shortfalls, the UCC did open up copyright relations with over eighty countries and offered protection that initially seemed adequate.

In the mid-1980s, however, United States government research indicated that American corporations were suffering staggering losses due to foreign copyright piracy. As a result, we finally joined the Berne Convention in 1989, accepting its life-plus-fifty duration of protection (which we had already adopted, as a preliminary step towards Berne accession, in the 1976 copyright act) and abolishing finally our system of formalities. This is why, for example, copyright notice is no longer a requirement when a work is published in the United States (although it is still wise to use copyright notice).

When there were more books written abroad, especially in Great Britain, than in the United States, international copyright protection would have created an unfavorable balance of trade. But as the economics change, political theories are usually not far behind. As cheap British knock-offs, published without advances or royalties, became competition for publishers and writers trying to market American literature, the first spark of interest in international copyright protection was kindled. Nevertheless, that spark has taken many years to ignite.

Today, more copyrightable works are produced in the United States than in any other country and these works represent a substantial portion of United States exports. The industries involved—film and computer companies, book, newspaper, and magazine publishers—are both large and profitable. Because a substantial and growing portion of these profits come from foreign sales (creating a bright spot in an otherwise dismal balance of trade), there have been loud and indignant calls for stronger worldwide protection. All over the developing world, piracy from the American computer and entertainment industries is a booming business. Allowing American publishing companies the opportunity to publish foreign works without having to pay advances or royalties was one thing; allowing the worldwide misappropriation of American literary property is clearly another.

Trade Sanctions, GATT, and Bilateral Agreements

The United States has vowed to use trade sanctions and other economic weapons available under the General Agreement on Tariffs and Trade (GATT) against any country that fails to protect adequately United States' intellectual property rights.

The issue of appropriate sanctions was initially addressed in a 1984 amendment to the Trade Act of 1974. This amendment, known as section 301, authorized the President to impose trade sanctions against any country that fails to protect American copyrights adequately or engages in unreasonable or unjustifiable trade practices. Further legislation created the "special 301," a beefed-up section 301 under which the United States Trade Representative (USTR) identifies and investigates pirate nations and then "must" recommend appropriate sanctions to the President who in turn "must" institute retaliatory measures. Sanctions, or rewards, can also be meted out under the Generalized System of Preferences (GSP).

The United States' adherence to the Berne Convention increased the likelihood of stronger protection for intellectual property under GATT because it helped the credibility of the United States which had suffered as a result of the "back door" activities pursued by American writers and publishers. The World Trade Organization (WTO), which evolved from the Uruguay round of GATT negotiations, came into force on January 1, 1995. One of the important aspects of the agreement establishing the WTO is that standards are included that dictate the minimum levels of protection that member countries must incorporate into their national intellectual property laws. This part of the overall agreement is titled: "Agreement on Trade-Related Aspects of Intellectual Property Rights" (abbreviated as "TRIPs") and impacts such areas as copyright, trademarks, industrial designs, patents, and trade secrets; it came into force on January 1, 1996. On December 8, 1994, the United States enacted a law to approve and implement the Uruguay agreements. Included in this law are a number of amendments to United States copyright law to conform to the obligations of the Uruguay requirements.

United States Goals

The United States had a number of goals with respect to copyright in the trade negotiations. As a leading source of intellectual property and a net exporter of copyrighted works, it wanted to encourage strong protection and enforcement provisions, fight piracy, and increase the flow of revenues to entertainment and information producers in the United States.

In addition, the United States wanted to incorporate the Berne Convention obligations as a requirement of membership in the WTO. The United States also sought to require the protection of computer software (with respect to both copyrightability and rental rights) and data bases for nations joining the WTO. And, for those nations that would join, the United States pushed for the Berne minimum term of copyright protection of life plus fifty years, and a minimum term of fifty years for works not granted the full Berne term or not protected by the Convention (such as "sound recordings," CDs, LPs, etc.).

In all of these respects, the United States succeeded in meeting its goals. The minimum protection and enforcement provisions that nations are obligated to meet are elaborated at length. Some of the basic requirements are that "Procedures concerning the enforcement of intellectual property rights shall be fair and equitable . . . Decisions on the merits of a case shall preferably be in writing and reasoned . . . Parties to a proceeding shall have an opportunity for review." The remedies are similar to those already existing under United States law—injunctions (to prevent or halt an infringement), damages (including the possible payment of expenses and attorney's fees), and other remedies (such as disposition or destruction of infringing goods and materials used to create such goods). While other substantive and clarifying provisions sought by the United States were not adopted, the overall effect should be beneficial in terms of protecting the value of United States copyrights around the world.

Restoration of Copyright

Of course, certain concessions by the United States encouraged adherence to its proposals. One such concession is the restoration of certain copyrights that have gone into the public domain in the United States but which are still protected in their country of origin, called the "source country" in this act. Works in the public domain no longer have copyright protection and may be freely copied by anyone. Because in the past the United States had numerous formalities that had to be followed in order to either obtain or keep copyrights, copyrights could enter the public domain for diverse reasons (such as being published without copyright notice). By degrees, starting in 1978 and especially in 1989 as part of the process of joining the Berne Convention, the United States had ceased to require these formalities (so that the failure to place copyright notice on a work today is not a fatal mistake that forfeits the copyright, but notice is desirable for other important legal and evidentiary benefits that it confers).

If nations that become members of the WTO have citizens who lost copyright protection in the United States, that copyright protection will be restored on January 1, 1996, and the copyrights will run for the term that they would have had if they had never entered the public domain. However, the provision does not necessarily work in reverse, so United States works will not be restored to copyright in the rest of the world (which is probably not as significant as it sounds, since United States laws were more likely to cause a loss of copyright than the laws of most foreign countries—especially those countries that belonged to the Berne Convention). But some important trading partners will be forced to reciprocate, namely China and Russia, which offered little or no copyright protection for older United States or other foreign works until very recently.

This does mean that some United States companies may find themselves in the awkward situation of planning to use or having actually already used public domain foreign works which are now being restored to copyright protection. With respect to certain future uses of restored works, such uses will be infringements subject to all the penalties that the copyright law provides. However, with respect to certain copies of works that have already been acquired or used and then are restored to copyright protection, the user will be considered what the law calls a "reliance party"—a party which used the work in reliance on its public domain status. For an owner of a restored work to gain full rights against reliance parties, the owner will have to file notice of intent with the Copyright Office and fulfill such requirements as the Copyright Office prescribed under its regulations issued on September 29, 1995. The law's provisions are complex and have some special cases, so both owners of restored works and reliance parties will have to seek expert legal advice to be certain that they choose the best course of action.

Enhanced Enforcement

China offers a good example of the impact of the WTO. China had a brand new copyright law which appeared adequate on its face, but its provisions were not enforced. The result was extensive piracy in China of copyrights originating in the United States. China and the United States both belonged to the Berne Convention, but the only resort for the United States with respect to China's failure to enforce would have been a proceeding before the International Court of Justice.

Because copyright is now an issue to be addressed pursuant to the WTO dispute settlement procedures, the United States can threaten trade retaliations against countries that fail to provide enforcement mechanisms for their copyright laws (although China is not yet a WTO member, its intellectual property protection has become a prerequisite for membership). In the case of China, the United States threatened to impose 100 percent tariffs on over $1 billion of imports of Chinese products if China continued its flagrant piracies. These threatened retaliations were under existing United States retaliatory trade provisions, which would be strengthened under the new WTO procedures if China is allowed to join and decides to do so. To avoid this retaliation, China agreed to take both immediate and long-term steps to put an end to these piracies. Included among these steps are the creation of a copyright recordation system, the use of coded merchandise, and the investigation of factories producing such merchandise (such as CDs and CD-ROMs) to make certain no infringements are taking place, regular consultations with the United States, and the provision of information and statistics about Chinese enforcement efforts. Similar successes have occurred in newly emerging markets in Russia and Eastern Europe.

So the increased international protection and enforcement resulting from United States membership in the WTO should work to the benefit of creators, producers, and distributors of works protected by copyright.

The threat of impending sanctions, or potential loss of concessions under GATT, can also be used to encourage bilateral treaties. Under the 1976 Copyright Act, the President has the right to extend copyright reciprocity where he determines that a foreign state is offering acceptable treatment to America copyrights. Bilateral agreements do not undermine Berne as long as they meet its minimum requirements without contradicting its provisions. A member country can set longer terms of protection than life-plus-fifty and those terms will then be durational minimums for copyright holders seeking protection in that country. This bilateral approach is used to avail the United States of immediate copyright protection in countries that have not yet begun the often cumbersome process of joining an international copyright convention and it was used as a stop-gap in some countries while the GATT/WTO was being negotiated. In addition, these agreements are used to obtain greater levels of protection than are possible under the UCC or even Berne. Effective treaties will tie protection of copyright to other trade or economic issues, including loan forgiveness and economic aid packages. The United States has entered into bilateral copyright agreements with more than seventy countries, most of which are already Berne members. Unfortunately, these agreements have so far proven difficult for local governments or the United States to enforce. Nevertheless, the GATT, trade sanctions, and bilateral agreements remain powerful weapons in the arsenal that can be brought to bear on those who pirate American copyrights abroad.

The United States has finally begun to shed its two-hundred-year-old notions of isolation in the area of copyright protection and is now moving toward a position at the forefront of the crusade for effective transnational copyright protection. This change is attributable to the fact that the United States has progressed from the piracy capital of the world to the foremost exporter of intellectual property. International protection of copyright requires us to reconcile contradictions—like the fact that we once practiced exactly what we now condemn. Details of the international copyright relations of the United States can be obtained from the Copyright Office in Circular 38a, "International Copyright Relations of the United States."

Protecting Electronic Rights

In September of 1995, "The Report of the President's Working Group on Intellectual Property Rights" recommended legislation "to accommodate the new technologies of the rapidly expanding digital environment" and to further clarify the application of copyright protection in the cyberspace of the Internet. The report found that:

> Creators, publishers and distributors of works will be wary of the electronic marketplace unless the law provides them the tools to protect their property against unauthorized use . . . Just one unauthorized uploading could have devastating effects on the market for the work.

The result, according to the report, is that investment, both creative and economic, will not flow into the information infrastructure unless adequate protections for the products of that investment are put in place.

In response to the Working Group's recommendations, a bill known as the National Information Infrastructure Copyright Protection Act of

1995 has recently been introduced in both the United States Senate (S.1284) and the House of Representatives (H.R.2441). The bipartisan support which it has gathered indicates that its passage into law is imminent.*

The purpose of the bill is to increase and clarify the scope of copyright protection as an incentive for copyright owners to make their works available on the Internet, for the benefit of the public at large. To that end, it clarifies that a transmission of a publication is a part of the distribution right for purposes of copyright protection. A transmission is defined in the new bill as something that is distributed by any device or process whereby a copy or phonorecord of the work is fixed beyond the place from which it was sent. In addition, the new bill bans de-encryption devices because of the important role encryption plays in protecting transmitted copyrighted content.

A variety of civil remedies are provided under the bill for frustrating encryption systems, including injunctions, impounding, actual or statutory damages, attorney's fees, or destruction of infringing products or devices. Damages are available even if the copyright owner has not registered his or her copyright prior to the infringement. The bill also includes criminal sanctions. If enacted, the Copyright Protection Act of 1995 will be a landmark of copyright protection in cyberspace.**

The Legacy of Copyright

At first blush, the copyright law appears to limit the freedom of the public to benefit from artistic and literary works. However, the purpose of copyright is to benefit the public as well as the author. Copyright laws are founded on the assumption that the stimulus to authorship provided by economic incentives ultimately bequeaths a richer cultural legacy to the public than would a system that allowed the public the liberty to pirate at will. This rationale applies to nations regulating international trade as well as to citizens making choices as to whether to seek permission or steal. Societies renounce piracy in the belief that the cultural wealth engendered by this abstinence will enrich future generations. Viewed in this way, the conflict between the writer and the public vanishes. For what is the writer but a part of society? And what are the writer's freedom and copyright but a reflection and record of society's intellectual liberty and cultural legacy?

7 Other Rights of the Writer

*C*ases regularly arise in which writers are aggrieved by conduct that cannot be prevented or remedied under the copyright laws.

> . . . The Defendant, a publisher, advertised for sale certain poems, which he represented by the advertisement to be the work of Lord Byron, on whose behalf a Bill was filed (His Lordship being himself abroad), for an Injunction to restrain the publication under the title described in the advertisement . . . Notice having been given pursuant to this Order the application was now renewed before the Lord Chancellor, who approved of the course which had been taken by the Vice-Chancellor, and, upon the Defendant declining to swear as to his belief that the poem in question was actually the work of Lord Byron, granted the motion (*Lord Byron v. Johnston*, 2 Mer. 29, 35 Eng. Rep. 851).

This success of Lord Byron's friends in restraining the publication of falsely attributed poems occurred in 1816. Doctrines and statutory rights other than copyright may prevent false attribution, failure to give authorship credit, unauthorized use of a title or character, or alterations made in the course of using a work. Each situation must be resolved with respect to its own facts, but this chapter will serve to alert the writer to general legal principles that provide protections beyond the scope of copyright law. Often these protections will overlap one another, so a lawsuit may rely on a variety of them.

Moral Rights

Moral rights are not economic. They are not based on the ownership of property. Instead they derive from the belief that the creative person should have certain powers over his or her work, regardless of who the owner of the property rights may happen to be. Thus, the moral rights provided by the Berne Copyright Convention state:

> . . . the author shall have the right to claim authorship of the work and to object to any distortion, mutilation or other modification of, or other derogatory action in relation to said work, which would be prejudicial to his honor or reputation.

France provides an example of a well-established system of moral rights. These moral rights (or *droit moral*) are perpetual and inalienable. They last forever and cannot be transferred by the writer. The right of disclosure gives the writer the sole power to determine when a work is completed and ready to be communicated to the public. Once the work has been disclosed, the writer has a right to reconsider or retract the work. This affords an opportunity to withdraw work that the writer no longer considers valid or worthy of being before the public. An important limitation on this right, however, is the obligation of the writer to pay in advance for any losses which such a withdrawal will cause the party owning the right of economic exploitation.

The right of paternity guarantees that the writer's name and authorship will be acknowledged with respect to any of the writer's works. An agreement under which a writer is required to use a pseudonym will not be valid since the right of paternity would be violated. Also, the writer may prevent the use of his or her name in association with a work created by someone else. Finally, the right of integrity provides that there shall be no alterations or distortions of a work without consent. The writer has the right to reshape the work—including rearranging, adapting, or translating it—and to prevent others from doing so. The power to enforce the rights of paternity and integrity can be transmitted to heirs or third parties under the writer's will, while the right of disclosure is enforced by the writer's executors, descendants, spouse, other heirs, general legatees, and, finally, the courts.

In the United States, moral rights have never been explicitly recognized with respect to writers. Even though moral rights are a major theme in the Berne Convention, the Berne Implementation Act enacted by Congress in 1988 made it explicitly clear that adherence to Berne did not bring to the United States any additional moral rights. In fact, it provides that Berne adherence does not:

> . . . expand or reduce any right of an author of a work . . . to claim
> authorship of the work; or . . . to object to any distortion, mutila-
> tion, or other modification of, or other derogatory action in rela-
> tion to, the work, that would prejudice the author's honor or
> reputation.

There is an ongoing disagreement as to whether doctrines available to protect writers in the United States amount to the equivalent of moral rights in countries such as France. The better view is that true moral rights offer greater protections than the doctrines explained in the balance of this chapter. But the importance of these doctrines should not be discounted, since often the writer will gain protections much like those afforded by moral rights. While moral rights as such are not recognized in the United States (except with respect to some works of visual art under the Visual Artists Rights Act enacted in 1990), they do provide a good starting point to discuss what rights a writer does have in the United States.

Unfair Competition

"The essence of an unfair competition claim is that the defendant assembled a product which bears so striking a resemblance to the plaintiff's product that the public will be confused as to the identity of the products . . . The test is whether persons exercising 'reasonable intelligence and discrimination' would be taken in by the similarity" (*Shaw v. Time-Life Records*, 38 N.Y. 2d 201).

The application of unfair competition can be even broader than this definition indicates. It can prevent the writer from being presented as the creator of works which he or she did not create; prevent the writer from being presented as the creator of distorted versions of the writer's own works; prevent another person from claiming to have created works in fact created by the writer; protect titles which, although not usually copyrightable, may become so well recognized that reuse of the title (such as *Gone with the Wind*) would create confusion of the new work with the original work; and generally prevent competitors from confusing the public to benefit unfairly from the reputation for quality of the writer's work.

Gilbert Patten, using the pen name of Burt L. Standish, wrote more than one thousand stories about an idealistic young man named Frank Merriwell (whose name appeared in each title). In 1934, nearly forty years after the first Frank Merriwell story was published, a motion picture company decided to produce and distribute a dozen three-reel featurettes titled *Frank Merriwell, Flash (The Talking Horse)*, and *Captain (King of Dogs)*. These films were about the Canadian Mounted Police and had nothing to do with the Frank Merriwell character created by Burt L. Standish, except that the name Frank Merriwell appeared in the title and designated a leading character. The court forbade such a use, stating:

> The plaintiff's copyrights do not cover the titles to the stories . . . But a name which has become descriptive, and is closely identified in the public mind with the work of a particular author, may not, during the life of the copyright, be used so as to mislead . . . Nor may such a name be used even after the expiration of the copyright, unless adequate explanation is given to guard against mistake . . . In the present case, the name "Frank Merriwell" has become associated in the public mind solely and exclusively with the plaintiff's authorship; it is a name which is highly descriptive of his work; and ordinary principles of unfair competition are peculiarly applicable (*Patten v. Superior Talking Pictures, Inc.*, 8 F. Supp. 196, 198).

Similarly, although the phrase "fifth column" was a common usage, Ernest Hemingway's play *The Fifth Column* acquired a sufficient secondary meaning associated with or suggesting his play to the public that the title *Fifth Column Squad* could not be used for someone else's film (*Hemingway v. Film Alliance of the U.S.*, 174 Misc. 725, 21 N.Y.S.2d 827).

Unfair competition does not merely prevent other literary uses, but also commercial uses. For example, the producers of the television series "Sesame Street" were successful in preventing "Sesame Street" from being used for commercial services or goods. In that case, however, the defendant children's schools were allowed to continue a limited use as long as a disclaimer showed the absence of any affiliation with the "Sesame Street" television series (*Children's Television Workshop v. Sesame Nursery*, 171 U.S.P.Q. 105).

Of course, the likelihood of the public being deceived can change as time passes and a title or name is forgotten (*International Film Service Co., Inc. v. Associated Producers*, Inc., 273 F. 585). And if a title or name is so little known that the public never associates it with a particular work, the doctrine of unfair competition would not be applicable at all. For instance, the writers of an unpublicized and unproduced play titled *Virgin Queen* about Queen Elizabeth could not prevent the use of the title *The Virgin Queen* for an independently conceived film based on her life (*Fishler v. Twentieth Century-Fox Film Corporation*, 159 F. Supp. 215).

A case involving the distortion of work arose when Norman Granz, a well-known promoter and producer of jazz concerts, sold the right to make "How High the Moon" and "Lady Be Good" into records for marketing under the credit line "Presented by Norman Granz." The music was rerecorded from a 78 rpm master to a 33⅓ rpm master, after which 10-inch 33⅓ rpm records were sold. The 33⅓ rpm master and records deleted at least eight minutes of the original musical performance. The court stated:

> Disregarding for the moment the terms of the contract, we think that the purchaser of the master discs could lawfully use them to produce the abbreviated record and could lawfully sell the same provided he did not describe it as a recording of music presented by the plaintiff. If he did so describe it, he would commit the tort of unfair competition (*Granz v. Harris*, 198 F.2d 585, 588).

One of the judges, in a concurring opinion, wrote:

> Under the authorities, the defendant's conduct here, as my colleagues say, may also be considered a kind of "unfair competition" or "passing off." The irreparable harm, justifying an injunction, becomes apparent when one thinks what would be the result if the collected speeches of Stalin were published under the name of Senator Robert Taft, or the poems of Ella Wheeler Wilcox as those of T. S. Eliot.

The theory primarily relied upon by the court, however, was that the required credit line, "Presented by Norman Granz," created a contractual obligation that the music in fact be as Norman Granz had presented it.

This leads to an important qualification of unfair competition: It does not by itself entitle a writer to authorship credit. There is no question that in the United States a contract is valid even if a writer agrees either to work under a pseudonym or not to receive authorship credit. If a work is published without using the writer's name, it would be difficult to contend that alterations or distortions were misrepresenting the writer's work to the public. So the writer, to use unfair competition in cases involving distortion, must be receiving authorship credit.

But if a contract is silent as to whether the writer will receive authorship credit, is there still an implied obligation to give such credit? An artist named Vargas entered into an agreement with *Esquire* to create "Vargas girls," but the contract had no provision for authorship credit for the artist. In fact, the contract transferred "all rights" in the work. *Esquire* chose to publish the work under the name "Esquire girls" and Vargas had reserved no right to be credited as the artist upon publication. Despite his argument that the phrase "Vargas girls" implied he would receive credit, the court decided that he would be entitled to such credit only if the contract expressly so stated (*Vargas v. Esquire, Inc.*, 164 F.2d 522).

The writer in the United States who does not contractually reserve authorship credit is taking a risk, although the customary trade practices in the relevant medium might conceivably be shown to require such credit in the absence of any specific contractual provision. The writer should ideally reserve authorship credit, especially since such credit can be a precondition to obtaining relief in an unfair competition case involving altered or distorted work.

It should also be pointed out that unfair competition—or the closely similar doctrines relating to trademarks and trade names—cannot enlarge the copyright protections available to a writer. Samuel Clemens used the pen name Mark Twain in publishing a number of literary sketches which appeared prior to 1880. He did not copyright these sketches, so they became part of the public domain. A publisher then brought them out in a book using the name of Mark Twain as writer. Clemens objected to use of the name Mark Twain on the theory that his pen name had become a trademark which no one could use without his permission (the same argument would seem to apply whether or not the name was a pen name). The court found in favor of the publisher, stating:

> Trademarks are the means by which the manufacturers of vendible merchandise designate or state to the public the quality of such goods, and the fact that they are the manufacturers of them . . . A writer cannot, by the adoption of a *nom de plume,* be allowed to defeat the well-settled rules of the common law in force in this country, that the "publication of a literary work without copyright is a dedication to the public, after which any one may publish it." No pseudonym, however ingenious, novel, or quaint, can give a writer any more rights than he would have under his own name (*Clemens v. Belford, Clark & Co.*, 14 F. 728).

The Lanham Act, section 43(a), the federal corollary to state unfair competition laws, also offers writers some protection against unfair trade practices. An interesting case arose under the Lanham Act when, early in his career, Ken Follett was hired to do a hard edit of a manuscript. In the end, the revisions became so extensive that Follett felt he should own the copyright in the work. When Follett moved to commence legal action, the parties came to a settlement that included "With Ken Follett" being placed in smaller letters below the original writer's name on the book jacket. Several years later, when Follett's name achieved widespread recognition, the publisher reprinted the work, using Follett's name as the principal writer and switching the "with" to the other writer, referencing best sellers by Follett as by the same writer and carrying only Follett's name on the spine. Follett objected and sued. The court held that the publisher could give equal but not greater billing to Follett because to do otherwise would violate the spirit of the Lanham Act, which was designed to protect the public as well as creators from the harms of false attribution (*Follett v. New American Library, Inc.*, 497 F. Supp. 304).

Another interesting case arising under the Lanham Act's section 43(a) involved the distortion of a copyrighted work. The writers of Monty Python sued the American Broadcasting Company (ABC) for airing unauthorized edited-for-television versions of their work. Under the contract with ABC, the writers had agreed to allow minor script changes prior to initial recordation.

A few years after the initial airing of the work, ABC aired a version that cut twenty-four minutes from the original. When the writers sued for a preliminary injunction, the court, although it did not grant the injunction because of the balance of harms in the particular case, noted that:

> . . . the Lanham Act . . . has been invoked to prevent misrepresentations that may injure plaintiff's business or personal reputation . . . It is sufficient to violate the Act that a representation of a product, although technically true, creates a false impression of the product's origin . . . [When] a television network broadcasts a program properly designated as having been written and performed by a group, but which has been edited, without the writer's consent, into a form that departs substantially from the original work . . . [it] present[s] him to the public as the creator of a work not his own and thus makes him subject to criticism for work he has not done . . . In such a case, it is the writer . . . rather than the network, who suffers the consequences of the mutilation . . . Thus, an allegation that a defendant has presented to the public a "garbled," distorted version of plaintiff's work seeks to redress the very rights sought to be protected by the Lanham Act . . . (*Gilliam v. American Broadcasting Company*, 538 F.2d 14).

The court held that a valid cause of action for distortion, based on an impairment of the defendants' work and a misrepresentation of their talents, had been stated under section 43(a) of the Lanham Act. The court further noted that even a disclaimer of the defendant's authorship might not have been sufficient to protect them because television viewers often tune in late.

At the same time, the court recognized that the derivative right under the copyright law could be used to prevent mutilation or distortion in the form of unauthorized revisions, editing, and rewriting which allegedly harm the writer. Unless ABC had purchased the right to make derivative works, which it had not, its copyright license did not entitle it to make substantial changes to the work. In addition to being a violation of the Lanham Act, exceeding the grant of rights was therefore also a copyright violation. And, clearly, it was also a breach of contract.

Protection Against Defamation

Defamation is an attack on the reputation of another person. Both libel and slander are forms of defamation, libel being expressed by print, writing, pictures, or signs, and slander being expressed by spoken words. For a writer to bring an action for defamation, the defamatory material must have reached the public. Also, the defamatory material must be false, since the truth of the alleged defamatory material will be an absolute defense to a law suit based on defamation (except in a minority of states that require, in addition to truthfulness, that the publication be made without malice or for justifiable ends).

In 1913 Antonio d'Altomonte, an Italian of noble birth and a leading authority on criminology and African life and politics, was represented to be the writer of a sensational article about cannibals which appeared in the *New York Herald.* The article, accompanied by a one-half page illustration and a biography of the alleged writer, recounted in the first person the remarkable exploits of D'Altomonte in "Stopping a Congo Cannibal Feast." The article went on to state that a young American rescued by D'Altomonte was named John Harris Walton and that he still lived in San Paolo di Loando. The court concluded that the false attribution of this article was libelous to someone of D'Altomonte's reputation, because "if false and a forgery, it is calculated to destroy his influence as a writer and a lecturer . . ." (*D'Altomonte v. New York Herald Co.*, 154 App. Div. 453, 139 N.Y.S. 200, *mod.* 208 N.Y. 596, 102 N.E. 1101).

It is probably more common for a false attribution to involve material at least partially written by the person claimed to be the writer. For example, a lawyer named Joseph Clevenger wrote and edited *Clevenger's Annual Practice of New York* from 1923 to 1956. In 1956 he terminated his editorship and revoked the publisher's right to use his name as editor of any subsequent editions. Despite this, the 1959 edition stated that it was "Annually Revised" without any indication that the revisions were done by the publisher's staff. Clevenger argued that numerous mistakes in the text would be associated by the public with his name in the title, causing irreparable damage to his reputation as a competent lawyer and legal commentator. The court concluded that a jury might reasonably find that the wording and arrangement of the title page were libelous, so Clevenger's complaint could not be dismissed (*Clevenger v. Baker Voorhis & Co.*, 8 N.Y.2d 187, 168 N.E.2d 643). But Clevenger presumably would have had no grounds for a libel action if there had been a correct indication that other persons had revised the book or that the book was only derived from Clevenger's (*Geisel v. Poynter Products, Inc.*, 295 F. Supp. 331, 353).

The writer may sometimes have to meet a higher standard in showing libel than would an ordinary private citizen. For instance, an important distinction is made between defamation and criticism. A writer who places work before the public invites criticism of the work. The criticism, no matter how hostile, fantastic, or extravagant, is not by itself defamatory. However, if untrue statements are made which disparage the work, or if the writer is attacked personally in a way unconnected with the work, the critic may well have crossed the border into the area of defamation. William Buckley and Gore Vidal, both writers and well-known personalities, engaged in acrimonious television debates during the 1968 presidential campaign. These and later exchanges in magazines led to Buckley's filing a libel suit. Vidal counterclaimed for libel on the basis of Buckley's calling *Myra Breckinridge* pornography, describing Vidal as "nothing more than a literary producer of perverted Hollywood-minded prose," and writing to *Esquire* to warn that an article Vidal had submitted there might be libelous to Buckley.

The court stated that the relevant issue was not whether *Myra Breckinridge* was pornographic (and Vidal therefore a pornographer) but whether Buckley's comments were reasonable or fair and within the extensive latitude allowed to critics. After briefly discussing the contents of *Myra Breckinridge,* the court concluded that Buckley had expressed his honest opinions, which were within the protection of the rule allowing fair comment. The letter to *Esquire* was found to be a reasonable exercise of the privilege to protect one's own reputation from threats of defamation (*Buckley v. Vidal*, 327 F. Supp. 1051).

Closely related to the fair comment rule is the concept that the writer may be a public figure. Pat Montandon, who had written *How to Be a Party Girl* and was to publicize the book on television, was found to be a public figure under the following definition:

> "Public figures" are those persons who, though not public officials, are "involved in issues in which the public has a justified and important interest." Such figures are, of course, numerous and

include artists, athletes, business people, dilettantes, anyone who is famous or infamous because of who he is or what he has done (*Montandon v. Triangle Publications, Inc.*, 120 Cal. Rptr. 186, 191, 45 Cal. App.3d 938, 946, *cert. denied* 423 U.S. 893).

In order to recover for libel, a public figure must show by clear and convincing evidence that the defamation was done with malice—that is, with the knowledge that the statement was false or with a reckless disregard as to whether the statement was true or false. Montandon, through a bizarre series of events, was presented in *TV Guide* as planning to speak on the topic of "From Party Girl to Call Girl." The obvious implication was that Montandon had experience as a call girl, which was utterly without foundation. The court found in her favor on the libel claim, since the jury could reasonably have found that the call girl reference had been published with reckless disregard for its truth or falsity.

The limitations of defamation actions are shown in a case involving four well-known pro-Soviet Russian composers who sought to prevent the use of their music and names in connection with a film allegedly having an anti-Soviet theme. This espionage film, eighty-seven minutes long, used as incidental background music forty-five minutes of public domain compositions by Dmitri Shostakovich, Aram Khachaturian, Serge Prokofieff, and Nicolai Miakovsky. A credit line indicated that the music was from the selected works of these composers. The libel charge was based on the idea that the public would believe the composers had consented to the use of the music and, therefore, had acted in a disloyal and unpatriotic manner. The court stated that work in the public domain can be freely copied by all, so no implication of consent can be found either from the use of the music or the credit line. The composers' reputations would not be damaged and distribution of the film was allowed (*Shostakovich v. Twentieth Century-Fox Film Corp.*, 196 Misc. 67, 80 N.Y.S.2d 575, *aff'd* 275 App. Div. 692, 87 N.Y.S.2d 430). But when suit was brought in France, the French court found that the film violated the composers' moral rights.

In another transatlantic case, a New York court decided that suit for a bad French translation would have to be brought against the French publisher in France—not against the United States publisher who sold the translation rights. Since no contractual right had been given to distort or alter the work, the court observed that:

> . . . sufficient evidence has been shown to establish such substantial alteration as would warrant the granting of some relief to a writer who was entitled to and interested in the preservation and integrity of his work, if the parties responsible for the alteration

of his work were before the court (*Seroff v. Simon & Schuster, Inc.*, 6 Misc.2d 383, 162 N.Y.S.2d 770).

The protection against defamation is personal and protects only the writer while he or she is alive, not assignees or heirs. Defamation and the next topic, invasion of privacy, are also discussed in chapter 8.

Right to Privacy

The right to privacy is the right to be free from unwanted and unnecessary publicity or interference which could injure the personal feelings of the writer or present the writer in a false light before the public. This right is recognized in varying forms by almost every state. New York's Civil Rights Law Section 50, for example, prohibits using "for advertising purposes, or for the purposes of trade, the name, portrait or picture of any living person without having first obtained the written consent of such person." Under Section 51, however, this right is specifically not applicable to use of "the name, portrait or picture of any writer, composer or artist in connection with his literary, musical or artistic productions which he has sold or disposed of with such name, portrait or picture used in connection therewith."

A professor's privacy was invaded when his name was used in the unauthorized publication of his course lecture notes. The use of his name implied the professor's consent when, in fact, he reasonably believed the publication might jeopardize his professional standing (*Williams v. Weisser*, 78 Cal. Rptr. 542). It may be that false attribution is an invasion of privacy, although the cases are not all in agreement on this. At least one decision indicates that no invasion of privacy occurs if a work in the public domain is published using the writer's real name, even though the book originally appeared under a pen name (*Ellis v. Hurst*, 70 Misc. 122, 128 N.Y.S. 144; compare *Ellis v. Hurst*, 66 Misc. 235, 121 N.Y.S. 438). And the courts have also determined that the right of privacy does not protect pen names, only real names (*Geisel v. Poynter Products*, Inc., 295 F. Supp. 331, 355).

The right to privacy diminishes when the writer gains stature as a public figure, particularly with respect to those areas of the writer's life in which the public has a legitimate interest. Ayn Rand's review of *Chaos Below Heaven* by Eugene Vale was accurately quoted on the book's jacket without her permission. The court viewed the use of her name not as a blatant commercial exploitation of her personality, but rather as a comment by a public figure on a matter of current interest. Her suit based on an invasion of privacy was denied (*Rand v. Hearst Corp.*, 31 App. Div.2d 406, 298 N.Y.S.2d 405, *aff'd* 26 N.Y.2d 806, 309 N.Y.S.2d 348, 257 N.E.2d 895). While theoretically the right to privacy might be used to protect the writer against distortions of the writer's work, the practical effect of the right to privacy in this area would seem quite limited.

The right to privacy is personal and only the living writer may assert it, not assignees or heirs.

Right to Publicity

The right to publicity is a relatively new right independent of the right of privacy. The right to publicity states that a person with a public reputation has a right to benefit from the commercial value associated with that person's name or picture. Sports figures, for example, have the right to financial benefits from use of their names and pictures on baseball cards or in a baseball game. But the right to publicity will be of little value to the writer who is not well known.

The right to publicity does not prevent advertising uses of a famous person's name and picture if such uses are incidental to a legitimate news article. For example, Joe Namath was the subject of many newsworthy articles on football in *Sports Illustrated.* However, when *Sports Illustrated* used photographs from the articles to illustrate advertising, Namath contended that his right to publicity had been violated. The court concluded that the use of the name and photographs of Namath were only uses incidental to establishing the quality and news content of *Sports Illustrated.* To allow damages might well violate the First Amendment guarantees of freedom of speech and press, so Namath lost the case (*Namath v. Sports Illustrated*, 48 A.D.2d 487, *aff'd* 39 N.Y.2d 897).

In 1984, California enacted a celebrity rights law to clarify the nature of the publicity rights developed by court decisions. A number of other states have followed California's lead. The basic approach of these laws is to protect the publicity rights of deceased people for up to fifty years after their death. This applies to people whose name, voice, signature, or likeness had commercial value at the time of death, whether or not that commercial value had been exploited during life. Prohibited uses cover commercial exploitation, including the sale of merchandise or services, as well as advertising. Typical exemptions from the coverage of these laws would include works in the public interest and material of political or newsworthy value.

These celebrity rights laws impinge on the freedom of expression guaranteed to writers by the First Amendment. Since creative works are likely to be disseminated nationally, it may be that the most restrictive celebrity rights law will govern whether a writer must seek permission from the people to whom the decedent has transferred the celebrity rights or, if no transfer has been made, the heirs of the decedent.

In any event, valuable as this right of publicity may be to well-known writers, the right will at present neither protect writers from being denied authorship credit if a contract is silent as to such credit nor protect works from distorting changes. The right to publicity, unlike the protections against defamation and invasion of privacy, can be assigned or enforced by heirs.

Protection Against Misappropriation

A misappropriation is a wrongful taking or use of someone else's property. Some cases involving literary property do not fit easily under copyright infringement or unfair competition, but can be decided under the designation of misappropriation. Such a case revolved around Amos Burke, a fictional detective created by Pulitzer Prize–winning playwright Frank D. Gilroy. Burke developed out of a television program, "Who Killed Julie Greer," and became the main character in the ABC series "Burke's Law," which ran from 1963 through 1966. Gilroy assigned only his television rights in the character to ABC, retaining the publishing rights for himself since he planned to write a series of detective novels using Burke as the protagonist. However, the defendants—ABC, Four Star Television, Barbety Television Enterprises, Simon & Schuster, and Dell Publishing Company—cooperated in publishing two paperback novels and three comic books using the character of Burke. In 1965 Gilroy brought suit in New York State Supreme Court based upon this misappropriation of his literary property.

Seven years later a verdict was handed down in Gilroy's favor. The court agreed that the defendants had misappropriated the character of Burke and awarded Gilroy $15,000 in damages, the amount of the profits realized by the defendants from their publications. Gilroy appealed, arguing that the value of his property had been far greater than $15,000. It was contended that a writer of his ability could have made far more than that by writing a series of detective novels, but that the books published by the defendants had been of inferior quality and ruined the market for sequels dealing with Burke. Moreover, it was argued that expert testimony should have been permitted to establish reasonable damages based on the profit potential of the Burke character if used in a series of books written by Gilroy.

The Appellate Division agreed with these contentions, stating that: "The proper measure of damages flowing from defendants' wrongful appropriation of plaintiff's literary property is the reasonable value thereof and 'Opinion evidence of the value of the property' is admissible." The case was remanded to the New York State Supreme Court for a new trial on the issue of damages. At the new trial expert testimony was given by Marc Jaffe, senior vice president of Bantam Books, and Henry Morrison, a literary agent. The jury, after listening to their appraisals of what a series of Amos Burke books would have earned, returned a verdict of $745,000 in favor of Gilroy. The addition of interest and costs increased the total award to $1,185,737.

The defendants appealed to the Appellate Division, arguing that the damages were speculative and not based on any reasonable certainty of what would have been earned. The Appellate Division concluded:

> We think that what the defendant misappropriated had value. To some extent, at least, plaintiff's difficulty in demonstrating the amount of value is due to what we have determined to be defendant's fault . . . We think, however, that the present verdict cannot stand for the reason that it rests on evidence that is wholly speculative, essentially an estimate of royalties without any "stable foundation for a reasonable estimate of royalties." . . . On the whole, we think the interest of substantial justice will best be achieved by reducing plaintiff's recovery to the principal amount of $100,000 together with appropriate interest thereon.

The principal with interest amounted to nearly $200,000. The Appellate Division's reasoning that the damages were speculative rested on the fact that Gilroy had never written a mystery novel, so the expert testimony had gone too far in assuming the sales and prices of a series of mystery novels to be written at the rate of two per year over a period of fifteen years. Yet the $100,000 award was far in excess of the $15,000 originally given Gilroy (*Gilroy v. American Broadcasting System, Inc.*, 47 App. Div.2d 728, 365 N.Y.S.2d 193 *aff'd* 46 N.Y.2d 580, 389 N.E.2d 117, 415 N.Y.S.2d 804). In suitable cases, therefore, expert testimony will be admissible to establish the reasonable earning potential of literary property which has been misappropriated.

Writers in the United States

The enlightened approach often found abroad which explicitly creates moral rights for writers has yet to be adopted in the United States. Instead, the different doctrines which protect the writer here focus far more closely on economic rights, while leaving risks that the writer may not receive proper authorship credit or will have no recourse to prevent alterations or distortions of his or her work. Carefully drawn contracts, the creation and terms of which are discussed in chapters 10–18, are the writer's best avenue to obtain protections similar to moral rights. Such contracts can resolve troublesome issues long before costly litigation arises, although resort to the courts may still be necessary if wrongful use is made of a writer's name or literary creations.

8 The Limits of Expression

The First Amendment of the United States Constitution provides guarantees of freedom of expression which apply to writers and their works. These guarantees are not unlimited, however, and the writer must be aware that the content of a written work can sometimes give rise to civil or criminal liability. For example, copyright, the doctrine of unfair competition, the rights to privacy and publicity, and protection from defamation safeguard not only the writer but the writer's competitors as well. Significantly, other private citizens also have rights protecting them from invasion of privacy or defamation which the writer will have to consider when creating work. In addition, the public at large, through governmental agencies, may seek to suppress works which are considered obscene or that might deny a fair trial to a criminal defendant because of excessive publicity. And school boards will sometimes act as censors of textbooks or library books thought undesirable for a student readership.

Defamation

Defamation is an attack upon a person's reputation through written or spoken words, in books, pictures, signs, on television, radio, or even the Internet. That attack must reach the public, since damage to reputation is a requirement for an action for defamation. Whether the defamation is a libel or a slander depends on the medium in which the defamation occurs. Printed materials and films give rise to actions for libel, while spoken words give rise to actions for slander. Whether television and radio broadcasts give rise to libel or slander is gradually being resolved by statutes enacted in the various states, the importance of the issue being that a libel suit is often easier for the plaintiff than one based on slander (in which damages to reputation sometimes have to be proven, instead of simply assumed from the nature of the defamatory statement). Generally, everyone who participates in publishing defamatory material will be liable to the defamed person. While the truth of an alleged defamation is a valid defense, the burden of proving truthfulness is on the person who asserts truth as a defense.

Injury to reputation is the essence of defamation. The writer who attacks a person's reputation, for example by representing a person as involved in unethical or criminal conduct, as physically deformed in an unnatural or obscene way, or as lacking manners or intelligence, may face a libel suit. One decision states: "Reputation is said in a general way to be injured by words which tend to expose one to public hatred, shame, obloquy, contumely, odium, contempt, ridicule, aversion, ostracism, degradation or disgrace, or to induce an evil opinion of one in the minds of right-thinking persons, and to deprive one of their confidence and friendly intercourse in society" (*Kimmerle v. New York Evening Journal*, 262 N.Y. 99, 102, 186 N.E. 217, 218). In a more recent case, where the defendant had accused the plaintiff of leaving his children alone at night, having a serious drinking problem, and failing to properly cloth his children, choosing instead to buy a car, the defendant's statements were held to be per se libel because they alleged criminal neglect. Nevertheless, the case was dismissed on the grounds that the libelous statements were legally justified on the grounds of truth (*Haynes v. Alfred A. Knopf, Inc.*, 8 F.3d 1222, 21 Med. L. Rptr. 2165).

Statements found to be defamatory per se include allegations that a person "has attempted suicide, that he refused to pay his just debts, that he is immoral or unchaste, or 'queer,' or has made improper advances to women, or is having 'wife trouble,' and is about to be divorced; that he is a coward, a drunkard, a hypocrite, a liar, a scoundrel, a crook, a scandal-monger, an anarchist, a skunk, a bastard, a eunuch, or a 'rotten egg'; that he is 'unfair' to labor, or that he has done a thing which is oppressive or dishonorable, or heartless, because all of these things obviously tend to affect the esteem in which he is held by his neighbors" (Prosser, *The Law of Torts*, 4th ed., pages 753-54). The injury to reputation need only occur in the eyes of any substantial and respectable group in society, rather than society-at-large. And a statement which is defamatory at one time and place might not be defamatory in a different context.

The words used must be interpreted as they were reasonably understood in view of all the circumstances, including the entire statement which was made. The court decides whether the words could reasonably be understood as defamatory, after which the jury decides whether the words in fact were understood in that sense. Humor, ridicule, sarcasm, questions, and insinuations can all be defamatory if they are reasonably understood to disgrace someone. A distinction is made between statements of fact and those of opinion. Opinion, such as abusive name-calling done in anger, may very well be considered not to contain any specific charge which could be considered defamatory. But just because a statement is made in the form of an opinion will not give protection against defamatory assertions of fact that may be included in the opinion (*Milkovich v. Lorain Journal Co.*, 497 U.S. 1, 110 S. Ct. 2695). A person who repeats a defamatory statement is liable for defamation, even if the person gives the original source, indicates that he or she does not believe the statement to be true, uses the customary newspaper phrase "it is alleged," or states the story is based on rumors.

The defamatory statement need not refer to a person by name in order to be actionable. It is enough that the depiction be recognizable to those acquainted with the person's reputation. The problems this can cause with fictional works based on real events or the writer's own experiences are substantial. For example, MGM made a film depicting Rasputin as the cause of the destruction of imperial Russia. In the course of the film, a character named Princess Natasha is either seduced or raped by Rasputin. Many other facts included in the film indicated that Princess Natasha in real life was Princess Irina-Alexandrova. The court sustained as reasonable the jury's finding in favor of the Princess and awarding her 25,000 British Pounds. One justice, in weighing the defendant's arguments, rejected ". . . the contention that no reasonable jury could come to the conclusion that to say of a woman that she had been ravished by a man of very bad character, when as a matter of fact she never saw the man at all and was never near him, is not defamatory of the woman. I really have no language to express my opinion of that argument" (*Youssoupoff v. Metro-Goldwyn-Mayer*, 50 T.L.R. 581, 584, 99 A.L.R. 864, 870). Thomas Wolfe, whose fiction was highly autobiographical, had publication of one book held up because of the threat of a libel suit by a former mistress and, in another case, was actually sued by a former landlady and had to settle out of court despite his desire to fight the suit.

Fictional works will often use a disclaimer such as, "All circumstances in this novel are imaginary, and none of the characters exist in real life." The problem is that such a disclaimer means little if, in fact, the characters are drawn from real life. According to a comment in *The Restatement of the Law of Torts:* "The fact that the author or producer states that his work is exclusively one of fiction, and in no sense applicable to living persons, is immaterial except as to punitive damages, if readers actually and reasonably understand otherwise. Such a statement, however, is a factor to be considered by the jury in determining whether readers did so understand it [and, if they did], whether the understanding was reasonable." Punitive damages are extra damages beyond what is necessary to compensate a plaintiff for injuries suffered. They are awarded because the acts complained of by the plaintiff are reckless or malicious. A carefully drafted disclaimer, relevant to the particular content of the book, can thus have value.

A different approach to the problem of libel in fiction is to alter the fictional characters that may be the basis for libel suits. This can work very well, since changing a work's locale, plot, and the facts surrounding the characters' lives—including appearance and mannerisms—can ensure that no real persons will suffer a libel. The problem, of course, is whether the fictional work retains its integrity after the alterations. Some writers will be able to work out a compromise between what they want to say and what they dare to say, and others will not.

A lawyer's advice is a necessity if a piece is to be reworked due to fear of a libel suit. Similarly, a lawyer should be consulted if a release is to be sought from the person who might otherwise bring the libel suit. A release form would indicate that the person knows he or she will be the model for a character who may have additional fictional characteristics or experiences. The person—in return for a consideration such as payment of money—agrees not to make a claim or sue for libel, invasion of privacy, or any other reason based on the content, advertising, or promotion of the work. A problem arises, however, if the person is approached but refuses to sign the release. If the publisher or producer proceeds, the person defamed can argue for punitive damages on the basis that prior knowledge of the defamatory content is shown by the request for the release.

A different problem with fiction can arise when characters and names are completely imaginary but happen to correspond closely with a real person. An English newspaper published a fictional article of humor about the double life of a Mr. Artemus Jones, a blameless church warden who lived at Peckham with his wife except when he was secretly across the Channel at Dieppe "betraying a most unholy delight in the society of female butterflies." A real Mr. Artemus Jones sued for libel. This Mr. Jones was an unmarried lawyer who lived in North Wales. He complained only of the use of his name. The jury gave Mr.

Jones a substantial award for damages. The defendant's appeals were to no avail, and the headnote to the final decision states: "In an action for libel, if the language used is, in the opinion of the jury, defamatory and people reading it may reasonably think that it refers to the plaintiff, damages are recoverable, even though the writer or publisher may not have intended to refer to any particular individual" (*Hulton and Co., Ltd. v. Jones*, 26 T.L.R. 128, 129).

The requirement of reasonableness, however, saves fiction writers from facing an impossible task in the choice of names. James T. Farrell wrote a novel titled *Bernard Clare* after the name of the main character. The novel, while clearly fictional, draws in part on Farrell's own experiences as a young man journeying from Chicago to New York in order to become a writer. The character's name derived from County Clare in Ireland and was intended to connote an Irish background. A newspaperman named Bernard Clare claimed that he had been libeled by the novel. This real Bernard Clare had worked in Minnesota, Michigan, and Wisconsin, and had nothing in common with Farrell's fictional character except sharing the same name. The court granted Farrell's motion for summary judgment, stating: "It would be an astonishing doctrine if every writer of fiction were required to make a search among all the records available in this Nation which might tabulate the names and activities of millions of people in order to determine whether perchance one of the characters in the contemplated book designated as a novel may have the same name and occupation as a real person . . . It is inconceivable that any sensible person could assume or believe from reading this book of fiction that it purported to refer to the life or career of the Bernard Clare who was a newspaper writer in Minneapolis" (*Clare v. Farrell*, 70 F. Supp. 276, 279-80).

Defamatory statements directed at a large group will not be considered to defame an individual member of the group. To avoid unchecked group defamation in attacks on various minority groups, some states have enacted criminal statutes to punish such defamation. An individual can sue for defamation when the group defamed is small. "All of A's sons are murderers" is a defamation for which each son can sue individually. But the statement that "Some of A's sons are murderers" would be a much more difficult statement upon which to bring suit because not all of the sons are defamed and the ones defamed are not identified.

The First Amendment provides important limitations on the extent to which actions for defamation can successfully be pursued. The right of a public figure, in particular, to sue for libel is limited to false statements made with actual malice or reckless disregard of the truth (*New York Times v. Sullivan*, 376 U.S. 254). The term *public figure* is itself subject to definition. For example, a woman successfully sued a magazine for unfavorably misreporting the grounds of her divorce decree.

Although the woman was often mentioned in society columns and actually gave news conferences because of the widespread reporting of her divorce proceedings, the Supreme Court reasoned she was not a public figure because she had no major role in society's affairs and had not voluntarily joined in a public controversy with an intention to influence the outcome (*Firestone v. Time, Inc.*, 424 U.S. 448).

Similarly, when a magazine accused a prominent lawyer of having framed a policeman as part of a Communist conspiracy to discredit the police, the attorney was determined not to be a public figure. The Supreme Court stated: "The communications media are entitled to act on the assumption that public officials and public figures have voluntarily exposed themselves to increased risk of injury from defamatory falsehoods concerning them. No such assumption is justified with respect to a private individual" (*Gertz v. Robert Welch, Inc.*, 418 U.S. 323, *cert. denied* 459 U.S. 1226).

The Supreme Court determined that the states should have discretion to determine the standard of liability for defamation where a private individual is involved in a matter of public interest, so long as the states require some negligence or fault on the part of the person accused of the defamation. Thus, where a matter of public interest is involved, a public figure will have to show actual malice or reckless disregard for the truth to recover for defamation, while a private individual will only have to show negligence (assuming negligence has been selected as the relevant state standard). The Supreme Court recently defined the actual malice test stating: "However, in place of the term actual malice, it is better practice that jury instructions refer to publication of a statement with knowledge of falsity or reckless disregard as to truth or falsity." The court found that even a deliberate alteration of a plaintiff's words did not amount to knowledge of falsity because it did not result "in a material change in the statement's meaning" (*Masson v. New Yorker Magazine, Inc.*, 501 U.S. 496). When a private person is defamed on a matter not of public interest, there is no requirement even to show an intent to defame. Recovery in such a case is allowed on the basis of the defamation alone and malice or reckless disregard for the truth is only relevant in fixing punitive damages.

In cases in which a public official is defamed as to private aspects of his or her life, the official will be treated as a person (*Crane v. The Arizona Republic*, 972 F.2d 1511, 20 Media L. Rptr. 1649). Individuals can become limited purpose public figures in a variety of circumstances, especially when they actively, voluntarily or wilfully seek the public eye. In such cases, courts will treat them as public figures (*Russo v. Conde Nast Publications*, 806 F. Supp. 603, 20 Med. L. Rptr. 2113).

Damages for defamation can be lessened by a retraction of the defamatory statement. The retraction must be a complete and unequivocal attempt to repair the injury to reputation which has taken place. The retraction should be given the same prominence and publicity as the defamation, and come as soon after the defamation as possible. Such a retraction can be used to show that the plaintiff's reputation was not so badly damaged or that there was an absence of the malice necessary for punitive damages. In many states statutes limit the amount of damages which can be recovered if a retraction is made or if no retraction is requested by the injured person.

A person with a notoriously bad reputation is not likely to win a libel suit even where the words are false and per se defamatory. This is because in order to state a valid claim for defamation the plaintiff must show damage. When a plaintiff's reputation is already sullied that may prove difficult (*Brooks v. American Broadcasting Co.*, 737 F. Supp. 431, *aff'd in part, vacated, remanded in part* 932 F.2d 495).

Defamation is also discussed in chapter 7. It is mentioned there that only a living person who has been defamed may bring suit for defamation because neither assignees nor heirs can have the requisite standing (*Gugliuzza v. KCMC, Inc.*, 606 So. 2d 790, 20 Media Law Rptr. 1866). Statutes in a number of states do make defamation of the dead into a crime, but these statutes have been held not to give surviving relatives a right to sue.

Invasion of Privacy

The right to privacy is the right to be free from unwanted and unnecessary publicity or interference which could injure the personal feelings of the writer or present the writer in a false light. Recognized in varying forms by almost every state, it has been said to protect four distinct types of interests: (1) the appropriation of a person's name or likeness for business or commercial uses; (2) the disclosure to the public of embarrassing private facts; (3) the placing of a false image of a person before the public; and (4) intrusion into a person's seclusion or private life, such as by invading someone's home or eavesdropping by the use of wire taps.

Protection against appropriation is exemplified by New York Civil Rights Law Section 51, which provides: "Any person whose name, portrait or picture is used within this state for advertising purposes or for the purposes of trade without . . . written consent . . . may maintain an equitable action in the supreme court of this state against the person, firm or corporation so using his name, portrait or picture, to prevent and restrain the use thereof; and may also sue and recover damages for any injuries sustained by reason of such use and if the defendant shall have knowingly used such person's name, portrait or picture in such manner as is forbidden or declared to be unlawful . . . the jury, in its discretion, may award exemplary damages." Exemplary damages are the same as punitive damages.

Appropriation involves the use of a name or picture which identifies someone. A picture of a person's hand or foot without further identification would not be an appropriation. The mere fact that by coincidence a name in a novel is the same as a person's name in real life is not an appropriation. Nor is there an appropriation if an incidental mention of a person's name occurs in a book or motion picture. And, as discussed with respect to Joe Namath in chapter 7, magazines and newspapers can use articles and accompanying photographs for advertising the newsworthy qualities of the publication.

When Betty Friedan, a feminist leader and well-known writer, did a series of pieces for *New York Magazine* titled "The Year We Entered Modern Times," part of the series described her life twenty-five years before, including an illustrative photograph of her with her son and former husband. The court held the former husband's right to privacy had not been violated because Betty Friedan had become a public figure and the course of her life twenty-five years before was of public interest. Moreover, television commercials for *New York Magazine* based on the article were not an invasion of privacy either, since ". . . it has long been held that, under New York law, an advertisement, the purpose of which is to advertise the article, 'shares the privilege enjoyed by the article' if 'the article itself was unobjectionable'" (*Friedan v. Friedan*, 414 F. Supp. 77, 79).

The public disclosure of embarrassing private facts is an aspect of the right of privacy which has been made largely ineffectual by the doctrine permitting the publication of newsworthy information. A leading case involved William James Sidis, a child prodigy who at the age of eleven lectured on four-dimensional bodies to distinguished mathematicians and at the age of sixteen graduated from Harvard College. But after his graduation he suffered a nervous breakdown, felt revulsion for his feats as a child, and sought obscurity. Nearly a quarter of a century after his youthful fame, a writer for the *New Yorker* sought him out for a brief biographical sketch that the magazine published in 1937. The article was admittedly factual, but appeared against Sidis' will. It discussed not only his early renown, but the failed efforts to prevent discovery of his identity, his choice of a clerk's position in which his mathematical skill would not have to be used, and his curious interests—collecting streetcar transfers and studying the lore of the Okamakammessett Indians. The writer accurately portrayed Sidis' peculiar manner of speech and laughter as well as his shabby and untidy living quarters. Despite all the time that had passed, the court affirmed the dismissal of Sidis' suit for invasion of privacy because he ". . . was once a public figure. As a child prodigy, he excited both admiration and curiosity. Of him great deeds were expected . . . Since then Sidis has cloaked himself in obscurity, but his subsequent history, containing, as it did, the answer to the question of whether he had fulfilled his early promise, was still a matter of public concern" (*Sidis v. F-R Pub. Corporation*, 113 F.2d 806, 809, *cert. den.* 311 U.S. 711). But the court did not make the doctrine of newsworthiness so unlimited as to prevent an invasion of privacy suit for an unusual or shocking public disclosure of private facts. The court continued: "Revelations may be so intimate and so unwarranted in view of the victim's position as to outrage the community's notions of decency."

Another case which followed this rule with respect to news-worthiness involved the well-known body surfer named Mike Virgil. He gave an interview to a writer for *Sports Illustrated* in which he frankly told of his "putting out cigarettes in his mouth and diving off stairs to impress women, hurting himself in order to collect unemployment so as to have time for bodysurfing at the Wedge during summer, fighting in gang fights as a youngster, and eating insects . . ." Virgil revoked his consent to the publication when he realized the article would include these juvenile transgressions as well as his prowess as a body surfer. But the revocation did not help him, since the court concluded that ". . . the personal facts concerning Mike Virgil were included as a legitimate journalistic attempt to explain Virgil's extremely daring and dangerous style of body surfing at the Wedge. There is no possibility that a juror could conclude that the personal facts were included for any inherent morbid, sensational, or curiosity appeal they might have." The court stated that the final test of newsworthiness or legitimate public interest depends upon the values of the community (*Virgil v. Time, Inc.*, 527 F.2d 1122, *cert. den.*, 96 S. Ct. 2215 and *on remand* 424 F. Supp. 1286).

One revelation which did violate a person's right to privacy involved a man who had been convicted of hijacking a truck eleven years before, but who had since reformed and hidden his criminal past from his friends and his daughter. *Reader's Digest* ran an article about hijacking which mentioned the man by name and related the hijacking incident without stating when it had occurred. The court concluded that ". . . identification of the *actor* in reports of long past crimes usually serves little independent public purpose . . . Unless the individual has reattracted the public eye to himself in some independent fashion, the only public 'interest' that would usually be served is that of curiosity" (*Briscoe v. Reader's Digest Association*, 4 Cal. 3d 529, 537, 483 P.2d 34, 40). The facts of the crime could be reported since past crimes remained newsworthy, but use of the name of the rehabilitated individual did not serve the public interest and constituted an invasion of his privacy. Of course, this rule only prevents the use of names in special circumstances. It would not apply if the criminal reattracted public attention—for example, by committing more crimes or running for public office—or if the crime itself had great notoriety like that surrounding the Saint Valentine's Day Massacre.

The placing of a person in a false light before the public is a form of invasion of privacy which is quite similar to an action for libel (except that a false light invasion could be laudatory instead of defamatory). It was probably this aspect of the right of privacy which enabled Lord Byron to prevent publication of poems falsely attributed to him. The false light cases frequently involve a personality or event of public interest which is presented to the public in a fictionalized form. If true, the account would be protected by the First Amendment as newsworthy. But if transformed into a version which is substantially fictional, its newsworthiness is lost along with the protection of the First Amendment.

The United States Supreme Court considered this issue in a case in which *Life Magazine* ran a fictionalized account of a true incident. The article truly stated that three escaped convicts had imprisoned a suburban Philadelphia family for nineteen hours, but it added fictional acts of violence and verbal sexual abuse. The family, which had since moved and sought obscurity, sued for invasion of privacy. The court held ". . . that the constitutional protections for speech and press preclude the application of the New York statute to redress false reports of matters of public interest in the absence of proof that the defendant published the report with knowledge of its falsity or in reckless disregard of the truth" (*Time, Inc. v. Hill*, 385 U.S. 374, 387–388). The case was sent back to the lower courts for a determination as to whether *Life Magazine* had published the article with knowledge of its falsity or in reckless disregard of the truth.

Another false light invasion of privacy case involved the well-known baseball pitcher Warren Spahn. The New York courts found that a biography of Spahn for a juvenile audience contained gross errors of fact, invented dialogue, and a manipulated chronology of events. The facts had been altered to fit a dramatic portrayal appealing to the readership but remote from Spahn's actual life. The writer never interviewed Spahn or anyone who knew Spahn, but instead worked from uncorroborated newspaper and magazine clippings. Although Spahn admittedly was a public figure, the court concluded that he had shown the biography to be published with knowledge of the falsifications or a reckless disregard for the truth. He was awarded $10,000 in damages and the publisher was enjoined from printing or distributing *The Warren Spahn Story* (*Spahn v. Julian Messer, Inc.*, 18 N.Y.2d 324, 221 N.E.2d 543, *vacated and remanded*, 387 U.S. 239, *aff'd*, 21 N.Y.2d 124, 233 N.E.2d 840, *appeal dismissed*, 393 U.S. 1046).

An obvious corollary of the Spahn decision is that an essentially truthful biography of a public figure will not be grounds for an invasion of privacy suit. In one case, Random House published a biography entitled *Howard Hughes* by John Keats. Hughes, a well-known public figure, sought to prevent publication on an invasion of privacy theory. The court noted that Hughes had not even proven that *Howard Hughes* contained false statements, so the issue of whether there had been knowledge of falsity or a reckless disregard for the truth could not be reached. Random House was able to proceed with publication of the biography (*Rosemont Enterprises, Inc. v. Random House, Inc.*, 58 Misc.2d 1, 294 N.Y.S.2d 122, aff'd, 32 A.D.2d 892, 301 N.Y.S. 2d 948).

The final category of invasion of privacy involves intrusions into another person's seclusion or private life. The intrusion may be physical, such as a trespass into someone's home, but often relates to unauthorized electronic surveillance. There need be no publication in order to recover damages based on intrusion, since the intrusion itself is the invasion of privacy. In a much publicized case, former employees of Senator Thomas Dodd (aided by some current staff members) entered his office, removed and photocopied documents, and returned the original documents to their place in the files. Copies of these documents were turned over to the syndicated columnists Jack Anderson and Drew Pearson, who published articles based on the information. Anderson and Pearson had no involvement in the plans to get the documents, but in fact knew of the intrusion into Dodd's office prior to publishing the articles. The court reasoned that ". . . in analyzing a claimed breach of privacy, injuries from intrusion and injuries from publication should be kept clearly separate. Where there is intrusion, the intruder should generally be liable whatever the content of what he learns . . . On the other hand, where the claim is that private information concerning plaintiff has been published, the question of whether that information is genuinely private or is of public interest should not turn on the manner in which it has been obtained." Pearson and Anderson could not be liable for injuries caused by the intrusion for they had no part in the intrusion. And, since Dodd was a public figure, they could not be liable for publishing truthful articles pertaining to his qualifications as a United States senator. The summary judgment granted against Dodd was affirmed (*Pearson v. Dodd*, 410 F.2d 701, 705, *cert. denied*, 395 U.S. 947).

An invasion of privacy did take place, however, when *Life Magazine* equipped two employees with hidden radio transmitters and cameras and had them pose as patients in order to gain entry to the private home of a quack doctor. The court observed that: "The First Amendment has never been construed to accord newsmen immunity from torts or crimes committed during the course of newsgathering." It also permitted the amount of the damages for intrusion to be increased because of the subsequent publication of an article based on information obtained by the hidden devices (*Dietemann v. Time, Inc.*, 449 F.2d 245, 249).

The complexity of the doctrines relating to invasion of privacy makes resort to a lawyer necessary if difficulties are anticipated. The lawyer may determine that a release from any claims for invasion of privacy should be sought from people who might bring suit. Privacy is also discussed in chapter 7.

Obscenity

The First Amendment protection of expression does not extend to works that are legally obscene. Historically, the censors in England sought to prevent sedition against the Crown or blasphemy against the Church. The suppression of sexually impure expression gained impetus with the Victorian era, and in this century has all but replaced the original concerns of the censors. Just a few examples of books challenged for obscenity in the United States include Giovanni Boccaccio's *Decameron*, John Cleland's *Memoirs of a Woman of Pleasure*, Gustave Flaubert's *November*, Henry Miller's *Tropic of Cancer*, James Joyce's *Ulysses*, D. H. Lawrence's *Lady Chatterley's Lover*, Eugene O'Neill's *Strange Interlude*, and Edmund Wilson's *Memoirs of Hecate County*. The crucial issue becomes the definition of what is obscene.

The United States Supreme Court has given the following guidelines for determining what is obscene:

> (a) whether "the average person, applying contemporary community standards" would find that the work, taken as a whole, appeals to the prurient interest . . . ; (b) whether the work depicts or describes, in a patently offensive way, sexual conduct specifically defined by applicable state law; and (c) whether the work, taken as a whole, lacks serious literary, artistic, political, or scientific value (*Miller v. California*, 413 U.S. 15).

These guidelines hardly seem to offer more guidance than the subjective reaction of the ordinary citizen as to what may be obscene. Also, the guidelines specifically refer to community standards and state laws. This means that standards for judging what is obscene will vary not only from state to state depending on the state laws, but also from community to community depending on the local standards. The United States Supreme Court has clarified that community standards apply to clauses (a) and (b) in the test for obscenity, but that a reasonable person standard is to be used for clause (c) (*Pope v. Illinois*, 481 U.S. 497). The reasonable man standard, while still difficult to ascertain objectively, is a national standard which should not vary from one community to the next.

Courts have contributed so little to a clear definition of what validly comes within the scope of the obscene that it is perhaps of equal interest to hear what writers have had to say on the subject.

Henry Miller's writing found audiences in France and Japan long before the original English-language versions of his books were permitted publication in his native Brooklyn, New York. In his essay "Defense of the Freedom to Read," which sought to prevent the suppression of his book *Sexus* in Norway, he wrote: "But it is not something evil, not something poisonous, which this book *Sexus* offers the Norwegian reader. It is a dose of life which I administered to myself first, and which I not only survived but thrived on. Certainly I would not recommend it to infants, but then neither would I offer a child a bottle of *aqua vite*. I can only say one thing for it unblushingly—compared to the atom bomb, it is full of life-giving qualities."

D. H. Lawrence criticized society's guidelines for obscenity in his essay, "Pornography and Obscenity," in which he said: "There's nothing wrong with sexual feelings in themselves, so long as they are straightforward and not sneaking or sly. The right sort of sex stimulus is invaluable to human daily life. Without it the world grows grey . . . But even I would censor genuine pornography, rigorously. It would not be very difficult. In the first place, genuine pornography is almost always underworld, it doesn't come into the open. In the second, you can recognize it by the insult it offers, invariably, to sex, and to the human spirit." Lawrence noted as well that concepts of obscenity change with different societies and epochs. But our contemporary legal definition of obscenity excludes both violence and insult to the human spirit. Instead there is a categorization of meaningless terms, such as prurient, lascivious, lewd, and vile, which connote no more than the word "obscene" itself.

In the final analysis, it is impossible for the writer or his or her distributors to know when and where a work containing sexual motifs may be found obscene. At the least, no violation of the obscenity laws will occur while the work is kept in the privacy of the study. But the obscenity laws, if applicable, can cover such uses of work as possession for sale or exhibition, sale, distribution, exhibition, mailing, importation through customs, and transmission over the Internet. The manner in which the material is offered to the public may be important in a determination of obscenity. If there is an emphasis solely on the sexual aspects of the works, this factor will increase the likelihood of a determination that the work is obscene. If minors have access to the work, an even higher standard than that applicable to pornography may be applied by the states without violating the First Amendment.

The First Amendment, however, offers important procedural safeguards to the writer whose work risks being challenged as obscene. Law enforcement agencies cannot simply seize such works upon their unilateral belief that the works are obscene. Rather, they must give notice so that a hearing can be held to determine whether the work may be seized as obscene. At the hearing, the writer can be represented by an attorney who will argue that the work is not obscene. The judge must consider all relevant evidence bearing on the obscenity question. Only after observance of these procedural requirements can the censors, if victorious, have their way.

Obscenity is a complex legal area. The writer who either fears that an obscenity issue may arise, or who faces such an issue, should consult a lawyer, especially since most contracts require a warranty against obscenity.

Censorship in the United States

The control of school boards over such matters as curriculum, textbooks, and library books can have a significant effect on the access of students to books and the ideas contained in books. While state statutes usually give school boards the authority to dictate these decisions free from outside interference, several cases have been fought over attempts to place First Amendment limitations upon these decisions, particularly with respect to the removal of books from school libraries.

In a 1972 case the Community School Board No. 25 in Queens, New York, removed Piri Thomas's *Down These Mean Streets* from all junior high school libraries in the district. The vote on the board was five to three in favor of removal of a work described by the Second Circuit Court of Appeals as ugly, violent, replete with obscenities, containing normal and perverse sex, and depicting the use of heroin. The court, noting that no one had argued against the right of the board to initially decide which books would be purchased by the library, stated: "It would seem clear to us that books which become obsolete or irrelevant or where improperly selected initially, for whatever reason, can be removed by the same authority which was empowered to make the selection in the first place" (*President's Council, District 25 v. Community School Board No. 25*, 457 F.2d 289, 293, *cert. denied*, 409 U.S. 998).

In a 1976 case the Board of Education in Strongsville, Ohio, refused to approve Joseph Heller's *Catch-22* and Kurt Vonnegut's *God Bless You, Mr. Rosewater* as either textbooks or library books, despite favorable faculty recommendations. The board also ordered *Catch-22* and Vonnegut's *Cat's Cradle* removed from the high school library. The Sixth Circuit Court of Appeals decided that there had been no constitutional or procedural violation in the board's decisions not to use *Catch-22* and *God Bless You, Mr. Rosewater* as textbooks. However, the court did feel that the removal of library books curtailed freedom of speech and thought, particularly since the board members apparently found the books personally distasteful. The court stated that: "Neither the State of Ohio nor the Strongsville School Board was under any federal constitutional compulsion to provide a library for the Strongsville High School or to choose any particular books. Once having created such a privilege for the benefit of its students, however, neither body could place conditions on the use of the library which were related solely to the social or political tastes of school board members" (*Minarcini v. Strongsville City School District*, 541 F.2d 577, 582).

Book censorship in the schools expanded in the mid-1980s and on into the 1990s. Sometimes the courts decided on literary issues involving obscenity and pornography, secular humanism and evolution. At other times, public opinion held the day. The attacks against literature came from the left as well as the right as highly organized groups and individuals of all kinds sought to preserve what they perceived to be their quality of life through censorship. In Los Angeles, a parent found *Catcher in the Rye* filthy, claiming that it had "absolutely no literary value" and that it was "blasphemous." Teachers and school officials disagreed and were able to keep the book in the school, but only after a bitter struggle. Waldenbooks, B. Dalton, and Barnes and Noble took *The Satanic Verses* off the shelves to protect their employees and patrons from anonymous threats. Feminists and state governments lashed out against pornography, both in pictures and in print, calling it discriminatory against women and trying to redefine the standards by which pornography should be judged—only to be rebuffed by the courts (*American Booksellers Association, Inc. v. Hudnut*, 771 F.2d 323, *aff'd* 475 U.S. 1226). Time Warner was convinced by public outcry to discontinue songs by the rapper Ice-T because the lyrics including references to killing cops. Viewing art as a source of violence against religious values, women, and society at large, the right to free expression was questioned time after time.

A new coalition, known as the Free Expression Network (FEN), has been organized to fight against the deterioration of the rights guaranteed by the First Amendment. Comprised of the Authors Guild, the American Civil Liberties Union (ACLU), the American Library Association (ALA), People for the American Way, the National Coalition for Freedom of Expression, PEN American Center, and others, the group is working to establish a clearinghouse for information about censorship so that attempts to censor will be widely publicized and met with a broad-based and effective response.

To find out more about book censorship in the United States, writers can contact the ALA's Office for Intellectual Freedom at (800) 545-2433 Ext. 4223. The ALA sells a booklet, entitled *Banned Books*, for $20 a copy. It shows that dozens and dozens of books were banned in 1994 and 1995, from the best-selling autobiography by Maya Angelou entitled *I Know Why the Caged Bird Sings* to William Faulkner's *As I Lay Dying*, mostly by elementary and high school libraries.

9 The Freedom of Information Act

$\mathcal{A}$n important aspect of many kinds of writing is acquiring information. Under the federal Freedom of Information Act (FOIA), introduced in 1957 and finally enacted in 1966, writers can access a wealth of information in the possession of the federal government.

Any executive department, military department, government corporation, government-controlled corporation, or other establishment in the executive branch of the Government (including the Executive Office of the President), or any independent regulatory agency is subject to the provisions of the FOIA.

The policy considerations behind the act were to ensure an informed citizenry, vital to the functioning of a democratic society, necessary both as a check against corruption and to hold the governors accountable to the governed. As one court put it: ". . . the basic purpose is to protect people's right to obtain information about their government, to know what their government is doing and to obtain information about government activities and policies and to remedy the mischief of arbitrary and self-serving withholding by agencies which are not directly responsible to the people" (*Westinghouse Elec. Corp. v. Schlesinger*, 542 F.2d 1190. *cert. denied* 431 U.S. 924). The amount of information that can be accessed is staggering. Borderline cases are generally adjudicated in favor of disclosure, and the act stands as a great tribute to the openness of our society. As one court observed, "Freedom of information is now the rule and secrecy is the exception" (*Wellford v. Hardin*, 315 F. Supp. 768).

Congress intended to open the door for disclosure of documents dealing with the structure, operation, and decision-making procedure of the various governmental agencies, including final opinions and orders, indexes, certain staff manuals and instructions, statements of policy and interpretations thereof. These documents are available to any member of the public who requests and 'reasonably describes' them. The fact that the information requested has special importance for the person requesting the information has no particular significance. In fact, the actual identity of the person requesting the information need not be revealed to the disclosing agency.

How to Make a Request

Although some agencies may accept an oral request, the general rule is that in order to obtain access to particular records, an individual must submit a written request that "reasonably describes" the particular records. Beyond that, each agency has its own, often highly detailed, procedures that must be followed to the letter. The request must often be made to a specific FOIA officer, in a specially marked envelope, and at a specific location. The writer seeking to obtain information should be ready to expend substantial time and effort to obtain the desired documents. The sample request below is merely instructive. The writer should be sure to obtain specific instructions from the agency involved.

To obtain an individual's files, the writer should insert that individual's full name in the first blank space and include all other names used by that individual in the second blank space. The signature of an individual requesting his or her own file must be notarized. No other types of requests need to be notarized. To obtain an organization's files, the writer should insert the full name of the organization in the first blank. The second blank space should include any other name used to describe the organization. To obtain files pertaining to a specific subject or event, the writer should insert the full name of the subject or event, including any relevant dates or locations, in the first blank. The second should have any other facts that would aid the agency in locating the requested information. The writer should be sure to keep a copy of the letter and to address it correctly. In all cases, the envelope should be clearly marked: "Attention FOIA Request." For the FBI, at least two letters must be sent—one to the FBI Headquarters,

SAMPLE REQUEST

Date:

To: ☐ FBI Headquarters   ☐ FBI Field Office   ☐ Other Agency

This is a noncommercial request under the Freedom of Information and Privacy Acts. I have attached a sheet setting out my application for a waiver of any fees in excess of those which are provided free because of my category.

My category for fee and fee waiver purposes is:
☐ request for personal file; no search fee and 100 free pages.
☐ journalist, academic or scientist; no search fee and 100 free pages.
☐ other noncommercial requester (group or person); 2 hours free search and 100 free pages.

I request a complete and thorough search of all filing systems and locations for all records maintained by your agency pertaining to and/or captioned:

_____

_____

_____

including, without limitation, files and documents captioned, or whose captions include: [describe records desired and/or insert full and formal name]

_____

_____

_____

This request specifically includes where appropriate "main" files and "see references," including but not limited to numbered and lettered sub files and control files. I also request a search of the Electronic Surveillance (ELSUR) Index, or any similar technique for locating records of electronic surveillance and OINTELPRO Index. I request that all records be produced with administrative pages. I wish to be sent copies of "see reference" cards, abstracts, search slips, including search slips used to process this request, file covers, multiple copies of the same documents if they appear in a file, tapes of any electronic surveillance, photographs, and logs of physical surveillance (FISUR). Please place missing documents on "special locate."

I wish to make it clear that I want all records in your office "identifiable with my request," even though reports on those records have been sent

➜

to headquarters and even though there may be duplication between the two sets of files. I do not want just "interim" documents. I want all documents as they appear in the "main" files and "see references" of all units of your agency.

If documents are denied in whole or in part, please specify which exemption(s) is (are) claimed for each passage or whole document denied. Give the number of pages in each document and the total number of pages pertaining to this request and the dates of documents withheld. I request that excised materials be "blacked out" rather than "whited out" or cut out and that the remaining non-exempt portions of documents be released as provided under the Freedom of Information Act. Please send a memo (with a copy or copies to me) to the appropriate unit(s) in your office to assure that no records related to this request are destroyed. Please advise of any destruction of records and include the date of and authority for such destruction. As I expect to appeal any denials, please specify the office and address to which an appeal should be directed.

I can be reached at the phone number listed below. Please call rather than write if there are any questions of if you need additional information from me. I expect a response to this request within ten (10) working days, as provided for in the Freedom of Information Act.

Sincerely,

_____
SIGNATURE

_____
NAME (PRINT OR TYPE)

_____
ADDRESS

_____   _____
TELEPHONE   SOCIAL SECURITY NUMBER (OPTIONAL)

FOR PERSONAL FILES:

_____   _____
DATE OF BIRTH   PLACE OF BIRTH

FOR ORGANIZATION FILES:

_____   _____
DATE OF FOUNDING   PLACE OF FOUNDING

_____
ADDRESS OF ORGANIZATION

the other to each relevant field office. For the Immigration and Naturalization Service (INS), the writer should send a request to each district office in the vicinity of the individual, organization, subject matter, or event in question. Notwithstanding the above, the writer should contact the agencies involved and ascertain if there are any other specific procedures which must be followed.

Once a request is properly filed, the government has an obligation to make records "promptly available" to any person, whether or not they are a citizen of the United States, requesting such records. The agency has a statutory obligation to notify the writer within ten days that the request has been received and is being processed or that some necessary procedure was not followed. The exact amount of time which an agency can take to disclose requested documents varies from case to case. Whatever the proper period of time in a particular case, an agency may obtain an extension in unusual circumstances where it makes a good-faith, diligent effort. The writer would do well to contact the agency from time to time to monitor the progress of the request.

Fees may be charged by the document producing agency as long as they are not arbitrary or capricious and do not deprive the person seeking the records of due process or equal protection. These fees can fluctuate wildly and in many cases, especially those involving computer searches by an agency, can be prohibitive. Writers are therefore advised to demand an estimate prior to embarking on the disclosure adventure. If the costs are too high, it might be possible to obtain an exemption.

If a writer is unable to obtain records to which he or she has a right, and negotiations for disclosure as well as the appeal process have proven ineffective, the writer has the right under the FOIA to file suit in federal court for an order of disclosure. If the writer wins, the government must pay all attorney's fees.

Exceptions

The policy considerations behind the FOIA are overridden in certain enumerated instances by such interests as national security, the right to privacy, or confidential source and the requirements of law enforcement agencies. In such cases, the agency involved may still disclose the information, but it cannot be compelled to do so. And while the language sounds extremely broad, neither the president himself, nor his staff, nor any of nine exempted categories of information, including information in the possession of most government funded projects, are subject in any way to the act.

A Case Study—*The Nation Magazine v. Department of State*

In October of 1992, just prior to the presidential election, Max Holland, a contributing editor to *The Nation*, attempted to obtain information concerning independent candidate H. Ross Perot from the Central Intelligence Agency (CIA) and other federal government sources. *The Nation* hoped to "contribute to the ongoing public debate about [Perot's] qualifications to become President of the United States" and noted that a similar request for information, about presidential candidate Bill Clinton, which was filed after the requests in issue, had already been expedited.

In response to Holland's written request, the CIA responded with a letter to the effect that, on privacy grounds, he must first obtain the formal, written consent of H. Ross Perot. Holland informed the CIA that he was unable to obtain this and requested all the documents not protected because of Perot's right to privacy and suggested that the right be circumscribed due to Perot's national prominence. When he got no response, he hand-delivered a request for expedited processing to the CIA, claiming an urgent need for the documents on the grounds that the presidential election was less than a month away. In denying his request, the CIA stated:

> . . . that it granted requests for expedition only in the rare instances where health and humanitarian considerations create circumstances of exceptional urgency and extraordinary need and that his request did not satisfy those criteria.

The other government sources, including the Department of Defense, the Federal Bureau of Investigation (FBI), and the Department of State, also denied Holland's requests either explicitly, on privacy grounds, or implicitly through silence.

In response, Holland and *The Nation* commenced an action against the federal government for violation of the FOIA, seeking a temporary restraining order that would compel the government to hand over the requested documents. The court denied the motion because the plaintiffs had failed to show the necessary "substantial likelihood of success on the merits." The court found that defendant government agencies and departments were processing requests with due diligence. Though the defendants had exceeded the time periods outlined in the FOIA, such periods were "not mandatory but directory" if the government could establish "exceptional circumstances," unless the party requesting documents could show "exceptional need or urgency." The defendants established to the satisfaction of the court that they were "deluged with FOIA requests" and the plaintiffs failed to show the court the requisite urgency.

Arguably, if Holland had been looking for specific documents, that he had reason to believe existed and which would have unveiled an inability by Perot to carry out the job of President of the United States, that urgency might have been shown. But a general request for documents, with the combined purpose of selling more magazines and adding to the political debate, was of questionable urgency. The court noted that if the information requested involved a deportation proceeding, a murder trial, or other criminal proceeding for a serious felony, the requisite urgency might have been shown. The court further noted that it had refused to expedite a FOIA request concerning "George Bush and his alleged connection to the Kennedy assassination even though the 1988 Presidential election was imminent."

Responding to the plaintiffs argument that the request for documents relating to Perot should be expedited because a similar request, in that case for documents about Bill Clinton, was expedited, the court stated:

> . . . no rule of administrative law requires an agency to extend erroneous treatment of one party to other parties, "thereby turning an isolated error into a uniform misapplication of the law" (citing *Sacred Heart Medical Center v. Sullivan*, 958 F.2d 537).

The court also pointed out that while the requests for Clinton documents were expedited, the government had admitted its wrongdoing, curtailed the action mid-stream, and now attested to the fact that no documents had ever actually been released. The Clinton requests were returned to their "proper places in the queue." Had the Clinton documents been released, the court stated that it would have required the Perot documents to be released as well.

Finally, the court found that in deciding on a temporary restraining order it had to balance the interests involved. While it recognized the public interest in knowing more about Perot, that interest was outweighed by the fact that at least some of the requested documents were protected by Perot's right to privacy, that the government had limited resources, and that the public interest would not be served by setting "an unworkable precedent [that] would severely jeopardize the . . . orderly, fair, and efficient administration of the FOIA" (*The Nation Magazine v. Department of State*, 895 F. Supp. 68).

Obtaining Assistance

Many states have their own Freedom of Information Acts which should be utilized to obtain state level documents. Writers wishing to find out more about the FOIA can purchase a government publication entitled the "DOJ Guide to the FOIA" which is available for twenty-one dollars. It can be purchased by calling (202) 783-3238 and requesting Stock No. 027-000-01351-1. Writers may also wish to contact one of the following organizations.

Freedom of Information
  Clearinghouse
P.O. Box 19367
Washington, DC 20036
(202) 833-3000

National Freedom of Information
  Coalition
c/o FOIFT
400 S. Record Street, 6th Floor
Dallas, TX 57202
(214) 977-6658

The following phone numbers will also be of use:

U.S. Department of Justice FOIA
  Office Public Affairs
(202) 514-4594

Libel and FOI Hotline
(800) F-FOI-AID

10 Contracts: An Introduction

contract is an agreement creating legally enforceable obligations between two or more parties. The writer's relationships with publishers, producers, and agents are all contractual. A contract provides the legal framework within which the rights and obligations of the writer and other party can be specified. While oral contracts can sometimes be valid, the better approach is to use written contracts (as discussed more extensively later in the chapter). This chapter develops a background of the law relating to contracts so that subsequent chapters dealing with such matters as agency contracts and negotiating literary rights can be more helpful. An excellent companion volume with respect to contracts is *Business and Legal Forms for Authors and Self-Publishers* by Tad Crawford (Allworth Press).

Offer and Acceptance

An offer invites entry into a contract. It is a promise which can be accepted by a return promise or, less usual, by performance based on the terms of the offer.

If a publisher says to a writer, "I am willing to pay you $250 for first North American serial rights in your story, 'The Doves of Peace,'" an offer has been made. The publisher has promised to purchase in definite terms, which can be accepted by the writer's return promise to sell the story. If the publisher says, "This story would be a gem in my upcoming anthology," or, "This story should sell for a fortune," or, "I'm going to keep this story for a few weeks," no offers have been made. If the publisher says, "You write this story and we'll agree later about the price," or, "You write this story and I'll pay you as I see fit," no offers have been made because a material term—the price—has been omitted. However, if the publisher says, "Write this article and I will pay you $250 if satisfied," a valid offer has been made. The writer should beware of such an offer, because the courts generally rule that a satisfaction clause means that a dissatisfied commissioning party may reject the work, even though a reasonable person would have been satisfied (*Crawford v. Mail and Express Publishing Co.*, 163 N.Y. 404, 57 N.E. 616, contract for newspaper articles; *Haven v. Russell*, 34 N.Y.S. 292, contract for a play). In other words, the writer is working on speculation, an arrangement which should be avoided if possible.

The person making an offer can usually revoke it at any time prior to acceptance. Another way in which an offer can be terminated is by limiting the time for acceptance—for example, "I will purchase your story for $250 if you will sell it to me within the next ten days." This offer would terminate at the end of ten days. If no such time limit is set, the assumption is made that the offer ends after a reasonable amount of time has passed. An offer is also terminated by a counter offer. For example, if the publisher offers $250 for a story and the writer demands $500, the original offer of $250 is no longer effective.

Acceptance is usually accomplished by agreeing to the offer. If the publisher offers to pay $250 to have a story written, the writer can accept by stating: "I agree to write this story for $250." The end result of the process of offer and acceptance is a meeting of the minds, a mutual understanding between the parties to the contract. If a final contract is ambiguous, a court may try to determine the parties' intentions by examining customs in the profession, prior dealings between the parties, and the conduct of the parties with respect to the particular contract. Once performance has been completed under a contract which is ambiguous, the court will try to rectify the ambiguities by a standard of reasonableness. If a writer does an article which a magazine publishes, the writer should be paid a reasonable compensation even if no price had been agreed upon. In one case, a contract which had not been fully performed was held unenforceable for a failure to specify royalty rates (*Hindes v. Wilmington Poetry Society*, 138 A.2d 501, 116 U.S.P.Q. 301).

Consideration

Every contract, to be valid, must be based on consideration, which is the giving of value by each party to the other. The consideration each party to a contract receives is what induces entry into the contract. When the publisher promises to pay $250 for a story which the writer promises to write, each party has received value from the other in the form of a promise. The consideration must be bargained for at the time of entering into the contract. If a publisher says, "Your story is so good that I'm going to pay you an extra $250 even though I don't have to," the publisher is not obliged to pay. The writer has already written the story and been paid in full, so the promise to pay an additional $250 is not supported by consideration.

The one situation in which consideration is not required occurs when a person relies on a promise in such a way that the promise must be enforced to avoid injustice. If a patron makes a promise and should reasonably know that the writer will rely upon it, such as offering $250 as a gift for the writer to buy a typewriter, the patron cannot refuse to pay the money after the writer has in fact relied on the promise and purchased the typewriter.

Competency of the Parties

The law will not enforce a contract if the parties are not competent. The rationale is that there can be no meeting of the minds or mutual understanding in such a situation. A contract entered into by an insane person is not enforceable. Similarly, contracts entered into by minors will, depending on the law of the specific state, be either unenforceable or enforceable only at the choice of the minor. The age of reaching majority has traditionally been twenty-one, but most states (including New York and California) have now lowered the age of majority to eighteen.

Legality of Purpose

A contract for a purpose that is illegal or against public policy is not binding. For example, the novelist Anita Roddy-Eden sued comedian Milton Berle for breach of a contract under which Berle would take credit as sole author of a book in fact written by Roddy-Eden. It was hoped the public would buy more copies of the book because of Berle's name. But after Roddy-Eden finished a satisfactory book, Berle refused to go ahead with the contract. The court held that Roddy-Eden could not recover damages because the goal of the contract was to perpetrate a fraud upon the public. The court distinguished this from the common practice of using a pseudonym: "In such a case, regardless of the pen name employed by the writer, he is, in truth, the real author and is not exploiting the ability, talent and authorship of another, palming it off under the false pretense that it is his own" (*Roddy-Eden v. Berle*, 108 N.Y.S.2d 597, 600, 202 Misc. 261, 264).

Written and Oral Contracts

While not all contracts need be written to be enforced, it is certainly wise to insist on having them in writing. The terms of a contract may come into dispute several years after the creation of the contract. At that time reliance on memory to provide the terms of the contract can leave much to be desired, especially if no witnesses were present and the parties disagree as to what was said.

A written contract need not even be a formal document. An exchange of letters can create a binding contract. Often a letter agreement is signed by one party, and the other party completes the contract by also signing at the bottom of the letter beneath the words CONSENTED AND AGREED TO. A check can create or be evidence of a contract—for example, a check from a magazine to a writer stating: "This check for $250 is accepted as payment in full for world rights in perpetuity to the story 'Doves of Peace.'" If such a check conflicts with a prior written or oral agreement, it should be returned to the magazine so that any terms on the check accurately reflect the prior understanding. Both parties may not have signed an agreement, but a memorandum signed by the party against whom enforcement is sought can be found to constitute a valid contract. Even where the parties merely show, from their conduct, an intention to agree, a contract—called an "implied contract"—can come into existence. But when part of a contract is in writing, the writer should not rely on an oral agreement to the effect that compliance with all the written provisions will not be insisted upon. Courts are reluctant to allow oral evidence to vary the terms of a written contract, except in cases where the written contract is procured by fraud or under mistake or is too indefinite to be understood without the additional oral statements.

The copyright law requires that any transfer of a copyright or an exclusive right in a copyright must be evidenced by a writing. While this would cover most of a writer's transactions, it does not apply to nonexclusive licenses. It also would not apply to literary property which might not be copyrightable—for example, an idea. However, the Uniform Commercial Code might still apply (in every state except Louisiana), requiring written evidence indicating price and subject matter and signed by the party against whom enforcement is sought. This pertains to a contract for the sale of intangible personal property if the amount being paid exceeds five thousand dollars (Uniform Commercial Code Sec. 1-206[1]).

The writer may often contract to render services, such as writing an article on commission. An oral contract for such services is usually enforceable if the services can be performed within one year. If the services will take longer than one year to perform, there must be a writing evidencing the contract and containing all essential terms of the contract. The ownership of the copyright of works for hire is discussed in chapter 4.

Warranties

Caveat emptor—let the buyer beware—expressed the traditional attitude of the courts toward the purchasers of property. Warranties, however, are express or implied facts or promises upon which the purchaser can rely. Warranties can be created orally, even if the contract must be written. They can be created during negotiations, at the time of making the contract, or, in some transactions not usually relevant to writers, after entry into the contract.

An express warranty is created when the writer asserts facts or promises relating to the character or ownership of the work which the purchaser relies upon in making the purchase. The writer will often be required to give a publisher an express warranty to the effect that the work does not infringe any copyright, violate any property rights, or contain any scandalous, libelous, or unlawful matter. If this warranty proves untrue, the writer must pay the publisher for any losses which result. However, sales talk or opinions by the writer as to the value or merit of the work will not create warranties. If, for example, the writer speculates that the work will earn a fortune over the next few years, the publisher cannot rely upon such an opinion and no warranty is created.

An implied warranty comes into existence by operation of law (rather than express representations of the parties) based on the circumstances of the transaction or the relationship of the parties. In some sales, for example, there is an implied warranty that the seller has title or the right to convey title in the goods being sold, but it has been held that no warranty of marketable title will be implied in the sale of literary property (*Loew's Inc. v. Wolff*, 101 F. Supp. 981, *aff'd* 215 F.2d 651).

Assignments of Contracts

Sometimes one party to a contract can substitute another person to take over the burdens or rewards of the contract. This is not true, however, for contracts which are based upon the special skills of one party to the contract. Where such personal ability is crucial to the contract—for example, in a contract for the writing of a story—the writer may not delegate the contractual duties for performance by another writer

(*Foster v. Callaghan & Co.*, 248 F. 944). But even though the writer is unable to delegate the performance of duties, assignment to another person of the writer's right to receive money due or to become due under the contract will be permissible. A well-drafted contract will state the intention of the parties as to the assignment of rights or delegation of duties under the contract.

Nonperformance Excused

There are a variety of situations where the writer's failure to perform contractual obligations will be excused. The most obvious case is that the death of the writer is not a breach of contract that would permit a recovery from the writer's estate. Similarly, because the writer's work is personal, disabling physical or mental illness will excuse performance by the writer (although a provision might be made specifically extending the writer's time for performance in the event of ill health).

Grounds other than the personal nature of the writer's work will also permit the writer to refuse to perform. If the other party waives the writer's performance or if both parties have agreed to rescind the contract, no performance will be necessary. If the writer is prevented by the other party from performing, performance will be excused and the writer will have an action for breach of contract (*Brockhurst v. Ryan*, 2 Misc.2d 747, 146 N.Y.S.2d 386). Similarly, no performance is required where performance would be impossible, as in the case of the interviewer who cannot conduct an interview because of the subject's death. Also, performance is excused if it would be illegal due to a law passed after entering into the contract.

Remedies for Breach of Contract

A party who refuses to perform a contract can be liable to pay damages. There must, however, be some detriment or loss caused by a breach of contract before the recovery of damages will be allowed. The damages will generally be the amount of the reasonably foreseeable losses (including out-of-pocket costs and lost profits) caused by the breach. Also, the injured party must usually take steps to minimize damages. Contracts will frequently set damages in advance to avoid the necessity of extensive proofs to establish proper damages at trial. The courts will enforce such provisions for damages, known as "liquidated damages," as long as damages would be difficult to establish and the amount specified is not unreasonable or a penalty.

The writer may wonder what happens when performance under a contract is either nearly completed or is completed but varies slightly from what was agreed upon. Unless the contract specifies that strict compliance is necessary to be paid for performing the contract, the writer should be able to recover the contract price less the costs necessary to pay for the defects in performance. For example, where an artist created stained glass windows in substantial compliance with the designs except that less light came through the windows than the parties had apparently intended, the court stated:

> . . . Where an artist is directed to produce a work of art in accordance with an approved design, the details of which are left to the artist, and the artist executes his commission in a substantial and satisfactory way, the mere fact that, when completed, it lacks some element of utility desired by the buyer and not specifically contracted for, constitutes no breach of the artist's contract (*Wagner-Larscheid Co. v. Fairview Mausoleum Co.*, 190 Wis. 357, 362, 208 N.W. 241, 242).

A similar rule should apply to a writer who, for example, does an article or book from an agreed-upon outline.

The question, however, of what constitutes substantial performance is an area where litigation is likely. The reason for this is another rule: that part performance under a contract will not allow recovery based on the price specified in the contract for full performance. Moreover, such part performance will not, in most states, even be paid for on the basis of reasonable value unless the part performance is of substantial benefit to the other party who accepts and retains the benefits of such performance. This rule would not apply, of course, if one party prevented the other from performing. Also, where one part of a contract can be separated from another part, such as a number of payments for a number of different articles, recovery will usually be permitted for the partial contract price specified for each partial performance.

In some situations, money damages may not be adequate to compensate for the loss caused by a breach of contract. If a famous writer is hired to do a story, the writer's refusal to honor the contract might be difficult to value in money damages. But since involuntary servitude is prohibited, the creation of the story cannot be forced on the writer. On the other hand, if a story with unique value is already in existence, a publisher might be able to require specific performance of a contract to sell the copyright. This would mean that a court would order the owner to transfer to the publisher the specific copyright for which the publisher had contracted (*Benziger v. Steinhauser*, 154 F. 151). Specific performance can only be used, however, where the payment of money would not be a sufficient remedy.

Statutes of Limitation

A statute of limitation sets forth the time within which an injured party must bring suit to have the injury remedied. After the limitation period has passed, no lawsuit can be maintained. The limitation period runs from the time of the breach. The limitation period for actions based on contracts varies from state to state, for example, six years in New York and four years in California (except that the period is reduced to two years in California if the contract is not written). The limitation period in many states is longer for written contracts than for contracts which are oral, partly in writing, or implied. The writer contemplating legal action is well advised to seek redress promptly so that no question will arise regarding statutes of limitation.

Bailments

A bailment is a situation in which one person gives his or her lawfully owned property to be held by another person. For example, a writer might leave a manuscript with unique art at the office of an agent, a publisher, or a printer. In all of these relationships, in which both parties benefit from the bailment, the person who takes the writer's property must exercise reasonable care in safeguarding it. If that person is negligent and the work is damaged or lost, the writer will recover damages. Even if the work has no easily ascertainable market value, damages would still be awarded based on the intrinsic value of the work. In one case, the court reviewed the relevant issues when a unique manuscript is lost by a printer (*Gerschel v. St. Crispin Bindery*, *New York Law Journal*, March 2, 1970, p. 23).

However, the reasonable standard of care required in a bailment can be changed by contract. The writer might, for example, be asked to sign a contract under which the writer would assume all risks of injury to the work. The writer should seek just the opposite—that is, to have the other party agree to act as an insurer of the work. This would mean that the other party would be liable if the work were damaged for any reason, even though reasonable care might have been exercised in safeguarding it. Of course, these considerations will hardly be significant if the manuscript is one of many copies and contains no valuable art work or transparencies. Another issue which might arise is whether all of the writer's bailments are for mutual benefit, or whether certain bailments would either be for the sole benefit of the bailor or the sole benefit of the bailee. If the bailment is for the sole benefit of the bailor, the bailee will only be liable for gross negligence. If the bailment is for the sole benefit of the bailee, the bailee can be liable even though reasonable care is taken with the goods. A bailment for mutual benefit will usually be found where the bailee takes possession of the goods as an incident to the bailee's business, even if no consideration is received.

Protection of Ideas

Ideas are denied copyright protection but can still be protected by contract. The idea may be a format, a theme, a situation, and so on. The problem comes upon submission of the idea, since the writer must feel assured of reimbursement if the idea is used. At the outset, it should be noted that many purchasers of literary property have release forms which must be signed by persons submitting ideas (and, often, unsolicited manuscripts) before any consideration will be given to the submission. Such release forms bar any claims by the writer based upon a subsequent use of similar material by the potential purchaser. In addition, if the writer should be able to sue and recover despite the release form, the maximum reasonable value of the material is stipulated (for example, $200) and the total recovery possible is limited to such an amount. These provisions are accompanied by a recital from the writer, such as "I recognize that there is always a likelihood that this material may be identical with, like, or competitive to material which has or may come to you from other sources. Identity or similarity of material in the past has given rise to claims and disputes between various parties and has caused misunderstandings. You have advised me that you will refuse to examine or consider material unless you obtain for yourself complete protection from me against the possibility of any such claims." The writer can expect to be bound by such provisions, so caution should be exercised before signing a release form in order to submit an idea or manuscript.

The writer will be best served by an express contract providing for payment in the event the purchaser does use the idea. This is likely to be difficult to obtain, but the writer who simply volunteers an idea is basically at the mercy of the other party. The express contract should specify the consideration and other details of the transaction. If a standard price is paid for such material, it should be stated. Otherwise, a reasonable standard of value should be required as compensation. The submission agreement need not be complex, although it must suit the individual circumstances. For example, the writer might use a brief letter:

IDEA SUBMISSION

Dear _____:

I understand it is your practice to entertain or receive program mate-rials, ideas, or suggestions for [specify the market]. I have developed such an [indicate what will be submitted] for submission and would like to disclose this to you. I understand that if you use it you will pay me a reasonable compensation based on current industry standards. Please advise me if I should send this to you.

Sincerely yours,

Alice Writer

It is not uncommon, however, for the writer to disclose ideas with-out having thought to obtain an express contract. Recovery may still be possible under a variety of doctrines which will only be mentioned here: implied contract (where the parties indicate by their conduct that a contract exists), confidential relationships (applicable to some cases in which the party with less bargaining power trusts in the other party's good faith and discloses the idea), and quasi contract (in which the law implies an obligation that the party receiving the idea pay for the benefits conferred). Especially for a confidential relationship or quasi contract, however, the courts may require that the idea be concrete, elaborated, or novel before recovery will be allowed. A written, express contract is by far the best way for a writer to protect an idea.

Contracts for Readings and Lectures

Writers frequently are offered the opportunity to lecture or read before groups interested in their work. The administrative efficiency of the host organization can vary greatly, sometimes leaving the writer with a vexing problem of how to insure receipt of a fee agreed upon before-hand. A good first step to resolve this problem is a written contract detailing not only the amount of the fee and any reimbursements for expenses, such as for travel and lodging, but also the time of payment. A good formula might be for travel expenses to be paid in advance, while the fee and other expenses are reimbursed upon completion of the first day of the engagement. The time which the writer will spend with the group and the nature of the services should be specified. In addition to giving a reading of poetry, for example, the writer might be required to read students' work and sit in on creative writing seminars over a period of several days. If the writer is lecturing or reading, there should be a reservation of the copyrights in any recordings made by the host organization. A contract for a lecture or reading must meet the needs of each occasion, but a simple model contract is shown here for use as a starting point:

LECTURE CONTRACT

Dear _____:

I am pleased by the invitation to address your group and would like this letter to serve as our contract with respect thereto. I agree to travel to [specify the location] on [specify the date or dates] and to perform the following services: [specify what is to be done]. In return you promise to pay my round-trip travel expenses in the amount of [specify amount] fourteen days prior to the date of said engagement, and pay me at the end of my first day of services a fee of [specify amount) and additional expenses in the amount of [specify amount and detail the reasons for the expenses, such as lodging and meals]. No recordings of my appearance shall be made without my express, written consent. Recordings shall include any electrical transcription, tape recording, wire recording, film, videotape, or any other method of recording voice or image whether now known or hereinafter developed. In the event permission to record my appearance is given, all copyrights to material contained therein shall be reserved to me and no use of said material shall be made without my written consent thereto and an appropriate placement of copyright notice in my name. If these terms are agreeable to you, please sign this letter beneath the words CONSENTED AND AGREED TO to constitute this a binding agreement between us. Kindly return one signed copy of the letter to me for my records.

Sincerely yours,

Alice Writer

CONSENTED AND AGREED TO:

Municipal University

By: _____
　　 AUTHORIZED REPRESENTATIVE

11 Negotiating Book Contracts

$\mathcal{T}$he definition of a "good deal" will vary from book to book and from writer to writer, but there are certain standards that apply to all books and all writers and certain types of issues that consistently arise in contract after contract. The owner of literary property has the powers belonging to any property owner. These include the right to option, sell, or license the property. The writer marketing literary property may deal in one or more of a number of markets, including book, magazine, newspaper, theater, radio, television, film, audio, multimedia, and so on. Each of these markets has further subdivisions too numerous to list, but fundamental concepts involved in the marketing of literary property apply to any of these markets. Because in most cases the writer and publisher are on uneven ground when it comes to negotiating a book contract, a solid understanding of these concepts is essential if the writer is to achieve an agreement that does more than reflect the relative strengths of the parties. These agreements are often complex, and any writer will benefit from the advice of a knowledgeable lawyer or agent.

The starting point for negotiations is the writer's ownership of literary property. If the writer has worked with a collaborator, a separate collaboration agreement must detail the parties' rights with respect to artistic decisions, control over the property, the sharing of income, and authorship credits—as discussed in chapter 16. Initially the owner, assumed to be an individual writer, can grant an option to the property, an option being the power within a limited period of time to purchase rights to use the property. The payment for an option is smaller than the payment to be made upon exercise of the option and actual use of the property. Often an option agreement—for example, an option to make a story or novel into a film—will have attached a completed purchase agreement to be used if the option is exercised. Or the writer may sell property outright, such as the sale to a magazine of "all rights" in an article. Far preferable to selling all rights is the practice of licensing certain specific uses of the property and retaining all others.

The writer giving a license makes a grant of rights to the licensee. This grant will encompass the rights to exploit a work in a specific medium or form (for example, paperback rights), territory (for example, North American rights), language (for example, English only), and time (for example, the duration of copyright, or, more commonly, for a period limited to a certain number of years if the book remains in print). The writer seeks to limit this grant narrowly, careful only to transfer rights that the licensee can effectively exploit. This is because the writer's income from licensing is usually not a fixed sum, but rather a variable amount that increases based upon the purchaser's success with and use of the property. The measurement of this success will often require carefully drawn definitions of price, profits, or proceeds.

The purchaser will try to insist on having both control of and a share in the income from subsidiary rights. Subsidiary rights are simply defined as rights of exploitation in markets not encompassed in the grant of rights to the licensee. For example, film rights would be subsidiary rights in a book publishing contract. And book publishing rights would be subsidiary rights in a film contract. The writer will seek to limit the licensee's interest in subsidiary rights, but the final allocations of control and income will depend on the parties' bargaining ability. Thus, the interaction of the grant of rights and subsidiary rights provisions must be understood if the writer is truly to know what the licensee has acquired.

The writer will wish to have the work copyrighted in his or her name, but practice varies on this from industry to industry. The licensee will want the writer to give warranties stating that the property is original and does not infringe any copyrights, and also does not contain material which is obscene, defamatory, or an invasion of anyone's privacy. The writer indemnifies the purchaser for losses resulting from a breach or, sometimes, an alleged breach of these warranties. The writer will naturally strive to blunt the impact of the warranty provisions.

Artistic control is another important point, although this often does not become obvious until the agreement has been signed and realization of the end product is well under way. If the licensee has full power over artistic decisions, the end product may be so alien to the original concept that the writer would want a right not to be named as writer. If the writer is familiar with the reputation and prior work of the licensee, an attempt may be made to restrict the licensee's power to assign the property to others. The writer presumably knows the financial and artistic resources upon which the immediate licensee can draw to guarantee successful completion of the project, while nothing is known about possible assignees of the licensee. Similarly, if the writer is to complete certain work under the agreement, the obligation to do the work cannot be assigned to another writer (although the right to sums due to the writer can be assigned). And the writer, whether marketing subsidiary rights or making a commitment to undertake a project personally, will want to have authorship credit specified in detail.

These typical considerations provide an overview of the marketing of literary property to various markets. The bulk of this chapter will be devoted to an examination of the provisions of book publishing contracts. First, the writer must learn which provisions in a publisher's contract are onerous. After learning this, the next step is knowing the form of more favorable provisions that should be sought in negotiation. If this chapter dwells too long upon what is ideal, it is in the hope that the increased awareness and demands of writers will gradually reform the publishers' contracts. Realistically, writers must recognize that bargaining strength will do a lot to determine the final form of the contract—assuming equally skilled and knowledgeable negotiators on each side. The Authors Guild (referred to as the Guild) has created a model contract which is accompanied by an explanatory guide. While publishers have not adopted this contract, its provisions are educational and will be referred to in this chapter. The National Writers Union has a similar guide available to members. A model contract with a negotiation checklist also appears in *Business and Legal Forms for Authors and Self-Publishers* by Tad Crawford (Allworth Press).

Once the thorough discussion of the book publishing agreement is completed, some of the special features of magazine, syndication, theater, television, and film marketing, as well as electronic rights, will be considered. However, the book publishing contract offers a good illustration of some general concerns and concepts present in the marketing of any kind of literary property.

Grant of Rights

After setting forth the names of the parties, their addresses, and the date, a book contract will detail the rights granted by the writer to the publisher. This grant of rights can be limited as to the form of publication, the language, the time during which the work can be used, and the territory in which the book can be sold. The writer should never transfer the work itself or title to the work, but only grant rights that are carefully circumscribed. The grant of rights varies between the contracts of different publishers, and often the subsidiary rights provisions must be examined in tandem with the grant of rights in order to be fully aware of the interest which the publisher is acquiring. The Author's Guild contract limits the publisher to using the work in book form in the English language. The publisher's exclusive right to distribute the book covers the United States, its territories and possessions, the Philippines, and Canada. The exclusive nature of the right means that the writer cannot give any other publisher permission to distribute in these areas. The publisher receives a worldwide nonexclusive right (except for the British Commonwealth) to sell the English language copies printed in the United States.

However, the contracts of most publishers provide either in the grant of rights or the subsidiary rights provision for the publisher to participate in distribution or licensing to the British Commonwealth (which may be included in a more general geographic designation, such as "world distribution rights"). Depending on the specific provisions, the publisher may demand the right to sell its editions printed in the United States to the British Commonwealth, license an independent publisher in the British Commonwealth to bring out an edition, or license a subsidiary in the British Commonwealth to bring out an edition. The writer must determine whether the publisher can market the book more effectively in the British Commonwealth than the writer or the writer's agent working directly with a British publisher would be able to do. Particularly if the writer has no agent capable of marketing abroad, limitations placed on the publisher's right to distribute to the British Commonwealth may be self-defeating. The writer might also want to retain Canadian rights if his or her agent could sell the book to a Canadian publisher.

If the publisher is to have rights with respect to the British Commonwealth, the Guild contract recommends giving the publisher the exclusive right to license to the British Commonwealth (and the republics of Ireland and South Africa) for a limited period of time such as twelve months (definitely no more than twenty-four months) after United States publication. If, after this period elapses, the publisher has not granted a license, the license has terminated, or the license is terminable, then the writer has the power to revoke the publisher's rights with respect to the British Commonwealth. In addition, if the publisher does successfully license British Commonwealth rights, the Guild points out that traditionally the publisher's share of proceeds is between 15 and 20 percent and the writer's 80 to 85 percent.

The Guild contract recommends that the publisher shall have the exclusive right to license translations (except into English) in all countries, except that this right can be revoked by the writer after a limited period such as eighteen months (definitely no more than thirty-six months) if the publisher has not licensed the work, such a license has been terminated, or the license is terminable. The Guild suggests that writers retain the right to terminate in cases where the licensee fails to pay proceeds due, remainders the work, or allows it to go out of print. In practice, most publishers will demand translation and foreign rights in either the grant of rights or subsidiary rights provision, whenever possible, and most writers' agents will seek to withhold them. If the right to license translations in all countries is given to the publisher, the Guild suggests that the publisher traditionally receives no more than 25 percent of the licensing proceeds.

The Guild contract suggests limiting the duration of the grant of rights to twenty years although most publishers seek to obtain a grant for the duration of the copyright and are usually successful. Even if the writer agreed to such contractual language, the publisher's rights would be circumscribed by the out-of-print clause and the writer's right to terminate grants of rights after thirty-five years under the copyright law as explained in the discussion of copyright in chapter 2.

Subsidiary Rights

Subsidiary rights will cover many, if not all, of the rights not conveyed to the publisher by the initial grant. First, the writer must determine which subsidiary rights are enumerated in the contract. Next, the control over each of the subsidiary rights must be specified. Will the power to license the right belong to the publisher or writer? Retaining rights is most useful when the writer has the ability to sell those rights, preferably through an experienced agent. However, since publishers often seek to retain the subsidiary rights as insurance against an writer's failure to earn back the advance, writers may in turn want to protect subsidiary rights revenues either contractually or by retaining the rights.

Licensings of subsidiary rights can be made for abridgments, book clubs, reprints by another publisher, first and second serializations (which are magazine or newspaper rights before and after book publication), syndication, advertising, commercial uses, films, plays, radio shows, television, audio, multimedia, and electronic uses. Foreign and translation rights may also be subsidiary rights, unless included in the grant of rights or reserved entirely to the writer. This illustrates the interplay between the grant of rights and the subsidiary rights provisions, both of which must be examined for the writer to be certain of the aggregate interests the publisher is acquiring.

Definitions of the different subsidiary rights can vary between contracts. Clarity is essential here, and the writer should scrutinize the definitions to make sure they are precise and sufficient. For example, reprint rights could include mass market paperbacks (for distribution through chain stores and news and magazine wholesalers), cheap hardcover editions, quality paperbacks, and so on. Commercial, merchandising, or novelty rights are often included without further definition in the subsidiary rights provision. Commercial rights can be defined to cover the use of the literary work, the title of the work, the names of characters, and characterizations of the characters as a basis for trademarks or trade names for toys, games, clothing, and other products. But these rights may also include the publisher's power to license the use of the writer's name or likeness in connection with such products—an association that the writer may find objectionable, particularly if the merchandise is not of high quality.

The Guild contract allows the publisher to license paperback and book club rights, as well as post-publication periodical (second serial) rights, as long as the publisher asks the writer for his or her prior approval, which cannot then be delayed or unreasonably withheld. Also, no paperback edition may be published until at least one year after the date of initial publication of the trade edition. Assuming the publisher has the power to license subsidiary rights, the time when the exercise of a given power may begin should always be considered. The writer may want to require the publisher to bring out a hardcover edition (perhaps from its first-line imprint) before the publisher can license subsidiary rights. Similarly, the publisher's power to license subsidiary rights can be limited with respect to the geographic extent and duration of each right. For example, the publisher might have the power to license commercial rights in the United States for ten years, but the writer would retain the power to license outside the United States and after ten years would also regain the power to license in the United States. The publisher should have no right to share in the proceeds from subsidiary rights if the publisher fails to carry through its obligations (especially to publish) under the contract. Publishers will often sell the subsidiary rights prior to publication, so this distinction can be more than academic. It would be anomalous if a publisher never lived up to its obligation to bring out a trade edition, but still shared as a broker in proceeds from book club, paperback, film, and other sales.

The Guild contract also permits the publisher to allow excerpts, condensations, or abridgements to be used in textbooks or anthologies after its initial hardcover publication. The work may also be used in its entirety for the blind or handicapped, such as in Braille or large type editions. However, any use in retrieval or storage systems shall be permitted only with the writer's prior written consent, which shall not be delayed or unreasonably withheld. The guide to the Guild contract notes that writers may wish to retain a right of approval over all reprints to prevent publishers from charging unreasonably low fees.

Some subsidiary rights provisions do not mention performing (as opposed to publishing) subsidiary rights. The Guild recommends that the publisher have nothing to do with stage, record, radio, motion picture, television, and audio-visual rights. The rationale here is that the publisher usually does not market to these fields and should not, therefore, control any rights or share in any proceeds. A similar rationale applies to commercial rights, multimedia, and electronic rights. Publishers' contracts, however, usually do not reflect this reasoning. In practice, writers, especially those without agents, may find that publishers are in a better position to market certain of these rights.

Once the subsidiary rights have been enumerated and the issue of control determined (perhaps with the writer effectively having a veto power over certain licensings or giving the publisher a right of first refusal if the publisher is active in that field—e.g., electronic media), the final step is to resolve the division of the proceeds received from licensing the subsidiary rights. Obviously the percentages will be negotiated and vary from contract to contract. The Guild believes that the following percentages are reasonable for the writer to receive: 100 percent of first serialization income (90 percent if the publisher acts as agent), and not less than 80 percent (which should only be agreed to if most or all of the book is serialized in one or two installments); for paperback licenses, book club licenses, abridgments and selections, and second serializations, 50 percent of the first $10,000 of income, 60 percent of the next $10,000, and 70 percent of any income over $20,000; 50 percent of income from licensing film strips, microfilm, computer uses, and so on; and 100 percent of income from licensing stage, motion picture, television, and similar rights, unless the publisher is to receive 10 percent for acting as agent, but the writer should never receive less than 80 percent. If the original publication is in paperback, the publisher may sell hardcover rights to another publisher and agree to hold off the paperback publication for a year. In such a case, the writer may receive up to 75 percent of the proceeds, and certainly no less than 50 percent.

The definition of licensing income is critical, since percentages mean little without reference to what they are distributing between the writer and publisher. The Guild contract permits no reductions at all from licensing gross proceeds prior to payment of the writer's share. Publishers' standard contracts, however, will generally reduce gross proceeds by various expenses, including agent's commissions. Some contracts simply refer to a term such as "net compensation" without any further definition. This is not satisfactory, since the writer who is to receive a share of something less than gross proceeds should know exactly what is being subtracted to reach the net amount. The writer should definitely have the right to receive copies of any licensing contracts negotiated by the publisher, as the Guild contracts provide.

Electronic and Multimedia Rights

Electronic and multimedia rights, subsidiary rights in a book contract, are the hottest new topic in publishing contract negotiations and must be dealt with carefully. Electronic rights allow a book to be read digitally on a computer (sometimes called an "electronic book") and multimedia rights allow a book to be transformed through the use of several media such as words, sounds, music, photos, videos, lights, into a game, interactive software, or CD-ROM (sometimes called an "electronic version"). Unless the publishing company actually produces electronic books or multimedia titles, or has unique access to companies that do, the writer should be entitled to retain these rights.

Too many writers have signed contracts that failed to protect their rights in emerging technologies. The estate of Theodore Geisel, writer of the Dr. Seuss books, for example, had tough negotiations with Random House over the sale of multimedia rights because the contract did not adequately address the prospect of newly discovered technologies. Alberto Vitale, chairman of Random House, claims that he will not sign book contracts that fail to secure electronic rights for Random House and at least a right of first refusal on multimedia rights. In contrast, Robert Gottlieb, a senior executive at William Morris Agency says that, to protect the interests of his clients, he will refuse to sign book contracts that grant electronic or multimedia rights to the publisher. No doubt these antipodal positions reflect the starting points from which writers and publishers will strive to achieve compromise.

For example, in a recent report, a consultant to publishers recommended that publishers obtain electronic rights by the use of work for hire agreements. Since copyright law does not allow most books to be work for hire, the consultant gives as a second choice the use of an "all encompassing clause" which would define all electronic rights currently known and add the phrase "whether now known or hereinafter invented." Most book writers should be able to resist such overreaching by publishers, in which case the consultant recommends that such rights be treated as subsidiary rights.

Once again, unless the publisher has a way to market electronic rights or multimedia products, the writer should not allow such rights to be considered subsidiary rights. It would be far better for the writer to have his or her agent sell the rights directly to the end user, in which case no fee would be payable to the publisher. However, if the publisher is insistent, then a compromise may have to be reached. For an in-depth discussion of electronic rights, refer to chapter 14.

Reservation of Rights

The grant of rights and the subsidiary rights provisions are likely to cover all the conceivable uses of the writer's work. However, the writer should anticipate unthought of, even uninvented, uses. This is done by insisting on a simple clause stating: "All rights not specifically granted to the publisher are reserved to the writer."

Delivery of a Satisfactory Manuscript

The Guild contract calls for the delivery of a complete, clean, typewritten manuscript of the book by a specified date. The Guide to the Guild contract also suggests that, if a book depends on "future events, availability of information or similar contingencies," a clause be added which allows for an extension, provided that prior written notice of such contingencies be given to the publisher.

Nevertheless, the Guild recommends that the writer's failure to deliver the manuscript on the specified date should not automatically permit the publisher to terminate the contract and recover any advances. Instead, the contract should require the publisher to wait three more months. If, after those ninety days, written notice has been mailed and twenty additional days elapsed, the publisher should have the right to recover any monies that have been advanced to the writer.

If the publisher's contract specifies that "time is of the essence," the writer should definitely deliver the manuscript on time. If the contract does not specify that time is of the essence, the writer should still deliver the manuscript on time, but a late delivery (of perhaps a month or six weeks) may not be a breach of contract that would permit the publisher to terminate the contract and demand the return of the advance. Caution dictates, however, that the writer always request as early as possible a written extension if the delivery date cannot be met.

Publishers' contracts usually require that the delivered manuscript be in "content and form satisfactory" to the publisher. This places the writer in a difficult position. In the final analysis, what constitutes a satisfactory manuscript may turn on the publisher's subjective determination. As George Orwell once noted, "Every book is a failure." When the publishing house signs up a book, it is accepting at least some risk along with the writer. The advance should not transformed into a repayable loan, nor should the contract be treated as an option. Taken to the extreme, satisfaction clauses might seem to render a publishing contract unenforceable.

Historically, publishing companies were allowed almost total discretion in this area. More recently, the courts have circumscribed the ability of publishers to reject the final product in a capricious manner. In a New York case, the court held that although there is a right to edit, revise, and demand a higher quality manuscript on the part of the publisher, there is also some obligation to offer editorial assistance and allow the writer a reasonable opportunity to conform the book to those standards (*Dell Publishing Co. v. Whedon*, 577 F. Supp. 1459). But that assistance need not be adequate and can even be inferior as long as it is not offered in bad faith (*Doubleday v. Curtis*, 763 F.2d 495, *cert. dismissed* 474 U.S. 912). Furthermore, when a manuscript raised legal issues and was twice as long as the contract provided, the publisher did not even have to provide any editorial assistance when rejecting it (*Random House v. Damore*, unreported decision, Supreme Court, New York Country, Index No. 144 6/85). Nevertheless, the satisfaction clause must not be allowed to justify unilateral, damage-free termination of a contract, when the real reason is a change in financial prospects or conditions, management, editors, business policies, or diminished appeal of the writer or subject matter.

If the manuscript is objectively unsatisfactory, it would usually be unfair for the writer to be allowed to retain the entire advance. However, the Guide to the Guild contract suggests that the writer should negotiate hard for a provision requiring only partial return of the advance, not only because the publisher should share the risk, or because the writer has invested time, labor and money, but also to encourage the publisher to work with the writer to complete the book satisfactorily. Some publishers might agree to a first proceeds clause under which the writer would only have to repay the advance if a new publisher picked up the book.

If the publisher has seen all or part of the work prior to signing the contract, it should be recited that what was seen was satisfactory. If a practice is followed of submitting portions of the work in progress, it might be provided that the publisher indicate that each portion is satisfactory within a reasonable time after receipt. The writer can also seek to have the word "reasonably" inserted before "satisfactory," so that the publisher's decision cannot be wholly subjective. The contract could also entitle the writer to have a written explanation of the reasons why the work was not satisfactory, with a specified time to make revisions. At the least, the publisher should be required within a limited time, such as a month or six weeks, to make a decision with respect to whether or not the manuscript is satisfactory. The Guild has an additional provision granting the writer an automatic extension if any delay is due to military service, illness, or accident, although certain maximum limits are placed on the extensions allowed under this provision.

Additional Materials and Permissions

Most publishers' contracts will require the writer to deliver with the manuscript all photographs, drawings, other illustrations, maps, tables, charts, the index, the bibliography, and permissions. The expenses incurred to obtain these materials will be the writer's. However, the writer should keep in mind the possibility of dividing these responsibilities and costs with the publisher. Thus, each item might indicate whether the publisher or writer is to provide it and, regardless of who must provide it, which party will be responsible for paying for it. The writer might also seek a provision that if he or she fails to provide any required materials within a reasonable time after submission of the manuscript, the publisher must give the writer thirty days written notice before procuring the necessary materials. This would contrast with the more typical requirement in publishers' contracts that the additional materials be submitted at the time of delivery of the manuscript. The writer might also seek a right to approve any materials which are supplied by the publisher.

The issue of payment for other materials can be especially important for a children's book. If the publisher is to pay for illustrations, this should be specified. The Guild advises that the writer who also does illustrations negotiate for a separate payment as illustrator.

The writer might try to negotiate for the publisher to obtain any permissions and, again, divide the responsibility for payment between the writer and publisher. The rationale would be that the publisher is better equipped to obtain permissions than the writer. However, publishers' contracts normally require the writer to provide and pay for all permissions. In any case, the Guild suggests that if the publisher is to pay for permissions for art books, anthologies, or similar works involving substantial additional materials and permissions, the amount of the payment be stipulated in the contract.

Another safeguard for the writer might be a provision that if the publisher must make payments on behalf of the writer for any additional materials or permissions, these payments shall be advanced by the publisher and deducted only from monies earned under the contract. Nor should the publisher be allowed to deduct the advances from monies earned under other contracts which the writer may have with the publisher. The writer should always seek to have each book be a separate enterprise. No advances or other sums owed on one book should ever be deductible from monies received from another book with the same publisher, although some publishers will not agree to this separation. Many publishers try to impose this provision on writers, but the best argument against it is that the writer would be in a better position by publishing with another publisher. No question could then arise of deducting sums owed on one book from monies earned by another book. References in any provision to payment of sums owed on one book with monies earned by another book should be stricken from the contract.

Royalties

Royalties permit the writer to share in the success of a book and are in almost all cases far more desirable than a flat fee because they increase the writer's income potential. Royalties also benefit publishers in that they allow them to risk less cash. The percentage of proceeds payable to the writer upon the sale of each copy should be based on "retail price" or "retail list price." This is an important qualification. If the royalty is based on a net price—that is the price after discounts to book stores and wholesalers—the royalties will be far lower (possibly as much as 50 percent less) than if based on retail list price. The royalty also should not be a specific amount, such as one dollar per copy, because the publisher invariably has the power to determine the selling price of the book. The Guild does, however, recommend an additional provision providing for a specified amount as a minimum royalty. For example, setting one dollar as a minimum royalty might protect the writer if the publisher were to set too low a retail price on the book.

Royalty rates vary, so the writer should have the advice of an agent or more experienced writer in trying to determine if an offered royalty is fair. The Guild model contract provides for a percentage scale of royalties, the percentage increasing as more copies are sold. The Guild also sets forth guidelines for royalties in a number of different categories. For example, the writer marketing an adult hardcover trade book traditionally receives a minimum of 10 percent of the retail price on the first 5,000 copies, 12½ percent on the next 5,000 copies, and 15 percent on all copies sold in excess of 10,000.

The Guild suggests that royalties for children's books also start at 10 percent and step up to 15 percent with increasing numbers of copies sold, although the practice varies widely here. The writer doing children's books should keep in mind that royalties may have to be divided with an illustrator, if the illustrations are a central part of the book.

For the publisher's own quality paperback, the Guild indicates the royalty starts no lower than 6 percent of retail list price and increases to 7½ percent for sales of more than 10,000 copies (or increases sooner to 7½ percent if fewer than 10,000 copies are printed). On the publisher's own mass market paperback, the Guild contract has the royalty start no lower than 6 percent and increase to 8 percent when sales exceed 150,000 copies. The Guild also provides that no paperback edition may be issued within a year of the original trade publication. After that, the publisher must give the writer 120 days notice of any intended paperback edition, so that the writer can seek a better offer from a paperback publisher. If the writer succeeds in obtaining a better offer, the publisher is bound to accept it. These royalty rates for quality and mass market paperbacks would also apply to books first published in paperback form.

Royalties for professional, scientific, or technical books are customarily based on a net price, instead of retail price. The publisher's discount to bookstores is in the range of 25 percent to 33⅓ percent, so the writer's royalty is calculated against this lower figure. A typical royalty rate might be 15 percent, but the writer should keep in mind that a substantial part of the sales are likely to be mail order, library, or export (which means the writer's royalties will be reduced). For college textbooks, the royalties are also calculated on a net price, and the standard discount to book stores is 20 percent (although some publishers offer as much as 33 percent). On a hardcover textbook, the writer should demand 15 percent of net price on sales up to a specified number of copies (perhaps between 7,500 and 15,000), after which the rate should increase to 18 percent. Publishers are likely to offer 10 percent with an escalation to 15 percent, but this should be resisted, especially if the book is a basic textbook designed for a widely offered undergraduate course. Textbooks often have their best sales in the first few years after publication, so escalation for sales over a given number of copies in any year is another possibility. An original paperback textbook might have royalties in the range of 10 percent to 15 percent of the net price.

Royalty Reductions for Certain Sales

Royalties will customarily be reduced for certain sales, such as copies sold at a greater-than-usual discount from the retail price. The Guild contract, for example, provides that copies sold at a discount of 66⅔ percent or more from the retail price will realize a reduced royalty on sales. The Guild warns that a reduction, for example to 10 percent of net, can be harmful if it fails to result in a sharp increase in the number of copies sold. If the reductions are based on retail price, the royalty rate should not go below one half of what it would be for a sale which is not at a special discount. The Guild advises that the writer of children's books give close scrutiny to the discounts for library bound editions sold outside regular book selling channels. The Guild also indicates that, if the discount is for a sale in large quantity, all copies in the sale should have to be the same title (to avoid different writers' works being cumulated). If royalties are based on net proceeds rather than retail price, the writer should try to avoid discounts (since the less the publisher receives, the less the writer receives).

The Guild contract provides that the writer must be compensated for every book that is sold, with a minimum of 10 percent of the gross price received, even if books are sold at or below manufacturing cost. It also provides that no sale of overstock (copies sold in the United States at a 70 percent or higher discount) may take place until at least eighteen months after publication in book form, and that the writer must have thirty days notice and the option to purchase the overstock if the sale is to be made at or below the cost of manufacture. If all of the overstock is sold, which is called remaindering, the Guild provides that publishing rights revert to the writer.

Another common provision cuts royalties in half on copies sold from a small reprinting, usually 2,500 copies or less, more than one year after the first publication. The rationale is to allow the publisher to keep the work in print even if demand does not remain strong. Although the Guild contract does not contain such a provision, the Guide to the Guild contract explains that the best option would be to delete the clause entirely. If this can not be done, the writer should bargain for a reduction to three-quarters of the stipulated royalty (two-thirds at a minimum) on all copies sold from a reprint of 1,500 copies or less. The Guild suggests that this should only apply if sales have fallen below 500 copies in the six-month accounting period directly preceding the reprinting and if the reprinting does not take place until at least two years after the first publication. The rationale for allowing this reduction in the writer's royalties is the increased unit cost involved in small printings. This rationale is made more reasonable by the increases in paper prices that have plagued the publishing industry throughout 1995. However, it is the Guild's understanding that new technologies have made it cheap and efficient to do small printings.

Finally, the Guild indicates that the royalty rate may be reduced to two-thirds for copies sold by mail order, coupons, radio or television advertising, or in Canada, but in no case should this figure fall below 8 percent of the retail price in the United States. This two-thirds figure could be used as well for other export sales, but the writer might seek a full royalty or at least more than a one-half royalty if possible. No royalties are payable on copies destroyed or given away without charge to the writer or for promotion.

An important point is whether copies sold at a discount or in Canada will be added to the copies sold at regular retail price for the purpose of determining when the royalty rate escalates based upon the number of copies sold. Adding such copies is advantageous to the writer who should always consider which sales will add to total sales for purposes of escalating the royalty rate.

It is important to note that publishers are legally bound to act in good faith in allocating royalties. In one California case, the court found that a publisher could be held liable for allowing large discounts in order to pay lower royalties (*Levering v. Addison-Wesley*, 12 Med. L. Rptr.

1807). As one final precaution, writers should attempt to include a clause in the contract which specifically limits the percentage of books upon which the publisher can pay a reduced royalty.

Reserve Against Returns

Publishers regularly retain a percentage of royalties as a reserve against returned books. Bookstores are free to return books which do not sell. Depending upon the kind of book published and the publishing house, actual returns will vary from 10 percent to more than 50 percent. Yet the publisher pays a royalty based on copies shipped during the royalty period despite the likelihood of at least some returns.

To make certain that royalties are not overpaid (that is, paid on books that are later returned), publishers may reserve a certain portion of the royalties. Some publishers have been known to retain as much as 60 to 70 percent, although more common might be 30 to 40 percent. The Guild contract would limit the allowable reserve against returns to 15 percent and for the shorter of the first three accounting periods or eighteen months. It is important to place reasonable limits on the amount and duration of the reserve, since its effect may be to deprive the writer of royalties that should be paid.

Advances

The advance is a sum of money paid to the writer that is then deducted from future book revenues. No royalties will be paid until the full amount of the "unearned" advance is recouped by the publisher. The advance may be paid in full at the time of signing the contract, but more commonly it is paid in several installments. For example, two installments might be paid, one upon signing the contract and the other upon delivery of a satisfactory manuscript. Or three installments might be used, the first on signing the contract, the second on delivery of the manuscript, and the last on publication—although the writer should try to avoid having to wait until publication for the final installment (or to provide for payment upon the earlier of publication or twelve months after delivery of the manuscript). The Guide to the Guild contract suggests that writers insert a clause in the contract providing for a monetary penalty in the event that advances are not paid on time.

The amount of the advance varies with the writer's reputation, the success of the writer's previous work, the nature of the book itself, the publisher's expectations with respect to the market, and innumerable other factors that indicate how financially rewarding the book is likely to be. If a writer is uncertain whether an offered advance is fair, it would be wise to consult with an agent or a more experienced writer for advice.

In most cases, the writer should seek the highest advance that can be negotiated. The writer's time, effort, materials, and travel expenses on a book can be great, even if the book is not successful in the market. While a high advance will not necessarily guarantee that the writer will earn extra income from the book, or even that the book will sell more copies, the advance does establish a floor, a minimum recompense for the writer's work on the book. And, to the extent that it signifies a serious commitment of cash on the part of the publisher, it is likely to induce the publishing company to back up its bet with increased advertising, promotion, and a larger first printing, all of which, taken together, are likely to add up to a self-fulfilling prophecy of success. Furthermore, money in the bank, earning interest, is worth more than money paid the following year.

Nevertheless, there are times when a writer may decide to accept a smaller advance. The writer who has written several moderately successful books may have a fix on the rate of sale and prefer to put off income until future tax years when royalties are earned and paid. The writer may also want to go with a smaller publisher. The fact that smaller presses traditionally pay lower advances may be outweighed by the increased personal attention, warmth, and returned phone calls that are a hallmark of the specialty publishing house. The writer who demands and receives a high advance may also force a publisher to overprint the market for a book. The result can be a remainder sale, a flood of deeply discounted books that then undermine the market and force bookstores to return their stock for credit. The fact is that although smaller houses pay lower advances and print fewer copies, they are often able to keep books, especially specialized books, in print longer and remainder them far less frequently than larger houses.

If the publisher complains that a high advance will cause a cash flow crisis, the writer should suggest a higher royalty percentage as an alternative. If the publisher is immovable on that subject, perhaps the subsidiary rights are negotiable. While it is difficult to get concessions with respect to primary subsidiary rights, such as paperback rights, book club rights, or reprint rights, which are the publisher's bread and butter, publishers are often more amenable to bargaining for secondary subsidiary rights. This would include such things as first serial rights (publication in a magazine, periodical, or newspaper prior to publication), performing rights, British rights, and translation rights, which, because they are more speculative, can often be reserved by the writer.

The Guild contract provides that the advance shall be nonreturnable unless the writer fails to deliver a complete typewritten manuscript of the work within ninety days after notice from the publisher with respect to failure to deliver. The writer should follow this model and never agree to return an advance except for failure to deliver a satisfactory manuscript (always attempting to qualify the term "satisfactory" as discussed under delivery of the manuscript).

If the advance is nonreturnable except for delivery of an unsatisfactory manuscript or a late delivery (which is also discussed under delivery of the manuscript), it follows that the writer will be able to keep the advance if the publisher rejects the manuscript for any other reason. Thus, the writer must judge the real reason for any rejection. Perhaps the project has become too expensive, a competing book has come out, or the subject now seems dated. If the publisher in fact is breaching its obligations under the contract, the writer can demand the balance of any advance due and be under no obligation to repay it (even if, for example, another publisher were later to publish the book). These factual questions surrounding the reasons for rejection of a manuscript often lead to a compromise of the disagreement.

In any case, the writer should never agree to permit the publisher to recoup the advance on one book by taking royalties from another book. Each book contract, as mentioned earlier, must be considered a separate venture. The Guild advises that the publisher should only be able to take a percentage of proceeds from book club, paperback, and other subsidiary publishing rights to pay back advances, and that no proceeds from licensing first serial rights should be applied to the repayment of advances. The Guild also indicates that if the writer is to be given funds to cover expenses, the clause should explain clearly whether or not those funds are to be repaid from royalties as well as whether they must be repaid if the project does not reach fruition. The reasons for the failure of the project would, of course, bear on whether the money should be refunded. If a publishing contract does not provide for the publisher to recoup monies owed under one contract against monies earned under another contract, the writer should resist any attempts by the publisher at offsetting sums between contracts (*Fugate v. Greenberg*, 16 Misc.2d 942, 945, 189 N.Y.S.2d 948, 952).

Payments, Statements of Account, and Inspection of Books

Most publishers render accounts and payments on a semiannual basis. The accounting provision should require a separate statement of account for each book by the writer, including copies of statements of account from sublicensees to the publisher. The writer should also seek to require the publisher to include the following information in these statements: the number of copies printed in each edition, the date of completion of printing and binding, the publication date, and the retail price; for each different royalty rate, the number of copies sold, the number of copies returned, the amount of current royalties, and the amount of cumulative royalties to the date of the statement; the number of copies given away free, remaindered, destroyed, or lost; a description of subsidiary rights sales in which the writer's share is more than one-hundred dollars, including the total amount received by the publisher and the percentage of that total which the writer's share represents; and the amount of reserves held for returns. If the publisher accidentally makes an overpayment to the writer, this can be deducted from future payments.

An important provision, which is included in the Guild contract, requires that the writer be paid within ten days for subsidiary rights income received by the publisher. This provision is fair, because the publisher is truly acting as an agent with respect to such proceeds. Moreover, the Guild proposes that such funds be designated trust funds—as was suggested for funds held by the writer's agent (see chapter 15)—in order to force separate accounts for these funds prior to payment and provide some protection against the publisher's insolvency or bankruptcy.

The writer will certainly want the power to examine the publisher's books upon written notice. Although the writer will normally bear the cost of such an examination, the contract should shift these costs to the publisher if errors in favor of the publisher amounting to 5 percent or more of the total amounts paid to the writer are discovered. Publishers will seek to restrict this right of inspection, but it should be present in every contract, even if in modified form.

The writer who is in a high income tax bracket may wish to spread income forward into future tax years. Publishers, however, will rarely pay interest on such withheld royalties. The writer runs the risk of the publisher's bankruptcy as well. Especially with the relatively lower taxes that prevail today, the writer should have the assurance of expert tax advisers that such a provision is necessary before utilizing it.

Duty to Publish and Keep in Print

The publisher should be required to publish the work within a specified number of months after delivery of the manuscript. Although it is not uncommon for contracts to allow eighteen months, the Guild contract specifies that the publisher must publish the work within twelve months of satisfactory delivery. The publisher must use its best efforts to sell both books and subsidiary rights. In the event of unavoidable delays, the publication date is extended to not more than six months after the end of the reason for the delay. The inclusion of a publication date raises the possibility that the publisher will breach the contract by failing to publish. The writer will often find damages difficult to prove in such a case (*Freund v. Washington Square Press*, 34 N.Y.2d 379, 314 N.E.2d 453, 357 N.Y.S.2d 857 *modifying* 41 App.Div.2d 371, but compare *Contemporary Mission, Inc. v. Famous Music Corp.*, 557 F.2d

918). And many publishers simply place the date of publication within their own discretion. But all rights should revert to the writer if the publisher fails in its obligation to publish within a specified period of time.

The writer should also have a right to regain all rights if the work goes out of print. In one case, a writer was awarded damages for a sale of rights by a publisher after the book had gone out of print (*Fugate v. Greenberg*, 16 Misc.2d 942, 946, 189 N.Y.S.2d 948, 953). Each contract defines out of print differently. The Guild defines out of print as the point at which the book is "no longer available through normal retail channels" and is not listed in the publisher's catalogue issued to the trade. The Guild contract provides that the publisher must notify the writer in writing when the available stock of the book in the publisher's warehouse falls below 250 copies and must give the writer the opportunity to buy the remaining stock. The writer may then formally request that the work be reprinted. If this request is not answered within sixty days, or if it is answered in the affirmative and then not complied with after a period of six months, the agreement is terminated and all rights revert to the writer.

Most out of print provisions are far less favorable to the writer. For example, some contracts provide the work is in print if any license for subsidiary rights is in effect. The writer should seek the narrowest possible definition of what will be considered keeping the work in print (such as at least requiring a United States edition be in print). Of particular relevance today is making certain that licenses for nonprint subsidiary rights (perhaps electronic, multimedia, or audio rights) are not considered to keep a book in print.

Once a work is determined to be out of print, the writer should have the option to purchase the production materials, such as plates, film, and offset negatives, at scrap value and any remaining copies at either the publisher's cost or at a remainder price, whichever is lower. The Guild's provision allows the writer to purchase the remaining copies of the book at their unit cost and to purchase the plates, offset negatives, or computer drive tapes at their scrap value. This kind of purchase provision exists in most publishing contracts, but the writer is usually required to pay more for the privilege.

Copyright

Copyright should be in the writer's name. This is an accepted practice that should be insisted upon by the writer. A notice in the publisher's name—even if the copyright were held in trust for the writer—could be harmful in such situations as the publisher's bankruptcy, the unauthorized sale of rights by the publisher, the bringing of suits for infringement, or a claim by the publisher that the work is for hire. The writer should also require the publisher to obtain appropriate copyright notice, preferably in the writer's name, for all exploitations of subsidiary rights.

Warranty and Indemnity

Most publishers' contracts require the writer to make several express warranties. The writer warrants that he or she is the sole creator; that the writing is original; that the work has never been published before (unless the contrary is understood by the parties); that the material is not defamatory, libelous, or violative of other rights (such as privacy); that the work is not obscene and; that the work does not recommend activities which are "harmful." The "sole author" warranty will usually include language to the effect that the writer has obtained all necessary rights, licenses, releases, assignments, and permissions legally necessary to publish the work. The originality requirement relates to plagiarism rather than to novelty; it requires only that the work owe its origin to the writer. Whether the work defames, libels, or invades privacy is, of course, important because of the possible liability involved.

Indemnity provisions are created to protect the publisher from suits for breach of the aforementioned warranties. They should never apply to parts of the book that were added as a result of suggestions, corrections, or additions made by an editor or any other agent of the publisher (as to which writer should be indemnified). Publishers want to be "held harmless," while writers want the publisher to provide insurance or at least limit the writer's liability to the amount of the advance and royalties received or some other reasonable amount. Publishers worry that limiting an writer's liability will increase the chances of lawsuits. Immunized writers, they argue, will surely be less vigilant.

Courts have often sided with the publisher on the theory that "to require a book publisher to check, as a matter of course, every defamatory reference might raise the price of non-fiction work beyond the resources of the average man" (*Geiger v. Dell Publishing*, 719 F.2d 515). Because the publisher is generally in a poorer position than the writer to know whether the characters are modeled after real people (raising the possibility of a libel suit), whether the work was plagiarized (raising the possibility of a copyright infringement suit), whether the book has been published before in any form, or whether the writer owns all the rights, one court held that to hold the publisher liable for the writer's inaccuracies was to find liability without finding fault (*Ortiz v. Valdescastilla*, 102 A.D.2d 513). Nevertheless, when a publishing company was "grossly irresponsible," ignoring facts that should have given notice of potential legal issues, the publisher was not allowed "to escape liability by showing that it relied upon the integrity of a reputable author" (*Weiner v. Doubleday & Co.*, 74 N.Y.2d 586, 549 N.E.2d 453, 550 N.Y.S.2d 251, 17 Med.L.Rptr 1165, *cert. denied* 110 S. Ct. 2168).

The publisher clearly would like the writer to be liable when there is a "claim," even if it's spurious, and certainly if there is a settlement. This means the writer has to pay for the publisher's expenditures even if the alleged breach is completely without merit and never even goes to trial. The publisher would seek the right to withhold royalties from all contracts with the writer until any suit or threatened suit is settled.

A warranty provision of that kind can be disastrous for the writer, especially since a frivolous claim can take years to resolve in the courts. The writer should seek to limit the scope of the warranty clause. The writer would want to warrant only that "to the best of his knowledge" the book does not contain libelous matter, does not violate anyone's proprietary rights, is not an infringement of an existing copyright, and has not previously been published in book form in any of the territories covered by the grant of rights. The writer would want to indemnify the publisher only for claims that are finally sustained, so alleged breaches that never result in a recovery would not be covered. The Guild provision goes further, providing that the writer only has to pay the publisher after all appeals have been exhausted from a final judgment based on an actual breach of the warranties. In addition, the Guild limits the writer's liability by stating that the writer will only pay the lesser of a percentage of sums due under the contract (30 percent is suggested) or a fixed dollar amount.

The writer will want the right to defend any suit with his or her own lawyers without being liable for the fees of the lawyers hired by the publisher. Under most standard publishers' contracts, the writer does have the right to pursue his or her own defense independently as long as sufficient collateral is given to the publisher, either through expected royalties and rights fees, or in cash.

The Guild would not permit the publisher to set up a reserve to cover possible damages arising from a breach of warranty, or at least would limit such a reserve to no more than 30 percent of sums due the writer (and never more than the damages claimed). The writer should certainly not agree to let sums due under one contract be held in reserve to pay for a breach or alleged breach of the warranty provision under another contract. Writers should also include language that prohibits settlement without the writer's consent, or at the very least consultation. Although many publishers are leery of the high deductible, it is important to note that some of the disagreements over this clause have been alleviated by publishers, especially the larger ones, carrying liability insurance for their writers. These liability policies often cover claims for libel and other forms of defamation, invasion of privacy or publicity, as well as infringement of copyright or trademark.

The publisher will often argue that the warranty provision cannot be changed because the publisher would lose its insurance against such claims. Writers so far have had little success in obtaining insurance similar to that of the publishers. But the writer should not accept this explanation, since the effect of the warranty provision is to make the writer the insurer of the publisher. If money must be paid because of a breach of warranty, the insurance company will pay for the publisher and then sue the writer to recover whatever sums were paid out. Even if the publisher will lose insurance coverage, it is far easier for the publisher to play the role of insurer. This is particularly true of a book which is likely to generate claims under a warranty provision. The writer might simply demand that the provision be stricken and the publisher assume all such risks, especially when the risks are clear at the beginning of the project and the publisher is still eager to go forward. Depending on the kind of book, it may be better to lose a book, when a satisfactory warranty provision can't be negotiated, than to risk expensive and time-consuming litigation.

Insurance

The warranty provisions contained in standard book contracts make the writer liable in suits by third parties for damages arising out the writer's breach. Publishers usually have their own insurance and the insurance company traditionally pays any judgement, or the amount of the settlement. The insurance company then has a right to sue the writer, which it may or may not exercise in a particular situation. The Guild suggests that publishers provide insurance coverage for their writers against suits for libel, invasion of privacy, and related risks, and notes that several of the larger houses have already begun to do so, although the deductible is usually split evenly. Publishers pay an additional premium to include their writers under the house insurance policy and the writer agrees to cooperate in the defense. For books that may cause libel suits, the publisher's lawyer reads the books and decides whether or not they raise legal issues (called vetting), so there is every reason for the risk to be shared.

Some publishers, as noted earlier, argue that fear of liability creates vigilance on the part of writers. The Guild strongly disagrees. Few writers will be more qualified than a publishing lawyer to ascertain whether a work is likely to cause a suit, except in the case of an writer who has taken someone else's work. Furthermore, the insurance company may become more involved and exercise its knowledge-based vigilance through advice and suggested precautions. For screenplays, film companies obtain error and omissions insurance which covers the writer, although a signed statement is required as to original authorship.

In practice, publishers often pay for legal expenses, settlements, and judgments resulting from suits for such acts as misquoting, misstating facts, or even plagiarism, despite the writer being clearly responsible. Publishers might be tougher as far as collecting their percentage of such costs when dealing with a highly successful writer; when the case involves an unknown writer and an unknown book, the publisher may very well just absorb the loss as a cost of doing business. On the other hand, some publishers may seek to recoup such costs from royalties.

Some insurance policies may also contain a large deductible which may not be excessive for a publisher, but could be oppressive for a writer. Even when the publisher pays the writer's insurance, the writer may still be responsible for the deductible which can run as high as $250,000. The Guild suggests that an indemnity clause be omitted and that the writer's share of the deductible be limited as follows: the lower of 50 percent of the first $3,000, or, for example, 5 percent of the advance.

Another problem for the writer is that, even in cases which are won by the publisher and the writer, legal expenses can amount to as much as fifty-thousand dollars or more, of which the writer might be contractually obligated to pay half.

There are several precautions that a writer can take in an attempt to safeguard against a breach of warranty. Keeping one's notes, tapes, photos, rough drafts, and the like can be helpful in a future lawsuit. This practice will be especially helpful in a lawsuit for libel, in which truth is an absolute defense, or in a copyright infringement case, in which prior independent creation can rebut the presumption of infringement created by access and substantial similarity. The writer may also want to retain legal counsel trained in the specific areas likely to be involved. Such specialists should be able to minimize the possibility of exposure to legal action although they are unlikely to give any guarantees.

If the writer is unable to negotiate for publisher-paid insurance coverage, the Guild can provide a list of insurance companies which offer such policies.

Artistic Control

Most publishers' contracts require that the manuscript be in "content and form satisfactory to the publisher," which means publishers can exert a negative form of artistic control. The writer should insist, however, on the opportunity to make any necessary changes in the work and to approve any changes done by other persons. Of course, subject to the writer's review, the publisher has the right to copy edit the manuscript in the customary manner. If the publisher wants major changes (for example, changing more than 10 percent of the manuscript), the contract might provide for additional payments to the writer, especially in the unfortunate case that the book is being done for a flat fee.

However, the writer who unilaterally decides to change the manuscript after production has started may be liable for the costs involved. Most publishers' contracts provide that the writer shall be charged for any changes in the galleys or page proofs in excess of 10 or 15 percent of the original cost of composition. The Guild contract allows the writer to be charged for such changes if in excess of the greater of $300 or 15 percent of the composition cost. Many publishers make the cut-off figure 10 percent. But the Guild contract also requires the publisher to provide promptly an itemized statement of the extra expenses as well as showing the corrected proofs to the writer. Of course such changes should only be deductible against income earned under the contract for the particular book, not other contracts the writer may have with the publisher.

Most publishers' contracts give the publisher the power to fix the book's retail price, title, form, type, paper, and similar details. The writer might try to negotiate to have a minimum retail price established, to allow the title to be changed only if the writer consents in writing, and to have the publisher consult with the writer about the format and style of the text, graphic material, and the dust jacket. Since the dust jacket presents the book to the public, the writer may very well wish to seek a voice in its content. Particularly with children's books, the writer may want to be able to approve rough and final illustrations and the accompanying captions. The writer's controls here will have to be added into the usual contract, as will any prohibition against advertisements appearing on the cover or in the text. Such advertising can demean a book, and the writer should require that his or her written consent be obtained. The writer should seek to have any advertising prohibition apply with equal force to licensees, such as book clubs or paperback publishers.

The writer should also insist on the power to approve any condensations or abridgments, so that the publisher will have to require licensees to obtain the writer's consent to such changes. If the publisher can license translation rights, the writer may want control over the choice of a translator and the final form of the translation. A writer with great bargaining power might even insist that the final form of a film script accurately reflect the original book (but a writer with that much bargaining power probably would not give film rights to the publisher in the first place). Artistic control should be recognized as an issue in every publishing contract. But writers should also be aware that, in practice, publishers will want to retain final control over production matters. Although they may grant "consultation" rights, it is rare that they will grant approval rights.

If the publisher has the right to revise the book in the future, the writer should have the right of first refusal. If the writer cannot do the revisions, however, another writer may be chosen by the publisher under most contracts. The Guild advises that the publisher should have the right to revise the book only at intervals of several years, subject to the writer's approval which cannot be unreasonably withheld. The use of such a clause will vary, of course, depending on the subject matter. The writer's royalties will be reduced if another writer does the revisions, so the Guild recommends placing a minimum base (perhaps two-thirds of the original royalties) below which royalties may not be reduced. Regardless of whether the writer who revises the book is paid a flat fee or given royalties, any charges made against the original writer on account of the revisions should only be deductible from income earned from the book being revised. Also, assuming the writer cannot have a veto power over revisions by someone else, the Guild advises the writer to reserve the right to remove his or her name from the book in the event the revisions prove unsatisfactory.

Credits

The exact nature of the writer's credit should be specified, including size and placement, especially if another writer or editor has also worked on the book. If the book may be revised in the future, the credit to be given to the reviser should also be specified.

Original Materials

The publisher should be required to return the original manuscript to the writer along with any other materials, such as artwork. For example, return of the original manuscript, galley proof, page proof, and any graphic material might be required within six months or one year after publication. The publisher will usually not agree to either insure the work or pay if valuable materials included in the manuscript (such as transparencies) are damaged or lost, although the writer might demand this if the work is of great value. A writer may want to add a clause to the contract which provides that the original manuscript, and all drafts and revisions, made by either the writer or the editor, are the sole property of the writer and must be returned. This is important not only because in some cases these documents may have substantial value, but also because the writer may wish to prevent subsequent disclosure of the manuscript. Also, the writer who delivers a book manuscript in electronic form may want to require not only the return of the disk submitted, but also the erasure of any copies made during the production process (although, in any case, the writer's copyright should protect against infringing uses).

Competing Works

Publishers often ask that a writer sign a noncompetition clause. Typically, such clauses restrict the ability of the writer to publish a book with another publisher while the book at issue is in print. The restriction prevents the writer from creating works that address the same or similar subject matter to the extent that such a book might conflict with sales of the prior book. The Guild indicates the writer should not agree to this. First of all, as the Guild notes, the publisher is unwilling to make a similar commitment. Second, if the writer publishes a work that is closely similar to that already licensed to the publisher, the publisher may be able to sue the writer for copyright infringement.

In essence, these clauses are an attempt by the publisher to violate the scope of protection statutorily provided to the writer under the copyright laws. Under such clauses, Ian Fleming might have been restrained by a first publisher from writing more books that contained the character of James Bond; the world's greatest chef could be limited to writing one opus cookbook; and a professor of intellectual property might not be allowed to express original thoughts in new books as his or her knowledge and understanding of the field developed. These outcomes clearly counter the policy considerations behind the copyright law and constitutional provisions which grant Congress the power to promote, not to limit, the progress of science and the useful arts. For this reason and others, courts have frowned on such clauses. One case held that noncompetition clauses must be limited in duration in order to be valid, and that the word "competition" should be narrowly construed because of the difficulty in ascertaining whether the subject matter of one book diminishes the financial success of another book (*Harlequin Enterprises Limited v. Warner Books, Inc.*, 639 F. Supp. 1081). Another held that the sale of rights did not include, unless specifically mentioned, the ownership of the right to publish sequels or other books using the same general characters (*Goodis v. United Artists Television, Inc.*, 425 F.2d 397). A third court held that the contract for the exclusive right to publish books in a children's book series which included Hardy Boys and Nancy Drew did not extend to the characters or to future books in the series (*Grosset & Dunlap, Inc. v. Gulf & Western Corp.*, 534 F. Supp. 606).

If the publisher insists on such a clause, however, the writer should narrowly restrict its scope with respect to subject matter, audiences, forms of publication (such as a book-length work), duration, and geographic extent.

Options

Another common provision gives the publisher the option to publish the writer's next work. Such a provision may well be unenforceable unless the terms of the future publication are made definite. Courts have often found option clauses to be too ambiguous or void on the theory that they constituted a mere "agreement to agree" (*Harcourt Brace Jovanovich, Inc. v. Farrar, Straus & Giroux, Inc.*, 4 Med. L. Rptr. 2625).

In any case, the writer should insist that the option provision be deleted from the contract. If the writer and publisher are satisfied with one another, they will want to contract for future books. If they are not satisfied, there is no reason why the writer should have to offer the next book to the publisher. Option clauses are problematic for the writer because they have the potential of limiting the freedom of the writer to benefit from past successes. If the writer has negotiated poorly in one contract, the option clause magnifies this mistake by carrying it forward to future contracts under which the writer might have expected a higher advance and better terms.

From the publisher's perspective, promoting the first book of an unknown writer is an enterprise fraught with risk. If the publisher stands to gain from the future writings of the writer, the investment begins to seem worthwhile. Knowing that writers are also business people, who may hasten to find larger publishers and higher advances, publishers often seek assurances. They may ask for a right to match the advance of any other publisher on the writer's later books (known as "matching" or as a right of last refusal), provide for an identical contract for the next book, or perhaps even ask to have a several-month-long "grace" period with which to negotiate exclusively with the writer. The publisher may also ask for the right to see the next finished manuscript before negotiating. The problem with all these demands is that they effectively cut off the writer's income potential during the process of writing and, perhaps more importantly, they discourage other publishers from bidding on the writer's work. Publishers will be reluctant to negotiate aggressively for a book when they know that their offer can be matched, the book snatched away from them, and their time and efforts wasted.

If an option provision must be agreed to, the writer should not give an option for more than one work and should require the publisher to make a determination with regard to that work within a reasonable time period after submission of a detailed outline, or at most, after the completion of the first chapter.

Free Copies

Most publishing contracts will provide for the writer to receive five to ten free copies of the regular edition and any subsequent cheap edition. These are traditionally referred to as author's copies. Additionally, provision is made for the writer to purchase unlimited copies for personal use at a substantial discount, such as 40 to 50 percent off the retail list price. The Guild believes twenty-five free copies with a 50 percent discount on all copies purchased thereafter is reasonable. The writer should be careful to include the royalty percentage when calculating the real price paid. If the higher discount pushes the purchase into a lower royalty category, it might not be as good a deal as it looks. The writer should be careful not to allow the publisher to restrict the use of writer's copies (whether free or purchased) to the writer's own use. There is nothing wrong with this writer selling copies of his or her own book and there may often be substantial profit in doing so. In fact, many writers find that they have access to a segment of the market which is not covered by the publisher.

If the writer has a newsletter, organizational affiliation, or other contacts that make selling large quantities of the book a certainty, it may be possible to negotiate for even higher discounts on copies explicitly purchased to be resold. For example, 500, 1,000, or 5,000 copies purchased should justify a far higher discount than 50 percent, especially if the writer joins the publisher's print run.

A look at the economics will explain why such a higher discount should be possible. For a typical book printing of 5,000 copies, the average unit cost of the printing might be $2. However, to print another 1,000 copies in the same print run might only cost $1,000 or $1 per copy. If the book retails for $16.95 and the writer offers to buy 1,000 copies at a 75 percent discount off the retail price (or $4.23 per copy), the publisher is still making an excellent profit from the add-on to the print run. Some publishers will give even higher discounts depending on the size of the order, while others will refuse to consider anything beyond the typical 40 to 50 percent (perhaps from concerns relating to other production costs, overhead, or the possibility of the writer's sales competing with the publisher's sales). If the writer might profit more from selling the book than from the royalties, serious consideration should be given to self-publication or, at least, to finding a publisher flexible enough to sell substantial quantities at high discounts.

Assignment

It is not uncommon to require the written consent of either party to an assignment by the other. The publisher would not wish to have another writer substituted under the contract, but neither should the writer have to accept a different publisher. Nothing should prevent the writer from assigning to another person money due or to become due under the contract. The publisher may require a provision permitting assignment to any new publisher who takes over the entire business.

Infringement by Others

If the book's copyright is infringed by someone else, the contract must specify each party's obligations and rights to any sums recovered. For example, the publisher and writer might both participate in bringing an infringement suit and split the expenses of the suit. If monies were recovered, the expenses could first be recouped, after which the balance of the recovery could either be divided equally or, with respect to the subsidiary rights, divided according to the specified percentages. If one party chooses not to participate in the suit, the other party might have a right to proceed and recoup all expenses from any recovery before the balance of the recovery is divided as if the parties had both participated. The writer should retain the exclusive right to sue for infringement of rights retained by the writer.

Termination

The Guild contract provides for termination by the writer if the book goes out of print. Additionally, the writer is given the right to terminate if the publisher fails to provide the semiannual statements of account or fails to accompany the statements with the required payments. The writer may also want to negotiate for the right to terminate if royalties fall below a minimum amount.

The writer should also require a termination power in the event of the publisher's failure to fulfill the material terms of the contract, including a failure to publish within ninety days of the writer's notice stating the publisher is past the specified publication date. There should be an automatic termination if the publisher has become bankrupt or insolvent. In the event of termination for any reason, the writer should have the option to purchase the production materials and remaining copies as discussed with respect to the out-of-print provisions.

Arbitration

The writer will generally benefit from an arbitration provision, because disputes under the contract can be quickly and easily resolved. A contract might provide for arbitration before the American Arbitration Association, but the writer should be satisfied as long as unbiased arbitrators would hear the dispute. The disadvantage of arbitration is that an arbitrator's adverse decision is very difficult to appeal to the courts, so the writer should feel certain the arbitration will be fairly conducted. The writer may choose to reserve the right to sue if the dispute relates to royalties due under the contract. One reason not to use an arbitrator is that some cases have held that arbitrators can award only compensatory and not punitive damages (*Garrity v. Lyle Stuart, Inc.*, 40 N.Y.2d 354, 353 N.E.2d 793). In most cases, however, this will be of minimal significance.

Agency

An agent may seek to incorporate in the publishing contract a provision that gives the agent authority to act on behalf of the writer in all matters arising from the contract. If, in fact, the agent's powers are limited, it would be wise to limit the agency provision. Also, the writer should always have the right to receive payment directly from the publisher of a minimum of 90 percent of sums due if the writer wants direct payment once the writer-agent contract has terminated. This can be accomplished by the use of a clause to the effect that: "The authorization of the agent to act on behalf of the writer and to collect sums due the writer shall continue in effect until the publisher shall otherwise be instructed in writing by the writer." The exact language of the agency clause will have to be negotiated in the writer-agent contract.

Collaborators

The writer may collaborate with another writer, an editor, an illustrator, a technical expert, or a well-known person who is the subject of the book. In some cases the collaboration may be with someone the writer never meets, but who merely contributes material for the book. In any case, the writer and any collaborator must have a contract between them (as discussed in chapter 16) and the provisions of that contract must be reflected in the publishing contract when relevant (such as the clauses governing authorship credit or special instructions for payment to the writer and the collaborator).

Advertising and Promotion

The writer also has a right to at least some book promotion. As in all contracts involving exclusive rights, the publisher has a duty to use its "best efforts" to promote and sell the book. What constitutes best efforts will vary between publishers. The courts are unlikely to second guess marketing decisions. What is clear is that no marketing whatsoever would breach the publisher's duty to promote. A contract to publish a book "implies a good faith effort to promote the book" and to expend advertising funds "adequate to give the book a reasonable chance of achieving market success" (*Zilg v. Prentice Hall*, Inc., 717 F.2d 671, *cert. denied* 466 U.S. 938. See also *Van Valkenburg v. Hayden Pub. Co.*, 33 App. Div.2d 766, 306 N.Y.S.2d 599, *aff'd* 30 N.Y.2d 34, 281 N.E.2d 142, *cert. denied* 409 U.S. 875).

Writers of works that are potentially very profitable to publishers may actually be able to require the designation of an advertising and marketing budget that would cover ads and promotional events such as book signings, readings, and mailings of publicity fliers. If this is done, the budget should only be expendable for the single title, not group ads including other titles. A further breakdown into the categories of advertising is difficult prior to publication, although in special cases it may be possible to pinpoint markets in which advertising should later take place.

The Guild suggests that if the writer has the negotiating clout, he or she can negotiate a clause providing that an amount of money equal to at least 10 percent of the publisher's projected first year's income from the book be spent on advertising and promotion and also that the publisher be required to consult, or if possible get the consent of, the writer regarding advertising, promotion, and publicity. A small company would be very unlikely to agree to either of these clauses. And, even from a large house, only a powerful agent representing a desirable book would be able to get these kinds of concessions. The more usual approach is to request the highest possible advance, and leave the publisher to its own ingenuity with respect to the level of advertising and promotion.

Most contracts require that the writer allow the publisher to use the writer's name, likeness, or photograph in advertising and promotion for the work. While the writer wants this, he or she may also want an assurance that a suitable decorum will be maintained. One way to accomplish this is by pre-approving the specific likeness or photographs that will be used.

Security Interest

Some publishers' contracts contain a provision granting the publisher a security interest in the work. This secures the publisher for any sums due it under the contract, including advances not recouped, by giving the publisher the power to attach the manuscript and all related materials and, upon demand, take immediate possession of these properties. The writer is required to execute such documents as are necessary to perfect the security interest. Needless to say, any situation in which a publisher can seize a writer's work to pay monies owed is highly undesirable. Mechanisms for the repayment of advances and other sums owed are provided in most contracts, including a right to monies received under a subsequent publishing contract for the same book, and should be sufficient to protect the publisher.

Other Provisions

Some publishers' contracts will permit withdrawal of the contract offer if the writer does not return the signed contract within a limited period of time, such as sixty days. Contractual modifications will have to be written. The state whose laws govern the contract will be specified. The contract may state that heirs, legal representatives, successors, and assigns are bound by its terms. Waivers and defaults under one provision will be restricted so as neither to permit future waivers or defaults nor affect obligations under other provisions of the contract. The manner in which notice can be given—to whom and at what address—will be indicated.

This concludes the examination of the book publishing contract. The principles described generally apply to the licensing or selling of literary property to other markets as discussed in the chapters that follow.

12 Magazines and Syndication

Licensing to magazine publishers involves many of the same considerations as licensing to book publishers, except that the contracts will be much simpler. Also, magazine articles are frequently sold without a contract. If the editor calls with a rush job, the writer is often more concerned with meeting the deadline than with paperwork. Syndication involves licensing work to an organization which disseminates the work to its subscribers around the country (usually newspapers for the print media) which then pay a flat fee for running it. The National Writers Union has developed a Standard Journalism Contract that sets standards for the field. Members of the Union and the publishing industry are encouraged by the Union to use this contract.

Licensing to Magazines

If the parties do not have a written agreement, then the copyright law governs the grant of rights. In such a case, the law presumes that the magazine acquires the

165

right to use the contribution in that particular magazine and any subsequent issue of that magazine. The magazine has no right to make other uses of the contribution (such as in a different magazine owned by the same company or in a "best of" anthology drawn from the magazine). Also, the usage rights are nonexclusive, so the writer is free to license the contribution to other magazines.

The lack of a formal, documented meeting of the minds is as bad for the magazine as it is for the writer.* Both parties will want to clarify the nature of the project, the due date, the fee to be paid, whether or not expenses will be covered, how and when payment will be made, the effect of cancellation, how revisions will be handled, and exactly which rights will be transferred. A telephone conversation is unlikely to be equal to the task of dealing with all of these issues. If the publisher offers a written contract, the writer should keep in mind that the terms are merely an offer and are open to negotiation.

The normal contractual negotiations between a magazine editor and a writer will begin with a telephone conversation in which the basic issues such as the topic, length, and fee will be discussed. This is usually followed by the editor sending the formal assignment. If the editor does not send a contract for the writer to negotiate, the writer should then compose a confirmation of assignment that spells out the rights and obligations of the parties and ends with a statement to the effect that the confirmation must be signed before any work will be commenced (refer to chapter 10 for a full discussion of how contracts are formed). If it's a rush assignment, the writer should fax the confirmation and have it signed and faxed back.

The Grant of Rights

The grant of rights is the writer's main concern when dealing with magazines. This is due in part to the likelihood of overreaching by the magazine due to superior bargaining strength. It is also due in part to the ambiguity of the grant of rights in most such provisions. Some magazines purchase all rights (sometimes called exclusive world rights in perpetuity) which means the writer retains no rights to the work. Obviously the writer should resist agreeing to all rights or work-for-hire contracts. If the writer does accept a work-for-hire contract, the payment should be substantially higher. Magazines may purchase all rights with the understanding that the copyright will be held in trust for the writer and transferred back after publication (subject, perhaps, to certain rights retained by the magazine). In such a case, a written contract should set forth precisely the rights to be retained and those to be transferred back. Even all rights is not clearly understandable, since it may mean all magazine rights, all print rights, or all rights in any medium now known or hereinafter discovered.

Many magazines purchase only first serial rights (sometimes called first rights), the right to be the first magazine to publish the work. After such publication, the writer is free to sell the work elsewhere. A variation of first serial rights would be first North American serial rights, which means that the writer conveys to the magazine the right to be the first publisher of the work in North America. Another type of rights is known as second serial rights, more generally referred to as reprint rights: the right to publish work that has appeared elsewhere, for example, in a book. A different grant of rights would be one-time rights: the right to use the work once but not necessarily first. Another way of expressing this could be the grant of simultaneous rights: granting the right to publish to several magazines at once.

The writer should limit the grant of rights with regard to exclusivity (whether the writer can sell the article to another magazine simultaneously), number of uses (the number of times the magazine can run the article), types of uses (the form in which the article can be published), languages (which languages the magazine can publish the article in and whether translations need to be authorized), duration (the length of time after which the article can no longer be run), and geographic scope (the countries in which the article can be published). The writer who so desires can define with extreme precision the nature of the permitted publication. The writer may want to include a provision that states that no rights are transferred until the writer is paid in full. In addition, there should be a provision reserving all rights not specifically transferred to the writer.

The Assignment and the Due Date

The writer should describe the assignment in as much detail as possible, including content and length, to ensure that there is no misunderstanding. The contract should name the magazine in which the article will be published. A due date, expressed either as specific date or as a number of days from the date that the client magazine signs the confirmation contract, is also necessary. In cases in which the magazine will provide reference materials of any kind, the due date might be expressed as a number of days from the receipt of any such materials. The contract should not make time of the essence. It should also provide that illness or other delays beyond the writer's control will extend the due date, but not beyond a specified period of time.

Fees and Payment

The fee should be specified along with whether the magazine will pay for expenses. If the expenses are going to be high, for example, when there is travel or extensive research involved, the writer should provide a list of the expenses which will be covered and should seek a non-returnable advance against such costs. If the publisher fails to warn the writer about necessary permissions or privacy releases, the contract should require the publisher to bear such extra costs and indemnify the writer against resulting liability. Payment should be made within thirty days of delivery of the article. The Writers Union takes the position, in its Standard Journalism Contract, that payment in full is owed upon delivery and no partial cancellation fees should be acceptable (although the Union would allow one revision of the assignment to be included in the original fee). If the magazine requires a budget, provide for a variance percentage, perhaps 10 percent, to allow for flexibility in the event of unforeseen costs. For extensive projects, a schedule of payments is especially important.

If the magazine has paid on acceptance, the writer should require a provision stating that no part of the payment need be returned if the magazine fails to use the work. If the magazine pays on publication, the writer should stipulate that a fee, known as a "kill fee," be paid in the event the magazine does not use the work within a specified time period. The amount of the kill fee should be tied to the stage of the work at the point of cancellation and the reason for the cancellation. Certainly the writer should be paid in full if the project is completed and the publisher's only reason for canceling the contract is the fact that an article on the same subject appeared in another magazine the day before. The writer should specify when cancellation fees will be paid and that he or she owns all rights in the work in the event of cancellation, regardless of the reason.

Other Issues for the Writer

The contract should specify what credit the writer will receive for the work. In the usual case, the writer should receive credit for the article under his or her own name. Copyright notice should also be in the writer's name. The writer may also want to specify the type size and placement of the credit and copyright notice he or she will receive for the work.

Successful writers may be able to stipulate that no changes whatsoever will be made to the submitted article, but the average writer is unlikely to have such a provision approved. If any changes can be made in the work, the writer should seek the right to approve such changes, with approval not to be unreasonably withheld. If extensive revisions are necessary, the writer should retain the right, or at least the first opportunity, to make them. If the changes are the fault of the writer no additional fee should be paid, but if the changes are due to a change in the nature of the assignment then an additional fee should be paid. If substantial revisions are made by someone other than the writer, the writer should retain the right to have his or her name removed from the work.

The writer may want to require the magazine to return the original manuscript and should certainly require the return of anything of value, such as photographic transparencies. The magazine should accept liability, in a stipulated amount if possible (called liquidated damages), in the event that valuable materials are lost. The writer may reasonably ask for several free copies of the issue containing the work.

The writer should resist giving a warranty and indemnity provision. Such provisions normally state that the work does not violate another writer's copyright or contain libelous statements. If the writer agrees to a warranty and indemnity provision, he or she should negotiate for it to take the form of "to the best of the writer's knowledge." The writer should not, under any circumstances, agree to pay for the client's damages or attorney's fees. Instead, the writer should try to arrange for coverage under the magazine's liability insurance policy. If possible, the deductible should either be covered by the publisher or, at the least, limited to a specific amount—perhaps the fee for the assignment.

The contract should also contain an arbitration provision which should only apply to amounts which exceed the limits of the small claims court in the writer's jurisdiction.

The protection of the copyrights in contributions to collective works is discussed on page 29. Generally, the writer should consider the refinements of the book contract when negotiating the simpler licensing of rights to a magazine.

Electronic Rights

Electronic rights are the newest and hottest issue for writers who publish articles in magazines and newspapers. To protect themselves, and also as a means of bargaining for higher payments, writers should resist clauses such as the following:

> Publisher may exercise, by itself or through third parties, the rights granted herein in any form in which the Work(s) may be published, reproduced, distributed, performed, displayed or transmitted (including but not limited to electronic and optical versions and in any other media now in existence or hereafter developed) in whole or in part.

> Publisher has the right to use and reproduce all such material and derivatives of it in various databases, and in conjunction with any other products, including, without limitation, microfilm and CD-ROMs.

> The publisher will own all right, title and interest, including copy-
> right, in the columns, for all purposes throughout the world (such
> material being provided as a "work made for hire" under the
> Copyright Act).

A writer who had written articles for the *New York Times*, *Atlantic Monthly*, and *Village Voice*, received payment for an article that he had written for *New York Newsday*. On the back of the check was language to the effect that, if he signed and cashed the draft, he would be giving up his electronic rights in the work covered by the payment.

The writer was Jonathan Tasini, president of the National Writers Union and a strong supporter of the rights of writers. Tasini crossed out the offensive language and then signed and cashed the check. When he found that Newsday had licensed electronic rights for his article to the Nexis on-line information service, then owned by Mead Data Central Corporation, he joined with nine other similarly situated writers and brought what may well turn into a landmark case against several of the most powerful newspapers, magazines, and on-line data base companies in the United States (*Tasini v. New York Times*, S.D.N.Y. No. 93-8678, see update for page 82).

Some magazine publishers contend that they have the right to reproduce and distribute the entire contents of each issue electronically. In a discussion of the *Tasini* case, Harry Johnston, vice president and general counsel at Time Inc., likened selling electronic rights in its magazines to selling a single copy to a public library. He noted that *Time* receives a flat fee rather than a royalty per use. To avoid litigation, however, publishing lawyers are advising publishers to insist upon clear language granting the publisher rights in "all media now known or hereafter invented" or "by any and all means, methods, processes, whether now known or hereafter invented." Magazine publishers are now sometimes requiring this kind of language.

The plaintiffs in *Tasini*, on the other hand, believe that free-lance writers should receive a royalty every time one of their works is accessed through an on-line service. When a subscriber to CompuServe calls up an article from *Forbes Magazine*, for example, a fee must be paid by credit card to CompuServe. If the *Tasini* plaintiffs had their way, the writer would receive a royalty on every such transaction. As Tasini notes: "Publishers are profiting by putting our work online and, if it's a penny or a million dollars, the point is they never asked our permission."

Until the *Tasini* case is decided, however, the Authors Guild warns writers to be extremely careful in negotiating magazine and newspaper contracts. The Guild stresses that "it is possible to get magazines to use contracts in which the author retains electronic rights." *TV Guide*, for example, recently stated that it will revise its standard electronic rights clause because "[w]riters and their agents across America slashed red pencils through this particular clause." Similarly, according to The American Society of Journalists and Authors' (ASJA) Contracts Watch, *American Health*, *New Choices*, and *Travel Holiday* are all magazines which offer writers a choice of either a share of the income from electronic rights or a flat fee for such rights. The ASJA also states that some *Penthouse* writers have reported successfully negotiating for 10 percent of the fee paid to the publisher for electronic rights in their work (although it seems this percentage should be higher to be fair).

Writers should keep in mind that magazines and newspapers are usually better situated to license electronic rights in articles than either the writers themselves or their agents. The optimal decision may not always be to retain rights. Often it will be to negotiate adequate compensation, preferably including a royalty, for them.

Writers should contact the Authors Guild (212-563-5904), the American Society of Journalists and Authors (212-997-0947), or the National Writers Union (212-254-0279) directly if they need specific information about electronic rights for magazine or newspaper articles, would like to discuss a specific clause in a contract, or have information which they would like to share with other writers.

Syndication

A syndicate gathers marketable features and columns for distribution on a regular basis to markets such as newspapers and magazines. Some syndicates purchase single articles much as magazines would, while others enter into an ongoing relationship with the writer. For a continuing series, the writer will normally be recompensed on the basis of the success of the syndicated material, rather than by payment of a flat fee.

A syndication contract involves a grant of rights, which the writer should restrict as narrowly as possible. The writer should keep the copyright and all other literary property rights in the material. Beyond the grant of rights, of course, will be the issue of subsidiary rights. The syndicate should not be given rights over or income from subsidiary rights in media which it cannot directly exploit. And the writer should weigh whether the syndicate's requests for control or a given percentage of income are reasonable with respect to each subsidiary right. Consultation with an agent or more experienced writer will help here, although the Guild guidelines for books can provide an idea of how to approach the problem.

The duration of the contract is particularly important and should be fairly short, probably no more than two years. This enables the writer to negotiate a better contract if the syndication is a success or to stop working on an unpopular venture. Since any kind of automatic renewal option would defeat the purpose of a short term, such a provision should be refused, or if given, should be accompanied by increased compensation. Also, the writer might consider reserving a right of termination if proceeds from the syndication fall below a specified level. This would permit entering into a new contract with a syndicate capable of more vigorous exploitation. In any case, the writer should not agree to either noncompetition or option provisions which might prevent dealing with others. If the syndicate insists, these provisions should be narrowly restricted in their application. If the writer is strongly identified with the pre-existing "flagship" newspaper or periodical, he or she may be able to exclude the work from syndication.

Payment is based on the receipts from the syndication, which in turn depend on how many publications carry the feature or column and what each publication pays for it (although the writer should demand as well the guaranteed minimum payment discussed in the next paragraph). The writer can expect to receive 40 to 60 percent of the syndication receipts. The most common arrangement is 50 percent for the syndicate and 50 percent for the writer. But care must be taken that the percentage is of gross receipts, not net receipts (which might also be phrased as "gross receipts less expenses"). If gross receipts are to be reduced prior to calculating the share due the writer, the reductions must be set forth and carefully defined. Package deals, where several features or columns are sold together, should be forbidden. Otherwise the writer won't know what would be paid if his or her own material were separately purchased. And, in fact, a more successful series may be carrying a less successful one, with both writers receiving the same income. If the syndicate is part of a newspaper chain, it must be specified that special discounts may not be given to newspapers in the chain. There should be a right to periodic accountings showing the source of all receipts and the exact nature of any expenses. The writer should also be able to inspect the books of the syndicate.

The syndicate should promise to use its best marketing efforts. In appropriate cases, the writer might even insist in advance upon an advertising and promotional plan and budget. A very important provision, however, is a minimum payment guaranteed to the writer regardless of the amount of receipts. The writer should seek this in every contract, both to insure that the writing will not go unrecompensed and to give the syndicate a greater stake in the enterprise.

The writer should seek control over the final form of the material. At a minimum, there should be a right of approval over any interpolations or changes by the syndicate. Warranties with respect to the material will invariably have to be given, although the writer should as always seek to limit their scope. Also, prior written consent should be required for any assignment of the contract, so the writer will always be able to choose the organizations and people with whom dealings take place.

The discussion of book publishing contracts should provide guidelines for the other provisions and considerations which may be relevant to the writer creating a feature or column for syndication.

13 Dramatic Productions, Films, and Television

Writers become involved with dramatic, film, and television contracts under a variety of circumstances. In the most common situation, the well-known novelist options his or her book to a production company. The price of the option can be anywhere from about $1,000 to a maximum of about $100,000, with feature film options garnering in the area of $40 to 50,000.

These option rights usually only extend for twelve months and then must be immediately renewed for comparable fees. Naturally, if the purchaser (an actor, director, independent producer, or a production company) decides to exercise the option and make the film, the purchase price kicks in. The writer could then receive from a few hundred thousand to several million dollars, plus bonuses once the production begins. But, in the common scenario of a well-known writer selling his or her work, the purchaser will usually buy the property outright rather than taking the tentative step of purchasing an option first.

Since film is more political than other forms of intellectual property, a writer would also do well to submit a book (or screenplay) to well-known actors, directors, or producers deemed well-suited for the film. As writers who option stories or novels will soon learn, such options are rarely converted into actual films. But tell a film producer that Dustin Hoffman wants to play the lead, and watch how quickly the wheels begin to turn. Another possibility is that a writer who is unable to sell a book directly to a publisher will attempt to sell it to a film company. If the book is optioned for the movies, it is then almost assured a sale to a publisher. For, if the film is made, the book will usually have strong sales. Such was the case with *The Horse Whisperer* by Nicholas Evans, which was first sold to the movies but also quickly reached the best-seller list for books.

Contracts for dramatic productions based on books, especially those that land at Broadway theaters, are even more difficult to consummate. The fact is that there are very few Broadway plays adapted from new books. A more common, though recent scenario, is for movie studios to turn successful stage dramas or musicals into feature films. For example, Columbia Pictures is currently producing a film version of the Broadway hit *The Fantasticks* and director Alan Parker is planning a film production of the highly successful *Evita*. In general, however, it is far more likely that a stage production will come from an original dramatic script than from any other source.

Dramatic Productions

Before negotiating any agreement for the use of his or her work, the writer should investigate the theater market in which the production is intended to be staged. By talking with writers and others who work in the industry, the writer can obtain important information about terms and clauses which are reasonable or unreasonable for the writer to expect. The Dramatist's Guild, Inc. (referred to as "the Guild") is also a valuable resource for those seeking information about certain theater markets. The Guild has developed many contracts for use by its members which in some instances are considered standard and in others are only references for the writer to consider. For example, the Guild's minimum basic production contract for an off-Broadway production was never completely negotiated between the Guild and the League of Off-Broadway Theater Owners. As a result, that particular contract is far from a standard indicator of what producers and writers deem acceptable for that market. In any event, every writer marketing a dramatic play or musical can benefit significantly by joining the Guild for both advice and information from which to start negotiations.

Generally, theaters are classified as one of three market standards: Broadway, Off-Broadway, and Off-Off-Broadway. These classifications reflect the overall theater market in New York City and are based on a theater's size and geographic location. Broadway theaters, also known as first-class theaters, are located in the Borough of Manhattan between Fifth and Ninth avenues from 34th Street to 56th Street and between Fifth Avenue and the Hudson River from 56th Street to 72nd Street. These theaters have a seating capacity of more than 499. For the Broadway market, the Guild and the League of American Theaters and Producers negotiated what is now known as the Approved Production Contract. This contract contains a range of minimum and maximum terms to be negotiated between the writer and the producer.

Off-Broadway theaters include all other theaters located in the Borough of Manhattan which seat no more than 499 people and are not located in the area defined for Broadway theaters. As mentioned earlier, there are no standard contracts which present guidelines for writers negotiating with producers in this market. While the Guild has a Minimum Basic Production Contract for Off-Broadway productions, writers should be careful, because many of the Guild's terms may be considered unreasonable or without precedent to producers.

Off-Off-Broadway theaters are generally all theaters that do not fall into the previous two classifications. These theaters include profit and non-profit theater organizations. Negotiating with such theaters typically comes down to what terms the theater can afford to give the writer versus what the writer will accept. This classification is, of course, too broad to give the writer much of an idea about the standard terms of contracts consummated in this market.

The three classes of theaters outlined above do not adequately categorize all types of theaters available to produce writer's works. Consider, for example, the Manhattan theater that seats more than five-hundred people and does not fit the Broadway description. However, taking time to understand the differences between these classes will help the writer to formulate a reasonable strategy to negotiate an agreement.

But how does the sale of dramatic material actually begin for the writer? In most circumstances, producers initially take an option to produce a dramatic play or musical. The option agreement should address important issues including: terms of payment, billing credits, script changes, usage rights for the script, creative approval rights (if any), travel and other expenses (in some circumstances), and reserved seating for productions of the play. An advance against future royalties is paid for the option, which is typically for anywhere between a six-month and one-year term (usually renewable for additional terms if certain conditions are met). If the producer successfully previews and opens the play before the expiration of a time period specified in the option or extensions of the option, the writer's compensation is then based on a percentage of the box office's weekly receipts (receipts being carefully defined). However, the producer who launches a production which runs beyond a stipulated number of performances gains additional rights—for example, a right to do first-class tours, to do an English production, to move from Off-Broadway to Broadway, to re-open the show after it has closed, to have a bargaining position with respect to motion picture rights, and to have a monetary interest in specified subsidiary rights. Typically, the producer acquires no control over the subsidiary rights. He or she merely receives a right to share in proceeds if the original play or musical has a long enough run. For example, subsidiary rights can include worldwide motion picture rights and the following rights in the continental United States and Canada: radio, television, second-class touring performances, foreign language performances, concert tour versions, condensed and tabloid versions, commercial uses, play albums or records, stock and amateur performances, and musicals based on the play. The producer's right to a percentage of subsidiaries (income from subsidiary rights) applies only to contracts executed within a specified number of years after the close of the production. Control over disposition of subsidiary rights is retained by the writer.

Films and Television

Film and television companies must draw together the financial and creative elements necessary to put together a finished product. This process is commonly known as the development stage. In it, the producer must obtain or control the rights to the project's storyline before the project can be presented to potential financiers or creative talent. As with theater, it is common for film or television producers to obtain an option to buy a particular script from a writer. An option allows the producer the exclusive right to shop the script, to see if there is sufficient financial and creative interest before deciding whether or not to actually purchase the script outright from the writer. Thus, the writer will negotiate a fee for the length of the option period and another fee for the purchase of the script in the event the option is exercised.

Before submitting his or her work to anyone, the writer would do well to register the work with the Writers Guild of America (WGA). Upon entering into any agreement, either with an agent or directly with a production company, writers are also advised to refer to the WGA's Theatrical and Television Film Basic Agreement which provides minimum compensation levels for the writer to consider prior to any negotiations. If the production company interested in a writer's work is a signatory to the WGA Agreement, then these minimum compensation levels, in addition to the other terms and conditions set forth by the WGA, will govern the writer's contract. Even if the WGA Agreement is not applicable, its terms and conditions are still considered important guidelines for writers in non-guild arrangements between the writer and the production company.

Writers employed in the creation of television and film scripts will usually be required to join the WGA. The WGA periodically negotiates revisions of its collective bargaining agreement with numerous production companies. The terms of this agreement are beyond the scope of this book but can be obtained from the Writer's Guild of America.

The complexities of television and film contracts require that the writer obtain the assistance of an attorney or agent. It is rare for literary property to be marketed to the television or film industries without an agent, intellectual property lawyer, or other representative acting as an intermediary. In fact, most production companies will not accept unsolicited materials and writers are strongly advised not to send any. Those who do accept unsolicited scripts or treatments usually require a signed release from the writer intended to protect the production company from, among other things, claims of unknown parties to the submitted material or claims by the writer that the production company has misappropriated his or her literary property.

In a writer's contract for film rights, the grant of rights will usually be quite extensive, although distinctions have to be made between television and film, which reach totally different markets. The practice with respect to artistic control is exactly the opposite as it is with dramatic plays and musicals. The writer can expect to have little control over changes in the property and the final form it takes. Usually, the writer seeks the right to perform the first and/or subsequent revisions of the property. Also, the writer will invariably have to give the production company the power to assign the contract (although the production company may remain liable if the assignee fails to fulfill its obligations), since financing arrangements require this. If the writer is to share in receipts from the film's distribution, it must be specified whose receipts (the producer's or the production company's) and how receipts are defined (a well-known writer who sells a novel to a film company will be granted up to 5 percent of the film company's income from the film). Billing credit will also require specification, because of the number of people and companies involved in creating the end product. The WGA has certain procedures whereby the WGA will arbitrate disputes over billing credits. This aspect, along with many other benefits, makes membership in the WGA worthwhile for writers.

One increasingly common scenario is the simultaneous sale of a writer's novel to a publishing company and a film studio. The writer, who has recently sold a novel to a publishing company, will have his or her agent or intellectual property attorney negotiate screenplay rights with a production company. If the novelist is a first-time screenplay writer, he or she will usually be paid WGA scale (anywhere from $35,000 to $50,000) to produce a first draft, and receive equal amounts for second, third, and final ("polish") drafts. The terms of such agreements give the producer or production company the option to reassign the material to another writer if they deem the first or subsequent draft unsatisfactory.

For a current list of scale rates in all theatrical and film deals, writers should consult the Writers Guild of America. For the addresses and phone numbers of the Writers Guild of America (East and West), see page 13.

14 Electronic Rights and New Media

*T*he extraordinary power of computers has transformed both the creation of information and the way in which information reaches the public. This transformation raises complicated issues regarding ownership of what is created. Technology has often pushed the boundaries of the copyright law. For example, photography did not exist when the first copyright law in the United States was enacted in 1790. Other inventions, such as phonographs, jukeboxes, radio, television, and communications satellites, have each raised the question of whether the copyright law must itself transform to ensure a proper balance between rewarding creativity and ensuring that the public enjoys the fruits of this creativity. If creativity is to be rewarded, how can the writer participate in the profits that producers and publishers will garner from electronic rights and the new media?

Today, the writer's work may be disseminated through a number of new media, including CD-ROM (which can store ten thousand pages of text), CD-Interactive, and electronic data bases (which might be accessed through the Internet or other on-line services). In the future, there may be print-on-demand bookstores which store the text of thousands of books and then print and bind the book while the customer waits. There may also be on-line electronic publishing whereby the entire texts of books, stories, and articles can be transmitted by modem into millions of homes. At this point, the greater part of electronic publishing involves works of non-fiction, including cookbooks, guidebooks, technical books, language books, dictionaries, encyclopedias, and textbooks. In all likelihood, the range of works which are published electronically will increase dramatically in the coming years along with the alternatives by which that content can be disseminated.

There is some disagreement about the number of individuals who have access to the Internet but, by all accounts, the number is already very large and is likely to become much larger in the near future. As reported in October of 1995, a well-respected survey company, Nielsen Media Research, interviewed members of three-thousand households to ascertain Internet use in the United States and Canada. That survey found that 10.8 percent of all adults in the two countries, or 24 million people, had accessed the Internet within the last ninety days. Of those 24 million, the survey found that the average time spent on-line per day was over five hours. It also found that purchasing over the Internet's World Wide Web had already become prevalent. According to the survey's findings, just under 10 percent of those who have accessed the Internet, or 2.4 million individuals, have used that access to buy goods or services. Writers can obtain a summary of the report by calling (212) 708-7714.

In December of 1995, however, the Nielsen survey's findings were questioned by Professor Donna L. Hoffman of Vanderbilt University. Professor Hoffman, who helped design the survey, claimed that the findings were based on "fundamental flaws," such as the fact that participants in the survey were older, better educated, and more affluent than the public at large. In contrast to Nielsen's 24 million, Professor Hoffman's findings indicate that there are fewer than 10 million adults who use the Internet.

Nevertheless, there seems to be little doubt that Internet use is expanding rapidly. This growing access to the Internet creates an opportunity as well as a threat for both publishers and writers. On the one hand, publishers have the opportunity to cut out suppliers, manufacturers, and wholesalers, and sell directly to consumers. The danger for publishers is that they will be unable to control access to their content and consequently payment for it. Furthermore, the lowered cost of entry into the field of publishing may increase competition among publishers—including writers who decide that they can now afford to be publishers on the Internet. The public, inundated with content, may become less willing to pay for some of it (although a more optimistic view would see content on the Internet as an additional choice rather than as a replacement). These same issues are important for writers. If anyone can access millions of consumers through the Internet, the number of writers, and especially self-publishing writers, is likely to grow substantially.

The Multimedia Paradigm

The market for multimedia works, like the audience for the Internet, is also growing rapidly. Because most new computers have the capacity to access multimedia CD-ROM, the future market size and audience should be very large. Much is being said about multimedia, which used to be a word defining exotic artworks that combined more than one medium. Multimedia offers a paradigm for the larger field of electronic rights and new media, because it is new, has momentum, is technologically driven, and is in a state of constant redefinition. To define multimedia today is like describing Proteus, but the hallmarks include some or all of the following features: (1) the use of more than one medium, such as combining still pictures, text, music, and film or video; (2) digital storage and retrieval of information; (3) delivery by new media, such as CD-ROM and computer networks, or by innovations in existing media, such as cable television; and (4) interactivity, which allows the end user to interact with the material in a variety of ways, such as choosing different viewing sequences or ordering additional products.

The digital nature of multimedia and the evolving delivery systems suggest the adaptability of multimedia works. Digital works suffer no loss of quality from one generation to the next. In addition, what may be stored in CD-ROM today may be delivered by cable tomorrow and by as yet unknown delivery systems in the future. Such works and delivery systems can easily flow across national boundaries, so to look only to the law of the United States may be inadequate in certain cases. Legal commentators speculate that the evolution of multimedia will prove "a full employment act for attorneys." Each multimedia work may require an incredible number of permissions. For example, it may be necessary to obtain licenses from the owners of copyrights in photographers, illustrations, designs, paintings, music, sound recordings, video, and film—all for a single work of multimedia. Each of these constituent parts may require releases from models, actors, performers, and directors, and perhaps involve union agreements (such as with SAG or AFTRA). Obtaining the materials may also raise issues pertaining to trademarks, unfair competition, trade secrets, and libel. If original work is created for use in multimedia, contracts will be needed with the creators. Once the multimedia work is complete, the developers will have to be able to negotiate with publishers or distributors to ensure placing the work in the proper channels of distribution. No wonder that lawyers look with delight on a field that will require so much of their labor to handle its complexities.

The creator who is contributing work wants to transfer the minimal rights that are needed for the work. The developer, on the other hand, wants to obtain the maximum in rights, perhaps by use of a work-for-hire contract. This may seem like old wine in new bottles, but multimedia seems likely to exacerbate the conflicts over rights between creators and developers or publishers.

Multimedia is an unfolding drama. It offers tools of heretofore unimagined power to the creator; yet it also attracts concentrations of capital that make for highly disparate bargaining strengths between creators, developers, and publishers. The creative and technological challenges require great ingenuity, but so do the business challenges. If the struggles of the past have taught us anything at all, it is that creators must be fairly compensated if they are to thrive and contribute to the dynamism that makes industries grow—including the promising industry of multimedia. This leads to a look at the larger set of issues presented by electronic rights, that is, the struggle between producers and creators over the ownership of the content of electronic works.

The Struggle Over E-Rights

In the summer of 1995 a number of creators' organizations (including the National Writers Union and the Graphic Artists Guild) and the Fashion Institute of Technology co-sponsored a fascinating program titled "Clients vs. Creators: The Struggle Over E-Rights." E-Rights, of course, are electronic rights. This symposium in New York City reflected the interest nationwide in the new issues raised by electronic rights and the new media. Because the concerns raised are becoming of ever greater importance and the points of view expressed will require mediation if creative enterprises are to flourish, the content of the program is worth elaborating here.

The panelists—who included Bruce A. Lehman, the Commissioner of Patents and Trademarks and Assistant Secretary of Commerce—represented an impressive range of expertise and viewpoint. In addition to Commissioner Lehman, other participants were Joseph S. Alen, President of the Copyright Clearance Center; Paul Basista, Executive Director of the Graphic Artists Guild; Ted Hill, Director of Business Development for Simon & Schuster Interactive; Maria Pallante, Executive Director of the National Writers Union; David Post, Associate Professor of Law at Georgetown University Law Center; Ken Richieri, Assistant General Counsel of the New York Times Company; and Richard Weisgrau, Executive Director of the American Society of Media Photographers. The panel moderator was Daniel Mayer, Executive Director of the Volunteer Lawyers for the Arts. Writers, artists, and photographers predominated in the audience.

Commissioner Lehman gave the opening address, stressing how important the copyright law is to protect creativity in commerce. He expressed his belief that the new information delivery systems could be "equally as important as the invention of the printing press" and could lead to a golden age for creators with more opportunities for employment, individual expression, and varied forms of distribution. Referring to his extensive work in developing the Administration's position on intellectual property rights in the digital environment, he pointed out how damaging to creators the new developments will be if creators' rights are not protected.

The Administration's position has now been finalized in the legislation discussed at the end of chapter 6. The proposed changes—for example, that putting a work on the Internet will be like a physical distribution and will give rights to creators, and that people who violate encryption or other protections for works on the Internet will be treated as infringers—are to serve Commissioner Lehman's goal of seeing that "creators continue to enjoy rights they ought to have" in electronic media. To stress the importance of these changes, his closing remarks pointed to how the diminution of public funding for the user community, such as librarians and teachers, is creating an environment in which stealing is more likely and creators are placed at greater risk.

Ted Hill of Simon & Schuster Interactive followed and gave the publisher's view with respect to rights. Pointing to the difficulties of assembling the many different types of rights necessary to do a multimedia work, he argued that "If it's hard to use rights, they won't be used." Since multimedia requires teams of creators, large investments, and may go out of date rapidly or have to be put on-line to recover the initial investment, he defended the publisher's desire for greater control while saying that publishers were not engaging in "a mad grab for rights." Echoing the publishers' line from the work-for-hire debates, he indicated that well-known artists will be able to retain rights while those creating incidental pieces will generally be asked to surrender all rights.

Collective Licensing

A more neutral position was espoused by Joseph Alen, the President and CEO of the Copyright Clearance Center. He started by emphasizing that, "We are not in a digital revolution. We are in a digital evolution." While he saw the future as holding continuous change, he felt the concept of a revolution came from referring to different time frames—what is likely to happen one or five or twenty years from now—as if they are all occurring in the present. Because millions of creators cannot locate millions of users who may be in different countries with different languages and laws, he felt that collective licensing agreements would play an important role in the short and long term. Such collective licensing agreements allow an agency to collect standardized fees and distribute these fees to participating owners. Stating that the Copyright Clearance Center handles hundreds of thousands of transactions a day, and may soon handle millions each day, he suggested the importance of such an agency to create markets that would not otherwise exist, lower transactions costs by allowing one-stop shopping, and preserve privacy and confidentiality.

Richard Weisgrau, the Executive Director of the American Society of Media Photographers and also Chief Executive Officer of its subsidiary, The Media Photographers Copyright Agency, viewed the new compensation paradigm as not being especially different from the old. In the old paradigm, creativity and information flowed up from the creators at the bottom of the pyramid to the corporate clients at the top while money flowed down from top to bottom. The new paradigm will be much the same, except that the possibility for lateral movement (such as creators distributing direct to consumers via the Internet) will be somewhat greater. Weisgrau observed that everything is built on the lowest layer where copyrights are created and expressed his belief that in electronic as well as other media creators must be paid for each use. If this is not done, then the system will not benefit all parties and creators will be forced to create information delivery systems of their own.

The pro-creator point of view was reinforced by Maria Pallante, then the Executive Director of the Writers Union, who observed, "Self-education is self-preservation." Noting that gentlemanly publishing is a thing of the past, she pointed out that the largest publishers are multinational corporate giants. While electronic media will allow minority voices more opportunities to be heard, such media will also be interdisciplinary in a way that will require different types of creative people to work together in a fair manner. Key to this development will be a centralization of records with respect to rights and knowledge about what rights should and should not be granted. For example, while selling all electronic rights would not be acceptable, selling nonexclusive nondramatic rights or selling electronic rights subject to a payment to be negotiated upon exercise of particular rights might be acceptable. Affirming her belief that creators "above all must respect copyright," she stressed her belief that antitrust issues around unequal bargaining strengths between creator and user will play a key role in the battles of the next decade.

Paying Revisited

Kenneth Richieri, the Assistant General Counsel for the *New York Times*, noted that the *Times* is a major player in electronic publishing. He felt that the roles of publisher and creator transferred well from the world of print to the on-line world. However, publishers that rely on advertising revenues, as the *New York Times* does, find the Internet poses risks since it is not yet advertiser friendly. He pointed out that the World Wide Web is 100 percent used for promotion and that "Consumers haven't weighed in yet." So we do not know what consumers want to find on the Internet. Nor do we know what they would be willing to pay, although the speculation is that they probably would not be willing to a pay a great deal. For example, would consumers be willing to pay extra to be able to access back issues of the *New York Times* on-line?

Next Paul Basista, Executive Director of the Graphic Artists Guild, gave a historical perspective which showed that since the Depression magazine and newspaper illustrators' fees have fallen in real dollar terms as well as tumbling dramatically as a percentage of publications' advertising revenues. Despite these downward trends, publishers are nonetheless seeking ever greater rights, including electronic rights. Yet graphics are becoming ever more important. The appeal of the World Wide Web is that it offers more graphics and is less text-based than other parts of the Internet. Arguing that publishers "have not adequately recognized the contributions of creators," Basista stressed the importance of improving the balance of power by giving knowledge to creators.

The World-Wide Copying Machine

The final speaker was David Post, Associate Professor of Law at Georgetown University Law Center and the writer of the "Plugged In" column for *American Lawyer*. His view of electronic rights mooted questions of the allocation of rights between publishers and creators, since he believes that copyright is unlikely to survive the digital age. Viewing the Internet as a "gigantic, world-wide copying machine," he expressed the belief that controlling copying in this environment is "fanciful." Arguing that those who take advantage of instant copying will flourish in this digital world, he predicted that content (including art and writing) would be given away and the price driven down. The giving away of what was once copyrighted will serve the purpose of attracting people to various sites on the Internet where other services or products will be sold to them. Observing that the number of World Wide Web sites is doubling every fifty-three days and that "Nobody on the World Wide Web is paying the slightest attention to copyright," he concluded by saying that the development of electronic media will only be hindered by a "wave of litigation over who owns what."

"Clients vs. Creators: The Struggle over E-Rights," offered a dramatic presentation of opposing points of view (video and audiotapes of the program are available from the Graphic Artists Guild: 212-791-3400). It clarified some issues and offered a great deal of information to those who are grappling with electronic rights issues. Divergent views of how rights should be shared between the creator and the publisher alert the creative community to the importance of these rights. And conflict over whether copyright is the way of the future or an anachronism in a world where information will be free suggests the need for us to stare into our crystal balls—or our computer screens after we log on to the Internet—and give some serious thought to the revolutionary evolution that is moving us step by step into a future filled with both risk and promise.

Contracting for Electronic Rights

The negotiation of electronic rights, for books and contributions to magazines, has already had some discussion in chapters 11 and 12. Here that discussion will be broadened to cover all sales, whether for electronic rights initially or as a possible subsequent use. The writer should use these general principles of limitation on the transfer of electronic rights as a guide and not as a dispositive resource. The market for electronic rights is growing so rapidly that settled principles of contractual fairness have yet to be defined. As a result, writers need to be especially careful about the rights they grant. In the worst case, a writer may be granting the primary use of a work to a publisher who not only lacks the contacts to license it for electronic use, but is also allowed to keep most or all of the profits realized on a sale of rights to an on-line service that will then license access, without a royalty, directly to consumers (with the writer sharing payment with the publisher or, even worse, receiving no payment at all).

The writer should be careful to avoid signing a contract that includes broad language under which "all electronic rights" are to be given to the publisher. Before the writer grants a publisher any electronic rights, he or she should be reasonably certain that the publisher has the ability to sell electronic rights effectively and that the contract provides for a sharing of all income from such sales.

In a position paper published in late 1993, the Authors Guild and the ASJA suggested that the writer consider retaining electronic rights. However, if the writer decides to grant some electronic rights, these organizations would limit the grant to "non-dramatic electronic versions of the Work" in certain electronic formats which would be limited by being listed. The publisher's right to license these electronic versions of the work would be subject to the writer's approval and the writer would explicitly retain all other electronic rights. In addition, the Guild and ASJA suggest that the writer need only allow the publisher a commission comparable to that of an agent—between 10 and 15 percent. However, many publishers are demanding a 50-50 split and forcing writers to try to negotiate for more.

Because the electronic landscape is changing so quickly, writers need to be certain not to give away too much. The most advanced technology of today may soon be superseded. In most cases, the writer should therefore seek to retain all electronic rights unless the publisher can show some particular ability to license such rights. The writer may want to find out from the publisher what sorts of electronic rights sales the publisher has closed in the past and should be sure to ascertain whether these sales were for writing in the same genre.

The writer should also retain the right to approve the "medium, format, and content" sold to on-line databases and for other electronic uses. This can be important in cases where the writer's reputation might be damaged by a use which essentially mutilates his or her work. There is every reason to believe that the kind of writing, especially the kind of technical writing, that is effective in print will be different from the kind that will be effective on the Internet. The writer should retain the some artistic control over any abridgements or alterations, much like the writer might try to do with a screenplay adapted from his or her novel. The writer may wish to include language to the effect that alterations, additions, or deletions can be done only with his or her express written consent. Publishers would probably require that such consent not be unreasonably withheld.

Furthermore, the contract should make clear how much content can be given to on-line services for promotional use without payment to the writer. The difficulty here is that a publisher may make a deal with an on-line service that allows use of a chapter from the writer's book when that use is not entirely to promote that particular book. For example, the on-line service might get content from a book in exchange for the publisher getting advertising space in a book marketing section which includes a variety of the publisher's titles. This may not help sell the particular title that has been excerpted.

Electronic Publishers

The writer must also understand the difference between selling electronic rights in the first instance and negotiating over electronic rights as a subsequent, or subsidiary, use. If a publisher actually intends to produce electronic products, such as CD-ROMs, rather than sell the right to do so to another publisher, the contractual language for the electronic rights should be more detailed. The National Writers Union has published three position papers regarding original publication on-line, covering CD-ROM (or disk), on-line book publishers, and self-publishing.

As the Authors Guild and the ASJA point out, electronic books are still books. Writers should therefore insist upon the same kinds of contractual terms that they would insist upon for a printed book. For details on negotiating book contracts, review chapter 11. The writer should receive an advance against royalties. The royalty should be based not only on sales of the CD-ROM but also on sales of access to the work afforded by on-line databases that license the CD-ROM. It should also include a per-use fee for rentals of CD-ROMs, which are likely to become as prevalent as rentals of video cassettes are today. Unlike printed book royalties, which traditionally escalate only after the sale of five thousand copies, the royalties for electronic publications and uses should escalate after a relatively small number. With printed books, the cost per book will never diminish below the cost of the paper. With electronic uses, however, the costs are all in the start-up. Once the work is transformed into an electronic product, the cost per use to the publisher or on-line service is extremely low.

The grant to the electronic publisher should be limited to uses now known and not extend to those hereinafter discovered. In addition, all rights that are granted but not exploited should revert to the writer after a certain amount of time. In many cases, the writer or the writer's agent may be able to sell such rights even though the publisher was unable or unwilling to do so. One way to get around this problem is to grant a nonexclusive license to the electronic publisher (although such a limitation can also limit salability) so that the publisher's failure to adequately promote and sell the electronic work will not limit the ability of the writer or the writer's agent to do so. But even these nonexclusive rights should revert to the writer if they are not exploited by the publisher. The writer should also consider giving the publisher a right of first refusal instead of an exclusive or nonexclusive license, because this will enable the writer to entertain other bids should the printed form of the work prove successful. If the publisher is granted any form of license for electronic uses, the publisher should be primarily responsible for ensuring that unauthorized uses do not occur.

The Author's Registry

Fifteen writer's organizations, including the Authors Guild, the ASJA, the Association of Authors' Representatives, and the Dramatists Guild, together with eighty literary agents and several well-known writers such as E. L. Doctorow and James Michener, have put together an electronic rights service that should do for writers what ASCAP and BMI have done for the music industry. With fifty thousand writers listed as this book goes to press, the Registry will simplify tracking and bookkeeping. It will collect monies owed from publishers for the licensing of electronic uses and distribute those funds to the appropriate agents or writers.

As a preliminary step, the Registry is negotiating with database publishers to provide information about the downloading of articles and chapters from books. Because paying up front for the use of content will prevent future litigation, database companies may find that providing such information is not only the correct moral and legal direction to take, but also that it is sound financial planning. The Registry hopes to begin to disburse payments to writers sometime in mid-1996. Writers who wish to find out more about the Registry can contact any of the above mentioned organizations involved or call Courier New Media, the company that is managing the database, at (508) 458-6351. In addition, the National Writers Union has an initiative with the CARL Corporation (owned by Knight-Ridder) for free lancers to be paid royalties when their articles are sold through CARL Corporation's Uncover Service (an index of magazine articles accessed through the Internet and delivered by fax).

Audio Rights

As with electronic rights, interest in audio rights has grown dramatically over the past few years. In the past, audio rights were nearly always granted to the publisher as a subsidiary right. The Authors Guild notes that established writers are now reserving such rights. With the recent boom of Books on Tape, writers and their agents are more and more likely to do so. The writer must always consider whether or not the publisher will be able to sell audio rights better than the writer or the writer's agent. In addition, the writer should consider whether the publisher has the capability of producing its own audiocassettes. If so, the writer may want to grant an option or a right of first refusal to the publisher of the printed book.

There are a number of issues that arise in all audio rights contracts which the writer would do well to bear in mind in order to avoid common and costly errors or omissions. The writer should first limit the grant of rights with respect to duration, territory, language, and exclusivity. The duration of audio rights is often shorter than the duration of book rights, which are usually tied to the term of copyright—provided, of course, that the book remains in print. The reason for this is simple. Audiocassettes will never go out of print because it is relatively inexpensive to make single copies. Printed books, on the other hand, even though new technology has increased the viability of small printings, usually must be printed in lots of at least one-thousand-five-hundred to two-thousand copies. The money laid out by the publisher in reprinting the book justifies the longer duration of book rights. If the publisher's grant was limited to a specific number of years, the company would be likely to let the book go out of print sooner than it otherwise would in order to prevent a forced remainder sale when its rights in the book expire. As a result, it is not at all uncommon for the grant of audio rights to be limited to a term of between seven and ten years after initial publication. The publisher will usually require the writer to grant an option, which the writer may be able to limit to a period of time not to exceed ninety days after the initial term expires, in which to negotiate in good faith for an extension or renewal term.

Publishers generally want the widest possible territory, such as worldwide rights, and all languages, but may settle for English-language rights, although they will likely insist upon the right to distribute such English-language tapes throughout the world. Once again, the writer should make certain that the publisher has access to all the markets included in the grant of rights. One way to do this is to ask the publisher for a breakdown of gross sales by country. Since this is an uncommon question, the publisher may be caught off guard and allow the writer access to this information if it is available.

The question of whether the writer should grant exclusive or nonexclusive rights turns on similar factors as the grant of territory and language. Is the publisher better situated that the writer, or the writer's agent, to sell audio rights? Here there are couple of additional issues. If the writer believes that the book will have strong sales, he or she may want to retain at least a nonexclusive right to make audiocassettes because the value of the rights, and the potential players in any sale, will change dramatically if the book is successful. Still, if this is the writer's rationale, he or she may do better to retain audio rights in full. Furthermore, a grant of nonexclusive rights may well prevent the publisher from trying to sell such rights at all because of the lower value and the greater difficulty in selling them. In addition, the publisher may decide not to make its own audiocassettes because of the relatively high start-up costs that would not be justified in the event that the writer went on to sell nonexclusive rights to other publishers as well.

The writer should specify that the audio version of the book will be stored on magnetic tape in the form of an audiocassette. This is important to ensure that there is no confusion as to rights in other possible forms of audio or audiovisual works, such as multimedia productions, the soundtrack to a movie, or even the movie itself. Indicating that the reading contained on the tape is non-dramatic will further ensure that future film rights are not jeopardized.

If the writer does enter into a contract for audio rights, he or she should receive an advance against royalties. Because the standard royalty rates in audio rights contracts are generally low, often escalating from 5 to 7 percent (sometimes with 1 percent added per 10,000 units sold), and are based on net receipts rather retail price, the writer may wish to negotiate for a substantial advance on the theory that there might not be much more money forthcoming.

Some of the issues involved in the sale of audio rights will be similar to those encountered when negotiating printed book contracts. For an overview and analysis of the contractual issues that arise between writers and publishers, see chapter 11. And, for a checklist of negotiation points for audio rights contracts, see *Business and Legal Forms for Authors and Self-Publishers* by Tad Crawford (Allworth Press).

Toward a Fruitful Future

No doubt we live in an interesting time. The Departments of Justice and Education have jointly issued a report to encourage the teaching of ethical use of computers and information technology in the nation's schools. This emphasis is certainly not misplaced. As the foundations shift beneath us, we must pay attention to what is fundamental. If some day the larger community will appropriate and own the creative expression of the ideas of its writers, then some mechanism must be provided to support those writers in their creativity and also preserve our democratic institutions. Until that day comes, the copyright law and fair contractual practices offer the best way in which to achieve the delicate balance between the rights of the writer/creator, the publisher/producer, and the community/user. Observing that law, and following the ethical standards developed from long experience in the field, offer us the best hope for a fruitful future.

15 Agents and Agency Contracts

An agency includes any relationship in which one person is given authority to act for or represent another person. Generally, any competent person of legal age may act as an agent. The agent is a fiduciary who must exercise good faith in dealing with the writer. For example, the agent should keep the writer promptly and regularly informed of the agent's activities and never give confidential information to competitors. The agent must not engage in self-dealing. An agent cannot represent parties with adverse interests unless both parties give an informed consent to the arrangement.

Authority of the Agent

The powers given to an agent can vary greatly. A general agent is usually empowered to perform all the acts connected with a particular trade, business, or employment. On the other hand, a special agent can only take limited action in accordance with particular instructions.

A literary agent normally can examine contracts,

negotiate modifications, and recommend that the writer either reject the contract or approve and sign it. Since the writer will probably wish to be certain that the agent obtains the writer's consent to any contract, a provision is often used in the agent-writer contract stating, "The agent shall submit to the writer any offer obtained, but no agreement shall be binding upon the writer without his or her signature." If the writer does want the agent to be able to make a binding contract for the sale of literary property, a power of attorney can be executed by the writer specifically indicating that the agent is being granted the power of disposition over enumerated rights in a work. A power of attorney is evidence to third parties of the agent's authority to act.

An agent acting within the granted authority obligates the writer. However, agents may sometimes act beyond the scope of their actual authority. Generally there can be no liability for the unauthorized acts of an agent. But if the writer acts in such a way that a third party, such as a publisher or producer, thinks the agent has more authority than the agent actually has, the writer can be bound if the agent concludes a deal based on this apparent authority. For example, the president of a printing company had also been acting as general manager. He contracted to print a book for a publishing house. Under the bylaws, the president lacked the actual authority to do this, although the general manager could have. However, the publishing house was justified in believing the president to have the authority of the general manager. The printing company was obligated by the contract to print the book, despite the fact that executing it was beyond the president's actual authority (*Condé Nast Press v. Cornhill Pub. Co.*, 255 Mass. 480, 152 N.E. 240).

A writer may also consent to the unauthorized acts of an agent, making the acts binding upon the writer by a process known as ratification. An unreasonable delay in repudiating unauthorized acts—or even inaction and silence in some cases—may be interpreted by the courts as a ratification.

The Value of Agents

An agent offers a number of services which can counter the traditionally weak position of the writer. Writers often lack experience, business knowledge, contacts, and the ability to negotiate effectively with respect to their own work. The value of an agent's services resides in the agent's greater ability to locate the right publisher, negotiate the best possible contract, and collect and account for all fees, advances, and royalties.

As a liaison between writers and editors, the agent's representation simplifies the search for a publisher. The agent can often tell immediately whether a book will sell in its present form within the channels to which he or she has access. Knowledge of the market for different categories of work, including fiction, non-fiction, textbooks, or magazines, helps the agent decide where to send a particular piece of writing. Agents know which publishers are buying which kinds of books. If they are any good, agents also have relationships with publishers and editors and have earned their respect over time.

These editors rely on the agents to screen manuscripts. As a result many editors, especially in the major houses, rarely even consider unsolicited books which are not sent to them by agents. Major trade houses sign up more than 80 percent of their books from agents and often return submissions with a form letter stating that they do not consider unsolicited materials. Smaller houses may read what comes in from all sources but are apt to make very quick decisions because they lack the cadre of readers that the larger houses possess.

Often an agent will have to make twenty to thirty submissions before the book will find a home in an appropriate publishing company; independently, the writer might well have given up hope long before that.

Once a publishing company expresses interest, agents are better situated than writers to negotiate deals without jeopardizing the writer/editor relationship. They can conduct auctions for specific rights which would be extremely difficult for the writer to do alone. The unwary writer, acting alone, might well grant an unduly wide array of rights, not knowing the going rates in the market or the trends in the specific sub-field, both of which can have significant effects on the value of literary property.

Writers write and agents make deals. The writer/agent relationship therefore involves a division of labor, an allocation of expertise, by which each party maximizes its benefits by doing what it does best.

Agents are more or less useful depending on the writing genre. Literary fiction is hard to get published and writers of such works would do well to find an agent. On the other hand, non-fiction "how-to" books may be as easy for a first-time writer to place with a small publisher as they would for an experienced agent. In the case of specialty books which would be better suited to a small publishing company than a large one, the need for an agent also becomes less pressing. Agents usually make contacts with the large houses because of the higher advances which these houses are able to offer.

Choosing and Dealing with the Agent

A writer in search of an agent should realistically evaluate whether his or her work is sufficiently commercial to interest an agent. The degree of commerciality of the work may also affect the choice of the agent, since many agents may have little interest in works of modest commercial potential. Another factor for the writer to decide is whether he or she wants to work with a large agency such as ICM or William Morris or one of the numerous, smaller agencies. The differences are much as one would expect and might be compared with the contrast between attending a small college and a large university. At a small agency the writer will receive more personal attention, calls will be returned faster, and there will be more overall access to people within the agency. Representation by a large agency may lend clout when dealing with a publishing house; but bear in mind that there are benefits to a long-term relationship with both an agent and a publisher. The clout may not be worth the emotional and psychological sacrifice of a less personal relationship. The larger agencies concentrate mainly on stars; if a writer is not a star, and assuming the agency is willing to take the writer on, he or she may get lost or be at the bottom of its list. On the other hand a good, solid writer might well be at the top a smaller agency's list. Nevertheless, it is undeniable that the biggest agents and the largest agencies do get the most money. Good sources for finding lists of agents include *Literary Market Place* (Bowker) and *Guide to Literary Agents and Art/Photo Reps* (Writer's Digest). The Association of Authors' Representatives, Inc., 10 Astor Place, 3rd Floor, New York, New York 10003; (212) 353-3709 makes available a "Suggested Agent Checklist for Authors," a list of member agents, and a Canon of Ethics. Another helpful resource is *Literary Agents: A Writer's Guide* by Adam Begley (Penguin).

Each writer must evaluate his or her unique needs before seeking an agent. First and foremost, the writer needs to decide what he or she needs. The next step is to find out as much as possible about the agent. What kind of personality does the agent have? If the writer needs a nurturing agent and the agent is simply not nurturing, then the courtship should be broken off. Is the agent respected in the field? What markets does the agent sell to? Does the agent run a business-like office? If a larger agency is involved, the important consideration is the individual with whom the writer will actually deal.

If a writer is thinking of sending work to a number of agents, the writer should make that perfectly clear to each agent with whom he or she deals. The industry is very small and the agents may find out anyway. They are unlikely to take on a client who has been dishonest with them. Since agents will seldom consider simultaneous submissions, the best approach is probably to submit to one agent at a time and withdraw the manuscript if the agent does not read it within a reasonable time (such as four to six weeks). The writer might also inquire up front as to how long the agent is likely to take for reading submissions from potential new clients.

If an agent indicates an interest in a writer's work, the writer should arrange a meeting. The best way to find out about an agent is to ask current clients about their agent. Agencies should be willing to allow a writer to contact some of their current clients for a recommendation, although it is important to bear in mind that they are unlikely to steer you towards those that are unhappy. The writer should also ask several editors and publishers whether the agent has a good reputation.

If more than one agent meets those criteria, select the agent who demonstrates that he or she will read and evaluate the work thoroughly, will return calls, fight for the success of the work, and respond within a reasonable time—such as four to six weeks. Always remember that the agent is in business and is not a therapist. Call the agent as if he or she were a doctor or a lawyer, not more. Agents want to know not only if the work will sell but if the writer be will agreeable to work with. If a writer takes too much of the agent's time, the agent will quickly do a cost benefit analysis and conclude that the relationship is not financially feasible.

Agents usually only take about 2 percent of unsolicited work in a given year. A writer should not seek out an agent unless he or she has an exceptional idea or a proven publication history. If the work is not the writer's best, he or she may be jeopardizing future chances of finding an agent and publishing work. If the writer can be recommended by a current client, that would be helpful. References are always helpful. The more authoritative the person making the reference the more it will help.

Agents are seldom willing to do more than a soft edit, such as offering an overall reaction, so the work submitted needs to be very clean. An outside editor or writing teacher should look over writing before it is sent in. The writer should avoid giving an agent more than one manuscript at a time.

The best agent is the one most suited to the particular writer. Chemistry is the key factor. The agent must truly feel enthusiastic about the prospects of selling the writer's work to the relevant markets. If the agent is not enthusiastic, or cannot effectively sell to those markets, the relationship will not be successful. The agent's reputation, credibility, and ability to sell other books is on the line when recommending a book, so he or she is unlikely to push a book without a strong belief in it. And that belief can make all the difference. It is not at all uncommon for one agent to give up on a book after many submissions, only to have a new agent place it almost immediately. For example, one agent in New York City recently took on a writer, then working as a bartender to support himself, whose prior agent had been unable to do anything with his work. Within two months the new agent had closed a sale on a combination book/screenplay/film deal with a major film company that set him up to the tune of $100,000.

It is important to keep in mind that the neophyte may not be able to obtain an agent at all. Agents make money on commissions and they cannot afford to take on writers who are unlikely to produce saleable works. Agents are selective and cautious about the clients that they accept. The most difficult question may not always be how to choose an agent; often it will be how to get an agent to choose the writer. Sound advice for a writer seeking an agent is to show the agent only the best possible work and never waste an agent's time.

Because the unpublished writer may not be able to get an agent at all, he or she may wish to hire the services of an entertainment lawyer who specializes in literary matters. These lawyers will negotiate a writer's contracts, although they will not generally attempt to place books.

Reading Fees

The beginning writer may be understandably perplexed when trade magazines carry advertisements by agents soliciting manuscripts and promising great sales and success. Upon responding to such advertisements, the writer discovers that a reading fee will be charged for each manuscript submitted. In return for the reading fee, advice will be given to the writer as to how the work can be made marketable. If the work becomes marketable, the agent promises to undertake placing it.

The reading fees are alleged to cover the costs of grooming a writer for the time when sales will generate commissions for the agency or, in some cases, to cover the agent's expenses so that the agency is able to afford to look over unsolicited manuscripts. If the writer earns money through the agency, then reading fees should no longer be charged. The important point is to be aware of what the agency is offering. If it is offering instruction in the craft of writing, the writer seeking instruction may be completely satisfied. If the same writer is seeking to make sales, the instructional activities may seem wasteful of time as well as money. There is absolutely no guarantee that such instruction will ever result in the sale of work. The writer must face this likelihood when considering whether or not to pay a reading fee to an agent.

The Association of Authors' Representatives, in its Canon of Ethics, states that reading fees are "subject to serious abuse" and bans the practice for all of its members as of January 1, 1996.

The Agency Agreement

A writer should always ask to see the agency agreement long before signing it. When looking it over he or she should consider the following points and, if necessary, seek the advice of an attorney.

The commission on domestic sales to a publisher should be no less than 10 and no more than 15 percent. The writer should be sure to know exactly what the commission will be. In the last few years many agents have increased their commission from 10 to 15 percent. Some agencies charge their old clients 10 percent and all new clients 15 percent.

Agents often work with subagents for foreign rights and so they may charge a 20 to 30 percent commission since the two agents split the money. The usual commission for film rights sold by a writer's agent is 15 percent. The agent customarily splits this with a film agent, who works as a subagent, with all monies to flow though the primary agent.

The agreement with the agent will often contain a provision to the effect that "The Agent shall make reasonable and good faith efforts to promote the writer and sell the writer's works." Some contracts may specify particular steps that the agent will take to do this, but specification is difficult and the writer must rely on the agent's acting in good faith.

Since the writer must trust the individual agent, it a good idea for the writer to provide for termination of an agreement with a corporate agency in the event of the cessation of employment or death of the individual agent.

While an agent's delegation of duties to others whom the agent employs may be permitted, assignment of the representation agreement by the agent is normally prohibited. For example, the writer might require use of language like: "This agreement may not be assigned by the agency without the prior written approval of the writer."

All information regarding the writer should be kept confidential by the agent.

The agency may request assurances of fair dealing on the part of the writer. These might take the form of warranties that the writer has title to the works and the power to enter into the agency agreement.

The agency's duty to the writer requires the agency not to represent adverse or competing interests. But every agent represents numerous writers who, at least in some sense, are competing with one another. Situations can also arise where the same agent has one client, such as a writer, selling to another client, such as a producer. When representing clients who are negotiating with each other, the agent must make full disclosure. The writer is well advised to have the right to obtain independent representation for that particular transaction and, therefore, not be under an obligation to pay the agent's commission.

The agency relationship is terminable at will as a matter of law but termination may create liability. That liability should be spelled out in the contract, if not to change the result at least to clarify it. The standard 10 or 15 percent commission must be paid to the agent as long as the book remains in print, regardless of whether the writer decides to work with a new agent on subsequent books.

The writer should make certain that the agent has a system to handle all subsidiary rights, including audio and film prior to granting those rights. Most agents will not handle magazine or periodical sales unless it is first serial rights for the book covered under the agreement.

Normally the writer will have to handle magazines because there is not enough money in it to split with the agent. Be certain that the contract is clear on this point, so that the writer does not end up owing the agent a commission for magazine sales made by the writer.

It may be best to sign an agreement that is on a per-book-project basis and not to agree to having the agent represent all works in all media. For that one project the agent should certainly be the exclusive agent.

The writer should retain the right to terminate the agreement at any time by giving thirty days written notice and allow the agent to do the same. If the agent has sold the one book under the agreement, he or she has a right to commissions on income from rights licensed under the contract (note that this may well include nonprint media), but all other rights should revert to the writer.

The writer should be certain to find out who owns the agency because, even though the agent may have signed the agreement, the agent may have to assign all executed contracts to the owner of the company in the event that he or she leaves the agency. So the writer should clarify whether the individual agent or the agency will handle the contract if the agent separates from the agency.

The writer should not automatically agree to let the agent represent other books in which rights may have reverted. First, the writer should ask the agent how he or she plans to sell the rights involved and be satisfied by the answer.

Many agency agreements are oral, although the larger agencies will generally use written agreements. Writers will be much better served by written contracts. The writer may well wish to alter an agent's standard contract or, if the agent has no contract, draft a simple letter agreement to resolve the more important issues which might create friction. Needless to say, the advice of a lawyer will be valuable here, despite the apparent simplicity of many of the dealings between writers and agents.

It is also wise to include an arbitration clause in the event of a breach of the agreement.

Scope of the Agency

The agent will probably want to be the exclusive agent throughout the world for marketing all rights in all the properties created by the writer, including but not limited to publishing, motion picture, stage, radio, television, recording, electronic, and multimedia rights. The writer, of course, may very well wish to limit the scope of the agency.

It is understandable that the agent wants the agency to be exclusive. If it were nonexclusive, nothing would prevent the writer from simultaneously submitting the same work through a number of agents. The duplication of effort and expenditures, not to mention the likelihood of confusion, make this anathema to any agent. But the writer must be aware that the word exclusive has two different meanings. This and other principles of agency law are well illustrated by a case in which an agent took a playwright to the courts in order to recover commissions. While the case is old, the legal doctrines remain valid today.

The playwright F. Hugh Herbert finished a new play early in August, 1939. He called up Laura Wilck, an old acquaintance and an agent in Hollywood (although she had not represented Herbert before) to ask her to sell the play. This play, titled *Quiet Please*, was immediately placed with a producer. The playwright was pleased and entered into an agreement dated August 17, 1939, appointing the agent as "sole and exclusive representative for the term of five years (5) years from the date hereof, for any play or plays which (I) may write" (*Wilck v. Herbert*, 178 P.2d 25, 28, 78 Cal. App.2d 392, 395). The agreement provided that the agent would decide whether or not to represent a play within ten days of receiving it. If she chose not to represent it, the playwright could submit it elsewhere. The agent was entitled to receive a 10 percent commission for monies received "under or by virtue of any contract effected, for which negotiations may have been carried on, within the term of this agreement."

Quiet Please didn't work out as well as had been hoped. The playwright cooled toward the agent and, on January 3, 1942, wrote a letter revoking her authority to act for him. A writer can always revoke an agent's powers. However, the writer must also have the right to terminate the agency or the agent will be entitled to commissions for sales after the revocation. In this case the term of the agency was for five years, so it would not terminate under the agreement until August 17, 1944.

Two months after revoking the first agency, Herbert entered into a two-year agreement with the Sam Jaffe Agency. By November 1942 he had completed a new play titled *Kiss and Tell*. Of course, he didn't show it to his old agent, but simply had the Sam Jaffe Agency sell the stage rights. The film rights were also sold, although it was not clear from the testimony whether the sale had been negotiated by Herbert or by the Sam Jaffe Agency. The play had a very favorable reception and earned substantial profits. And the original agent, under the terms of the representation agreement, demanded her 10 percent of the playwright's income.

The court refused to award her 10 percent of the income from the sale of the film rights, unless a jury determined that the sale had been made by another agent and not by the playwright himself. This illustrates the difference between an "exclusive agency" and an "exclusive sale" contract. "A contract to give an 'exclusive agency' to deal with specified property is ordinarily interpreted as not precluding competition by the principal personally but only as precluding him from appointing another agent to accomplish the result ... A contract to give the 'exclusive sale' of specified property ordinarily indicates that the agent is to have the exclusive power." The court concluded that the representation was for an exclusive agency, not for an exclusive sale. If the playwright had really sold the film rights by himself, he wouldn't owe his agent a commission. But if he had used another agent to do the selling, he would have violated her exclusive agency and the commission would definitely be owed. This issue was returned to the lower court to be decided by a jury.

So a writer should be certain whether his or her agreement with an agent is an exclusive agency, leaving the writer free to sell work elsewhere as long as no other agent is used, or an exclusive sale arrangement under which a commission must be paid the agent regardless of who sells the work.

Unhappily for Herbert, he had negotiated the stage production through the Sam Jaffe Agency, and the stage production was earning most of the income. But his revocation of the powers of the agent made no difference with respect to his obligation to pay her commission not only on the past profits of the stage production but on a reasonable estimate of the future profits as well (established by expert testimony). One lesson here is that the term of the agency was too long. If an agent wishes to stop representing a writer, it is almost impossible to force the agent to live up to a "best efforts" or "good faith" provision. But if the writer wishes to stop being represented by the agent, the unhappy end result may be the obligation to pay double commissions as Herbert had to do. The writer will usually be well served by an agency which can be terminated at any time upon thirty days notice to the other party. An agreement for longer than one or two years, if all the writer's work is to come within the agreement, seems too restrictive. One possible compromise might be to give the writer a right of termination if the agent fails to generate a specified minimum amount of income over every six-month or one-year period. If the agency is only to represent one or more specified works, the writer may be comfortable in agreeing to a longer term. If no term is agreed upon for the agency, it can be terminated by either party upon giving notice of termination to the other party. The death of the writer automatically terminates the agency, even if the agent is unaware of it.

Agents will sometimes provide that they have an "agency coupled with an interest" for literary property which is sold. While the legal efficacy of this provision is not completely certain, it may well prevent any revocation or termination of the agency with respect to these contracts. So the agent would collect monies due even after termination of the writer-agent contract—which is standard practice in any event. It is far better for the writer to have the right to receive payments directly from the publisher after termination (although the writer would still have to pay commissions due on contracts entered into during the term of the agency). If the agent insists on having an "agency coupled with an interest," it should be limited to the agent's commission so the writer will definitely be able to receive the balance of payments due directly from the publisher.

The scope of the agency can be limited to specified works. But assuming it is for an ongoing representation of the writer, another kind of limitation would be with respect to different types of work. For example, the agent might represent the writer with respect to fiction, but not nonfiction, or with respect to novels, but not plays. Or the limitation might be with respect to different types of rights. For example, the agent might represent publication rights, but not film, stage, or other rights. The geographic scope of the agency can also be limited. Instead of granting the agent the right to represent the writer throughout the world, the representation could be only for the United States or North America.

If the agent is representing all the writer's work, does this include work created prior to the commencement of the agency? What about work created during the agency but sold after the agency has terminated? The agent may want to provide for a commission if, within a limited time period after termination of the agency, the writer sells a work to someone with whom the agent had conducted negotiations during the term of the agency. And will the agent have any claim to commissions if a publisher or producer approaches the writer directly? Or if the writer receives speaking fees, grants, or prizes?

The distinction between an exclusive agency and an exclusive sale agreement is an important one. The writer must also consider limiting the scope of the representation agreement with respect to the types of works or rights covered, duration, and geographic scope. The innumerable details which can crop up in this area indicate that the simplicity of the agent-writer relationship can be singularly deceptive.

Agent's Commissions and Expenses

The customary commission for literary agencies had long been 10 percent on domestic sales, but many agencies have now increased this rate 15 percent. For foreign sales, the rate is likely to be 20 or 30 percent, which the domestic and foreign agents share.

The writer will want to resolve whether the agent is entitled to the full commission if another agent must be used. For example, many agents in New York City will associate with an agent in Hollywood in order to sell works more effectively to the film industry. Presumably the writer should not have to pay a double commission in this situation. But what if the writer sells a work through another agent? Again, if the agency is exclusive, the writer will have to pay the full commission to each agent.

All commissions should be deducted by the agent from the gross proceeds and the balance remitted within ten days. The writer should warn the agent or the accountant involved in advance and in writing of any special accounting procedures that he or she desires. In some cases, the writer may want a special account set up. At the least, all funds owed to writers should be kept in an escrow account which is separate from any of the agency's own accounts.

The writer may find that the agent wants to charge for expenses incurred on the writer's behalf, such as faxes, long distance telephone calls, photocopying, manuscript retyping, copies of books for use in the sale of rights, legal fees, and so on. The writer should clarify all costs for which the agency will bill back and get an estimate of how much these things will amount to. The writer should then examine each charge, determine whether it is fair, and attempt to negotiate a better deal. Many writers make their own photocopies because it is cheaper. Agencies usually charge for messengers, faxes, and overseas mailing. Determine whether the agency will charge the writer even if the agent fails to place the work. In that event, the agent would send an invoice for such fees. The agent should supply an accounting for all charges. The charges on this accounting should be itemized.

Payments and Accountings

Traditionally, the agent collects all the proceeds from the publisher and oversees the publisher's compliance with the contract. This allows the writer to avoid administrative difficulties and spend more of his time writing. The agent's standard practice should be to deduct commissions and expenses, if any, and promptly pay the balance to the writer. This payment should be made from a separate bank account, according to Association of Author's Representatives, in order to avoid commingling of the writer's funds with the working funds of the agency. The writer might consider asking that the funds due the writer be termed "trust funds" in the contract with the agency. If the agent will consent to this, the writer may even gain some protection against the agent's creditors (although this is far from definite).

An accounting is a record of income received during a given period of time. The agent should examine royalty statements and, if necessary, obtain corrections from publishers. Of course, royalties may come from other sources as well, and the writer should be able to rely upon the agent to check these accountings.

The writer will usually be satisfied simply with receiving the accountings rendered to the agent from the various income-yielding sources. However, the writer should have the right to receive an accounting from the agent with respect to funds received and, upon reasonable notice, the right to inspect the agent's books relating to the writer. In this way the writer can protect against unscrupulous conduct on the agent's part. And, as the Association of Authors' Representatives advises, the writer can expect the agent to keep the writer's financial affairs confidential.

A sample agent-writer agreement follows, but it must be adapted to the individual writer's unique needs. The relative bargaining strength of the parties will influence the terms of the contract as well. The writer will usually be well served in having the advice of a lawyer when such an agreement must be negotiated.

AGENCY AGREEMENT

Dear Alice Writer:

This letter will confirm your appointment of me as your exclusive agent throughout the world and my acceptance of such appointment to advise you professionally and market all your literary rights, including but not limited to publishing, motion picture, stage, radio, and television rights, in such works as you submit to me during the term of this agreement, including the following works:

I agree to exercise my best efforts in marketing your work and promoting your professional standing.

I agree to collect and receive for you all monies due you from the marketing of your literary rights and hold same as trust funds for you in a bank account segregated from the working funds of the agency. I agree to remit all monies due you promptly as collected (and in no event more than two weeks after my receipt of such monies), and provide an accounting and permit inspection of my books and records upon your written request. Nothing contained herein shall obligate you to submit all your works created during the term of this agency to me, nor shall you have any obligation to pay commissions to me with respect to works sold by you directly, regardless of whether or not I am representing said works. You agree that I am to retain _____ marketing of literary rights in the United States, its possessions, and Canada, and _____ percent of monies so collected from the marketing of such rights in the rest of the world. I shall not take any reimbursement for expenses incurred on your behalf without your prior written consent.

It is mutually agreed that this agreement shall have a term of one (1)

→

year, commencing on the date hereof, and renewing automatically for additional one (1) year terms unless terminated. Either party may terminate the agreement by giving thirty (30) days prior written notice to the other party. In the event that within sixty (60) days after the date of termination an agent representing you enters into a contract for the sale of literary rights with respect to which I had been negotiating prior to said termination, and the terms obtained by said agent are no more favorable than the terms which I could have obtained, the said contract shall be deemed to have been entered into during the term of this agreement.

I agree to submit to you any offers received, and no agreement shall be binding upon you without your consent and signature thereto. It is mutually agreed that this agreement shall not be assigned by either party hereto without the prior written consent of the other party. Modifications to this agreement shall be in writing. The agreement shall be governed by the laws of New York State.

Your signature beneath the words "CONSENTED AND AGREED TO" shall constitute this a binding agreement between us. Kindly return the duplicate copy enclosed to me for my records.

Sincerely yours,

Catherine Agent

CONSENTED AND AGREED TO:

Alice Writer

16 Collaboration Agreements

*C*ollaboration—two writers working together on a single project—presents both challenges and rewards. A collaboration agreement is necessary to ensure that the challenges are overcome and that the rewards are shared. To that end, the collaboration agreement specifies the respective obligations and rights of each contributor.

A variety of problems arise in the drafting and structuring of such an agreement: ownership and use of the copyright in finished, unfinished, published, or unpublished work; how to split the advance and royalties; authorship credit; arbitration and mediation clauses; and liability in the event of various types of lawsuits.

Copyright and Authorship

Under the copyright law, a joint work is a work prepared by two or more writers with the intention, at the time the work is created, that their contributions be merged into inseparable or interdependent parts of a unitary whole. The term of copyright for a joint work is the life of the last surviving coauthor, plus fifty years. In the United States, a jointly owned work can be licensed on a nonexclusive basis by either party as long as the proceeds are equally shared, but an exclusive license requires the consent of all co-owners. So, for example, an editor commissioning an article might contend that he or she was a joint author with a writer, in which case the writer could lose control over the work—or, at least, have to share that control.* Co-authors own equal shares in a work, regardless of who did the majority of the work. These results—the ownership of the copyright, the right to license, and the sharing of profits—can all be altered by contract. The parties should be certain to state either that each retains copyright in his or her own contributions or that the work is only to be considered a joint work if each party completes his or her portion. The writers can provide in the collaboration agreement that the duration of the contract is the same as the duration of copyright, but they are not required to do so.

Authorship credit will require elaboration. The collaboration agreement as well as the publishing contract should include the order, size, and color of the names that will appear on the jacket of the book, as well as in all promotional materials and advertisements. A co-authored work should usually be copyrighted in both authors' names and this should be clearly delineated in the contract. If a work is unpublished and co-authored it should still be co-registered for copyright in the name of both authors. The proposal should also be copyrighted in the name of its author or co-authors.

Income and Expenses

The usual royalty split is 50/50 if the authors are equal partners in the project and in the percentage of work required; although quality may certainly substitute for quantity, though probably not for fame; and creativity should be more highly valued than research time or administrative tasks. The division of the advance and monies from subsidiary rights usually mirrors the division of royalties. The writers, however, are free to share both the advance and the royalties in any manner they wish. In some cases, writers decide to divide various forms of income, for example income from electronic or audio rights, differently than income from other rights.

Often, an issue arises as to which co-author, or which writer's agent, should be the primary recipient of money owed from the publisher. While some contracts provide that all funds will pass through one of the writers, or agents, and then be distributed to the co-author or his or her agent, each collaborator would do well to demand direct payment, if only for the uncertainties and distrust that such a contractual clause will circumvent.

The agreement should specify if there will be an introduction, who will write it, and if there is a separate fee for this. If the introduction is supplied by only one of the authors or by an outside party, it should be copyrighted in the name of its actual author. Well-known authors who write introductions, whether a co-author or an outside party, can sometimes use their increased bargaining power to extract a small royalty percentage of between ½ and 2 percent for writing the introduction. Similarly, one of the authors may be given a flat fee, over and above the division of proceeds, for writing the proposal.

The parties must also devise a system for authorizing and sharing expenses. An easy way to do this is to set a budget that lists specific expenses and allows for some miscellaneous costs.

Expenses are usually shared in the same manner as income from the work. If the expenses are to be shared, the agreement should deal with the issue of who will own the products that were purchased, such as tape recorders and cassettes, notebooks, and film, as well as the results of such expenditures, recordings of interviews, research notes, and photographs. Another common expense is the obtaining of releases on, or licenses to use, copyrighted work. Some agreements require each collaborator to pay for releases or licenses necessary for their portion of the work.

Control of the Work

Artistic decisions could be made jointly by the coauthors or they could be the responsibility of one party. In either case, artistic control—and an orderly plan to complete the work—should be decided upon. The collaboration agreement should define the nature of the project, and the responsibilities of each participating party, in as much detail as possible. It should also specify a due date for the portions to be contributed by each writer. The parties may want to specify a schedule with a sequence of deadlines for each section. This can help avoid misunderstandings about both the progress and quality of the work being done by a collaborator.

In the absence of a provision giving control over uses of the work to one party, all collaborators will normally have the power to authorize nonexclusive licenses for the United States and the income will be shared equally among the collaborators. The contract can provide that all the writers must consent to a licensing of rights. It can also give the right to negotiate the licensing of a specific right to a single party, although usually the other party or parties would retain the right to veto any proposed agreement. In any case, each collaborator should receive a copy of any license or contract that is entered into. If each collaborator can sell his or her interest in the work, the other parties may desire a right to have the first opportunity to purchase the interest on the same terms being offered by outsiders.

The collaboration agreement should also deal with the possibility of the work never being completed or being completed but never placed with a publisher. If the collaboration fails to reach fruition, a determination must be made as to the rights each collaborator will have in the incomplete work. The writer who does complete his or her portion of the work should have the right to finish the work independently or to find another writer to complete the incomplete sections. If the work is such that contributions by each writer are merged into inseparable portions, the parties should determine who will own the rights in such sections if the work is not completed or sold. One possibility is that the parties could share nonexclusive rights in such sections. The writers may also want to fashion a buyout clause under which one writer would get the rights in return for a flat fee or a reduced royalty on future publication of the work. Similar language could deal with the situation in which one collaborator becomes disabled or dies. Each writer will probably want to retain the right to publish his or her portion of the work independently in the event that the joint work is not published after a certain amount of time.

The collaboration agreement should also address the issue of whether the writers can publish works which compete with the collaboration. In the normal collaboration, the parties decide upon a period of time during which no competing works can be published by the collaborators. A mutual understanding of what competition means in a particular case should be reached and included in the contract so that both parties are adequately protected but neither is barred from earning a livelihood.

The parties should also provide for possible future editions or sequels. What if the writers no longer wish to deal with each other after the project? What if a sequel takes off from sections written by one coauthor and does not even touch upon sections written by another coauthor? The issue of sequels will be especially important if the work creates popular characters, such as a James Bond or Superman.

The Publishing Contract

It is important to realize that the collaboration agreement is not a publishing contract. Therefore, consideration should be given as to whether the collaborators should have a joint contract with the publisher or whether each should have a separate one. If one collaborator is not a signatory to the publishing agreement, the collaboration agreement can reference the publishing agreement and indicate that the nonsignatory has read and approved the contract. The writer will usually have to agree to a warranty and indemnity clause. If the contract is joint, and signed by all the coauthors, each coauthor will be liable for breach of contract (unless they have agreed in the collaboration agreement that a particular party is liable for breaches based on particular sections or content).

If only one party signs the agreement with the publisher, the signatory might have the right to get rid of one of the other coauthors at his or her option. One reason that a coauthor might not want to sign the publishing agreement is the issue of liability. For example, only signatories will be liable for breaches of a warranty, unless the parties have formed a partnership under which one can legally bind the other. For this reason, coauthors may decide that they do not want to sign the publishing agreement and to clarify that they are not partners by stating in the collaboration agreement that they are independent of each other. However, few collaborators would agree to accept sole liability for the warranties contained in a publishing agreement. In fact, many collaboration agreements require each party to give a warranty and indemnity to the other collaborators. In this way each party has some protection against copyright infringements, invasions of privacy, libel, and other unlawful acts committed by the other collaborators. For more on publishing contracts, see chapter 11.

Agents

Coauthor agreements are often set up by an agent, although this is not necessary. If the project is done through an agent, or through two agents, the agent of the author who originated the project is usually the one to set up the agreement and that agent is usually listed as a party to the agreement in the agency clause of the contract. All sums of money due the coauthors will usually flow through the primary agent who will commission and disburse the appropriate portion to his or her client and then forward the remaining amount to be commissioned and disbursed by the coauthor's agent. Some agents may insist on having the money due their client sent directly to them, instead of through the primary agent, because of the control gained and the time saved. This should be spelled out clearly in the agreement.

Dispute Resolution

The contract must include a method for resolving disputes, such as a disagreement over publishers to which the completed work should be submitted or a disagreement arising between a surviving writer and the estate of a coauthor who has died. An agreement to arbitrate disputes that arise can save the writers considerably in both time and legal fees. In addition to arbitration, writers should include a mediation provision for the initial forum. Through the use of an independent mediator, whose decisions, unlike those of an arbitrator, are not binding on the parties, amicable solutions to disputes can often be found. For information on avoiding disputes, and resolving them once they have arisen, see chapter 24.

17 Packagers

Packagers, also known as book producers, book developers, or content providers, are independent companies that produce books to be sold to publishers. The number of packagers listed in the *Literary Market Place* has risen steadily from just over a dozen in 1962 to over three-hundred today. And while most of these companies are relatively small operations with under a dozen employees, increasingly they are becoming full-service operations with all the latest digital technology at their fingertips. Since an increasing number of books are packaged, packagers can be a good source of work for writers.

Usually packagers work for many different publishers. They take ideas that publishers do not have the time or inclination to pursue. As one packager, Steve Ettlinger, put it: "I take half-baked ideas and bake them." The impact of the packager producing the entire book is to eliminate the need for staff at the publishing house. Depending on the contract, the packager may deliver a copy-edited manuscript, mechanicals (on boards or, more likely today, on disk), or printed books. Often packagers will even design the jacket, although the publisher will have a strong interest in the end result. Packagers are particularly useful if the book involves many illustrations, usually in four color, for example a natural history book or an art book, or when a book requires a great number of permissions, as compilations do, or when it needs a lot of coordination, as does a multimedia project.

A packager is paid by the publisher, usually in two sets of fees. One is the production budget, marked up to help cover the overhead of the packaging firm, which has its own staff and may also use free-lance editors and graphic designers. The publisher will evaluate the production budget to be sure that it could not be done cheaper in-house.

The other bill the packager submits is negotiated and similar to what a writer would expect—an advance against royalties pursuant to a publishing contract. In the contract, the packager is effectively the writer. If the packager has an agent, money will flow through that agent and commissions will be deducted. If there is no agent, the publisher pays all monies owed directly to the packager who, in turn, pays the writer and any free lancers.

Because packagers are likely to offer writers terms inferior to those offered by publishers, it is important for the writer to understand something of the nature of the packager's business.

The problem for writers is that the packager is quite likely to want to keep a substantial portion of what the writer would typically receive. By adding a third party, the packager, to the writer-publisher relationship, the rewards for the writer diminish.

There are many instances of younger writers anxious to be in print for the first time, happy to have some work come out under their name, signing a work for hire agreement with a packager, who then offers them a few thousand dollars. In a number of cases, such books have gone on to sell hundreds of thousands of copies to book clubs and overseas. In other cases, the packager pays a very small royalty that escalates if the book sells more than twenty-five-thousand copies. Writers should be especially careful that the contract does not include a clause which provides that the twenty-five-thousand only includes trade sales, which in many cases will be a very small percentage of the market for a packaged work. Finally, the packager will often pay the royalty on net receipts from the publisher and net receipts may be just a fraction over manufacturing cost. The writer may be getting 10 percent of 20 percent of the cover price. On a $19.95 book, the writer would then get roughly forty cents a book, in contrast to the $2 that he or she would have received from the sale of a hardcover book sold by a trade publisher.

While more experienced writers are often able to negotiate with packagers for higher fees, the packager's offer should always be compared to what a publisher might offer for a comparable work. If the advance or royalty is substantially lower, the writer may want to reconsider his or her options. If the packager seeks to pay a flat fee in return for all rights or work for hire, the writer should consider whether it is fair for the packager to own the entire work as if the packager had in fact written it. The writer should also review the grant of rights and consider whether the packager will have the capacity to deal adequately with the rights which it is being given. In many cases, packagers will not be able to sell or license certain subsidiary rights as well as the publisher, the writer's agent, or even the writer acting alone. If this is the case, there is no special reason for the writer to agree to split income from such rights with the packager.

Under no circumstances should the writer work without a guarantee of payment. This situation arises when a packager is developing ideas and pitching them to publishers. In such a case, the contract with the packager must provide for payments to the writer regardless of whether the project is placed with a publisher. Furthermore, whether the work is satisfactory must be determined by the packager, not the publisher. A final issue that often arises is authorship credit. The writer should be clear that his or her name will appear on the book, since packagers often wish to be credited as the writer.

A writer dealing with a packager should also carefully review chapter 10 on contracts generally and chapter 11 on negotiating book contracts in particular. Many of the same issues that arise in dealing with a publisher will also arise when negotiating with a packager. For example, the writer dealing with a packager should have a general overview of contract law in order to be certain that the contract itself is valid. And the writer will also want to develop an understanding of the negotiable points in a publishing contract, such as ownership of copyright, the percentage split on subsidiary rights, royalty rates, artistic control, the schedule of payments, accountings, the right to inspect the books, out of print clauses, and the like.

Working with packagers, though it clearly involves risks, is an important option for writers to consider. The trade association for packagers is the American Book Producers Association, 160 Fifth Avenue, Suite 604, New York, NY 10010; (212) 645-2368. The Association has an annual display of the work done by its member packagers. For writers interested in working with packagers, the Association's membership list is a good starting point, although not all packagers are members.

18 Vanity Presses and Self-Publication

*C*ommercial publishers cannot possibly print and market all the books submitted to them. Of necessity, many books make the rounds of the publishing houses only to return without being placed. The writer must not only wait for this slow process of disappointment to play itself out, but must face the fact that his or her work may never find an audience. And the verdict of the editors will frequently not be that the work lacks merit, but rather that there is an insufficient likelihood of earning a profit to justify underwriting the investment necessary for publication, distribution, and promotion.

If rebuffed, the resourceful writer will seek alternatives to commercial publishing. These exist in the form of university presses, small presses, writers' cooperatives, self-publishing, and vanity presses. University and small presses require the same submission procedure as commercial publishers, while writers' cooperatives require joining a group and contributing money for publication. The most direct route for the writer is to pay for either self-publication or publication by a vanity press.

Self-Publication

Self-publication encompasses a number of different methods of bringing out a book. The writer may buy a printing press, following the examples of Anaïs Nin for *Winter of Artifice* and Virginia Woolf for "The Mark on the Wall." An easier alternative is that taken by Stephen Crane for *Maggie: A Girl of the Streets* and by D. H. Lawrence for *Lady Chatterley's Lover.* They contracted with printers to publish a specified quantity of the bound book. Here, of course, the writer's concern must be with the quality, price, and promptness of the printing job. Once the book is in the writer's hands, the hurdle of distribution must be overcome. The ingenious writer will find many avenues open to promote and distribute the book, including such efforts as direct mail or selling books to customers on the street, which is legal in New York City as long as certain simple regulations are followed.

Some recent self-published books have achieved widespread success. *The Celestine Prophecy* by James Redfield, for example, has remained on the *Publisher's Weekly* best-seller list for well over a year and there are nearly 2.5 million copies in print as we go to press. Self-publishing, if successful, can also lead to big deals with large publishers. Often these publishers are unwilling to take the initial risks themselves. However, when they see that something is working, they are often quick to react. Such was the case with Marlo Morgan's self-published *Mutant Message Down Under* which Harper-Collins recently paid $1.7 million to acquire.

In any case, there should be a realistic appraisal of the total cost of self-publication before any project is undertaken. That appraisal should be followed by an examination of the market for the book and the likelihood of the writer reaching that market. Relevant to that analysis is the competition in the specific field and the degree to which grass roots selling, such as bringing running books to races or political satires to the Democratic and Republican National Conventions, will be effective. Most writers who self-publish probably do not earn back their investment, yet the experience of reaching an audience can still be rewarding. And if others criticize a book because it is self-published, their ignorance of the venerable history of self-publication makes silence the only polite response.

The writer who decides to self-publish does not give up control of his or her creative product upon its completion. Instead, the self-publishing writer will need to oversee the process of designing, printing, and selling the book. In the course of these endeavors, the writer will need to enter into contracts with a book designer, a printer, and, in some cases, a book distributor, and will also need to fill out and file an application for copyright registration and obtain an ISBN number.

Unless the writer decides to use one of a variety of desktop publishing programs, he or she will need to deal with a book designer. That relationship will be less strained if the writer looks at samples of the designer's work and talks to prior clients before entering into contract negotiations. When the writer is ready to go forward, he or she should keep certain issues in mind. The contract should state explicitly the name of the book, the specifications, including its dimensions and the number of pages, and whether the designer will work on the cover (front, spine, back, and flaps), the interior, or both. The next issue is the form in which the designer will deliver the finished product. If the designer is going to deliver mechanicals (whether on boards or a computer disk) ready for printing, rather than mere specifications to be followed by another designer or the desktop publisher, the cost will be lower. The writer should consider whether the designer should be allowed to handle the printing and, if so, the proper mark-up on the printer's bill. Most self-publishers will want to be able to approve the cover design, and even the interior, as the work progresses. The more involved the writer is in the process, the less likely it becomes that disagreements will arise. Artistic rights and a stage-by-stage approval process should be clearly spelled out in the contract.

The writer should be certain that the grant of rights in the design (and any interior art or photography) includes all uses, including promotional and advertising, that will be necessary. To the extent that the writer intends to create promotional items, such as T-shirts, post cards, cups, and tote-bags, the contract should specify that these are included in the term "promotional uses." If such items will be sold, the designer may argue that a re-use fee is appropriate. Whatever is included in the grant should be spelled-out definitively and any fees for other uses should be negotiated and included in the contract.

The fee for the work must be specified, along with a determination of whether tax will be charged (in most states it is not required on mechanicals or other materials used for book production, since books are for resale), and a schedule of expenses, including a maximum amount, that will be reimbursed. Some designers mark up their expenses as much as 15 to 20 percent to cover the interest on the money laid out, the time it takes to obtain such materials, and the paperwork involved. The specific amount or percentage, if any, that will be added to the expenses incurred by the designer should be included in the contract. The writer should retain the option of cancelling the contract at any time without being liable for any expenses that have not yet been incurred. Revisions that are caused by the designer's errors should be the responsibility of the designer to correct, regardless of how much extra time they take. On the other hand, last minute changes by the writer will probably cause the self-publisher to incur additional costs.

The writer should retain the right to terminate the agreement if the designer fails to deliver a finished product within a certain amount of time. Once the book is produced, the writer should be allowed to keep the physical materials necessary to re-use its design. Finally, the writer should include an arbitration clause for amounts higher than that which can be obtained in Small Claims Court.

Contracts with printers are usually less complex than those with designers. Nevertheless, the writer should learn as much as possible about the printing process before he or she undertakes to negotiate with a printer. The self-publishing writer may want to read *Pocket Pal* (International Paper Company, P.O. Box 100, Church Street Station, New York, New York 10008-0100) and *Getting It Printed* by Mark Beach, Steve Shepro, and Ken Russon (Coast to Coast Books, distributed by North Light Books). In choosing a printer, the self-publisher should consult the *Directory of Book, Catalog, and Magazine Printers* by John Kremer (Ad-Lib Publications, P.O. Box 1102, Fairfield, Iowa 52556-1102).

The self-publisher's first problem when dealing with a printer is to get the right price. As a first step, the writer should send the book's specifications, such as quantity, paper stock, trim size, number of pages, and desired binding, to a number of printers for a price quotation and a length of time for which the quote will be valid. When the writer determines the best price, he or she should then check the quality of the printer. This can be done by examining the printer's camera work, looking at the result of several of the printer's prior jobs, talking to some prior clients, or even hiring a specialist or consultant. The self-publisher who is happy with the price and quality of a printer should attempt to lock in that price by prescheduling the job and prepurchasing the paper if it will not be supplied by the printer. Since trade custom allows printers a 10 percent swing on the press run, meaning that they can print "overs" or "unders" of up to 10 percent, the writer should consider printing a slightly higher quantity, especially if a significant portion of the intended press run is presold (sold prior to publication).

In the contract with the printer, the self-publisher should indicate a delivery date, the terms of delivery (for example, who pays shipping and who bears the risk of loss), the price for the quantity ordered, and payment terms. The printer should agree to show proofs (often called "blue lines") to the self-publisher for both the cover and the interior of the book before going to press. The writer should retain the option of terminating the agreement at any point and for any reason before the printer begins work on the project, and if the printer fails to meet the production schedule or the quality level. The contract should have an arbitration clause under which the printer's damages should be limited to costs incurred up to the point of the disagreement. The self-publisher should not allow the printer to limit damages for late shipment, or failure to deliver the books at all, to the cost of the books because there may be significant other losses involved; nor should the printer be allowed to limit the time within which defects or other damages can be reported, since cartons are not traditionally opened until books are unpacked by bookstores and defects are often not discovered until the books are actually read.

Finally, the self-publishing writer may want to find a book distributor with the power to reach the book's market. This distributor might be a publishing company, preferably one that sells books in the same fields, or it might be a distribution company that handles books from a variety of publishers. In either case, the self-publisher will want to go with a company that seems committed to selling the book and will do much more than merely list the book in its trade catalog. Before entering into a distribution agreement, the writer should look closely at the other books distributed by the same company to determine both compatibility and whether or not competition might be a problem. In addition, the writer should speak with the sales manager for the distributor to get a sense of the type of marketing effort to expect.

When the self-publisher has decided upon a distributor, several issues will arise. The distributor will likely want to buy the books on consignment, meaning that no money will be owed to the writer unless the books sell to consumers, whereas the writer, and certainly writers self-publishing for the first time, will want to sell the books outright. The amount paid to the self-publisher is usually in the area of 25 to 40 percent of the retail price (which can also be stated as 60 to 75 percent of the net proceeds received by the distributor from its retail accounts), tending towards the lower end if the distributor buys outright and towards the higher if the books are taken on consignment. If the distributor is buying the books, it will be more cautious about what quantities it buys. As a result, the writer may have to print less, and therefore pay a higher unit cost, or bear the burden and expense of storing books in a warehouse. On the other hand, if the distributor takes large quantities on consignment, the writer will not get a nickel until books actually sell and may have all or most of the books returned at some later date.

Whether the contract is for the sale or consignment of books, the self-publisher should be careful to limit the grant of rights to the territory within which the distributor sells. If the distributor sells to regular bookstores in the United States, the contract should only give the distributor the right to sell to such trade bookstores in the United States. The writer would then be free to enter into separate agreements with mail-order companies, foreign distributors, specialty wholesalers, military stores, and the like. The writer would also be free to sell books for corporate premiums or to book clubs. However, if the distributor does have the unique ability to reach other markets, the writer would do well to grant the distributor the right to do so. If the books are to be sold on consignment, the distributor should not have the right to sell them at higher than a specified discount off retail price (perhaps 55 or

60 percent). In fact, the distributor might be allowed a reduced percentage on sales made at higher discounts.

For further information regarding contract negotiations between self-publishers and book designers, printers, or distributors, as well as for information on other types of contracts that may need to be entered into, see *Business and Legal Forms for Authors and Self-Publishers* by Tad Crawford (Allworth Press). For information on filling out copyright applications, see pages 42–43. And for information on obtaining an ISBN number call Bowker's, a division of Reed Reference Publishing, at (908) 464-6800 and ask to speak to an ISBN agent.

Vanity Presses

Vanity presses usually undertake to distribute books which they have published at the writer's expense. Writers usually seek out a vanity press, or are enticed to do so, when they have been unable to find an agent, have received dozens of rejection letters from trade publishers, and feel that they have nowhere to turn.

Nevertheless, vanity presses do publish thousands of books so it is worthwhile to have a look at the issues that arise when dealing with such companies. As with any other contractual negotiation, the writer should contact several companies and compare the fees that they charge and the services that they offer. When the writer is comfortable with a particular company, it is time to negotiate. In the contract, the writer should first arrange for a schedule of payments that he or she can meet, with the largest amount due as close to publication as possible or even afterwards. The writer should require at least some editorial assistance and certainly copyediting, and should retain the right to approve the cover and interior design and to review galleys.

As in a distribution agreement, or a publishing agreement with a trade publisher, the writer should not grant the publisher the right to sell in any markets except those that the publisher can properly exploit. In general, all subsidiary rights should be retained. If possible, a promotion budget should be agreed upon with a detailed account of how it will be spent. This clause may be more likely to be accepted by a vanity publisher, whose risk of loss in doing any project is substantially lower, than by a trade publisher. The writer should retain the right to approve major marketing and promotional decisions, especially if those decisions have a likelihood of adversely affecting the writer's reputation. Since the marketing effort of most vanity publishers is weak, the writer might also try to retain the nonexclusive right to sell books even into the markets granted to the publisher. The writer should be sure to negotiate a high discount on all copies that he or she purchases from the publisher. This discount should reflect the fact that the writer has already paid for the books once.

The royalty rate given by vanity publishers is often as high as 40 percent of the retail price, but this is more a reflection of the fact that the publisher has already made a profit than it is an indication that the writer is likely to make money off the deal. In fact, few vanity press writers ever do make a profit.

The main risk in dealing with a vanity publisher is that the distribution and promotion will be a passive affair, since the publisher makes most of its profit from the writer. Moreover, vanity presses are scorned by the majority of people who have ever published in another way. Yet vanity presses do offer the public a heterogeneity of style and subject matter which is beyond the scope of commercial publishers. But these presses must repair their image before they can be accepted as a valid publishing vehicle. One way to combat the poor image of vanity publishers may be to convince the publisher to allow the writer to use his or her own imprint on the book. For an analysis of the contract negotiations involved in publishing with a vanity press, see *Business and Legal Forms for Authors and Self-Publishers* by Tad Crawford (Allworth Press).

A Case Study: *Exposition Press*

In the leading case involving vanity presses, a company called Exposition Press published the following advertisement in a variety of newspapers and magazines:

> Free to Writers seeking a book publisher. Two fact-filled brochures tell how to publish your book, get 40% royalties, national advertising, publicity and promotion. Free editorial appraisal. Write Dept. STM-3. Exposition Press, 386 4th Ave., N.Y. 16.

From the language used, according to the Federal Trade Commission (FTC), at least some writers would assume that there were large profits to be made in publishing with Exposition Press. As a result, the FTC ordered Exposition to cease and desist using the word "royalty" in its advertisements because such use had the "tendency and capacity to deceive a substantial portion of the purchasing public." According to the FTC, the use of the word royalty indicated that the writer would receive income "free and clear." In fact, the writer was receiving a partial repayment of the printing, promotional, and sales expenses that were, in large part, paid by the writer.

Exposition Press appealed. It argued that use of the word royalty was not deceptive because every individual who responded to the advertisement was immediately sent information making it clear that the writer would have to pay the expenses incurred in connection with publication.

The court addressed the issue of whether or not the wording was deceptive. It first noted that less than 10 percent of Exposition Press's writers had earned a profit. In fact:

> Of the authors published by Exposition, Dr. Cleere, for example, advanced $2,100 for publication of his book . . . and received back $24 in "royalties." Mrs. Royall . . . paid Exposition $2,600 and got $239 back. Miss Claytor . . . paid $1,150 and got $53 back.

The court agreed with the FTC that the advertisement was deceptive. Furthermore, it held that Exposition Press's initial deception could not be overcome by making it clear that the writer would have to pay for the publication of his or her work: "The law is violated if the first contact is secured by deception, even though the true facts are made known to the buyer before he enters into the contract of purchase." Exposition Press, like many other vanity publishers, was using misleading words to obtain business contacts that it would not otherwise have obtained (*Exposition Press, Inc. v. F.T.C.*, 295 F.2d 869).

When dealing with vanity publishers, writers should be careful that they know up front what the project will cost. As with gambling, they should not bring to the bargaining table more than they are willing to lose.

19 Taxes: Income and Expenses

 humorist once wrote that "To produce an income tax return that has any depth to it, any feeling, one must have Lived—and Suffered." The truth of this quip by Frank Sullivan is felt most vividly in April when many writers scramble to see whether they have the information needed to fill out their tax returns and the funds to pay any taxes due. Chapters 19 and 20 are designed to help the writer keep proper records on a regular basis and pay estimated taxes on time. Since the writer may be able to take steps at the end of each year to lessen the tax burden, tax information should be kept up to date on a current basis rather than waiting for April 15th. If the writer follows these guidelines, taxes won't be more work than they have to be, there will be that much more time to devote to creative work, and the tax bill may very well be smaller.

The writer's professional income includes income from sales of writing, advances, royalties, wages, prizes, awards, and even certain grants. This income is taxed as ordinary income by the federal government and by the state and city where the writer lives, if such state or city has an income tax. The business expenses of being a writer, however, are deductible and reduce the income which will be taxed. Both income—as gross receipts—and expenses are entered on Schedule C, Profit or (Loss) from Business or Profession, which is attached to Form 1040 (except that prizes and awards can be entered directly on Form 1040 as "Other Income" which avoids having to pay self-employment tax on these amounts). A sample Schedule C is reproduced on pages 242–3.

The writer must also determine whether other state or local taxes, such as an unincorporated business tax, must be paid in addition to the personal income tax. These taxes vary with each state and city, so guidance must be obtained in the writer's own locality.

General guides to federal taxation are Internal Revenue Service Publication 17, *Your Federal Income Tax*, for individuals and IRS Publication 334, *Tax Guide for Small Businesses*, for businesses. These and other IRS publications mentioned here can be obtained free of charge from the IRS. The IRS also has a Tele-Tax service that allows taxpayers to use the telephone to check the status of a refund or listen to recorded tax information on about one-hundred-and-forty topics. IRS staff are also available to answer questions made by phone to local IRS offices, but the writer should keep in mind that this advice is sometimes erroneous and is not binding on the IRS.

It is also important to be aware that IRS publications and tapes represent the views of the IRS and are sometimes inconsistent with precedents already established by the courts. It may be advisable to purchase one of the many privately published guides, such as J. K. Lasser's *Your Income Tax*. Also, the tax law is frequently revised. A major tax bill is pending in Congress as this book goes to press. Whether any or all of this revision will be enacted into law is impossible to know at this time. However, this annual addiction to tax-code tinkering requires writers to consult a tax guide which is updated annually. Nonetheless, the chapters on income and estate taxation in this book will provide a valuable overview of taxation as it applies to the writer.

Record-Keeping

Good record-keeping is at the heart of any system to make the task of filling out tax returns easier. All income and expenses arising from the profession of being a writer should be promptly recorded in a ledger regularly used for that purpose. The entries should give specific information as to dates, sources, purposes, and other relevant data, all supported by checks, bills, and receipts whenever possible.

It is advisable to maintain business checking and savings accounts through which all professional income and expenses are channeled separate from the writer's personal accounts. IRS Publication 552, *Recordkeeping Requirements and a Guide to Tax Publications*, and 583, *Recordkeeping for a Small Business*, provide details as to the "permanent, accurate and complete" records required.

A good ledger might be set up like the following example. The first column is for the date, the second column shows the nature of the income or expense, the third column specifies the check number and the receipt number, the fourth column shows the amount of income, the fifth column shows the amount of the expenses, the sixth and subsequent columns are designated for different expenses based on the writer's special needs. This means that each expense is entered twice, once in the expense column and again under the particular expense category into which it falls. This will help in filling out Schedule C and, if the writer's expense categories fit easily into the expense categories shown on Schedule C, the task will be even easier.

SAMPLE LEDGER

DATE	DESCRIPTION	CHECK/ RECEIPT	INCOME	EXPENSE	EXPENSE CATEGORIES					
					1	2	3	4	5	6 etc.

If the writer paid $24 for office supplies on January 8th, the date would be entered as January 8th, office supplies as the description, a check number if payment was by check as well as a receipt number if a receipt was given (the writer can number the receipts to locate them easily). The amount of $24 is then entered twice—under expense in Column 5 and again in the column for Office Supplies (one of the columns from Column 6 to the last column). The benefit of entering the amount twice is that the arithmetic can be checked easily. If the total of Column 5 is added, it should equal the totals of Column 6 through the last column. If $250 is received on January 11th for an article, this would be entered as January 11th with the title of the article, the name of the publication, and perhaps the month of publication, and showing the $250 in Column 4. If payments are received from many sources, income categories can be created (such as royalties by book title, articles by name of publication, speaking appearances, etc.) which allow a review of the sources of income and allow the writer to double check the total of the income column against the total of the columns showing the various types of income.

Accounting Methods and Periods

Like any other taxpayer, the writer may choose either of two methods of accounting: the cash method or the accrual method. The cash method includes in income all income actually received during the tax year and deducts all expenses actually paid during the tax year. The accrual method, on the other hand, includes as income all that income which the writer has earned and has a right to receive in the tax year, even if not actually received until a later tax year, and deducts expenses when they are incurred instead of when they are paid. Since most writers operate on the simpler cash method, the chapters on income taxes will assume that the cash method is being used.

Income taxes are calculated for annual accounting periods. The tax year for the vast majority of taxpayers is the calendar year: January 1 through December 31. However, a taxpayer could use any fiscal year (for example, July 1 through June 30), although there must be a reason to change from a calendar to a fiscal year. Since most writers use the calendar year as their tax year, the income tax chapters will assume the use of a calendar year.

The cash method of accounting may, in a few cases, include income not actually received by the writer, if the income has been credited or set apart so as to be subject to the writer's control. For example, income received by an agent for the writer will be taxable to the writer when received by the agent unless substantial limitations or restrictions exist as to how or when the agent will make payment (James Gould Cozzens, 19 T.C. 663).

One valuable tax-saving device for the cash basis, calendar year writer is to pay expenses in December while putting off receipt of income until January when a new tax year has begun. The expenses reduce income in the present tax year while the income is put off until the new tax year. On the other hand, if the writer anticipates that a sharp increase in income in the next year will push the writer into a higher tax bracket, it might make sense to take additional income in the present year and defer expenses until the next year.

Further information on accounting methods and periods can be obtained in IRS Publication 538, *Tax Information on Accounting Periods and Methods.*

Types of Income

The writer must be aware of the different types of income.

The first distinction is between ordinary income and capital gains income. Ordinary income is realized from all the incomeproducing activities of the writer's profession. Ordinary income is taxed at the regular income tax rates, which go up as high as 39.6 percent. Capital gains income is realized upon the sale of capital assets, such as stocks, real estate, or silver bullion. Capital gains from assets owned more than one year are classified as long-term gains and receive preferential tax treatment (by being taxed at a maximum rate of 28 percent, which may be lowered if pending legislation is enacted).*

The substantial tax discrimination in favor of long-term capital gains as compared to ordinary income will cause the writer to wonder why a copyright or a manuscript is not an asset that receives favorable capital gains treatment. Congress, when enacting the tax laws, specifically stated that "a copyright, a literary, musical, or artistic composition, a letter or memorandum, or similar property, held by the taxpayer who created it" cannot be an asset qualifying for capital gains treatment (Internal Revenue Code, Section 1221[3]). And if the writer gives a copyright or a manuscript to someone else, that person will own the work as the writer did—as ordinary income property rather than an asset qualifying for capital gains treatment.

Another distinction to be kept in mind is between ordinary income that is earned and that which is unearned. The professional income of the writer is considered earned income, but income from stock dividends, interest, rent, and capital gains, for example, is treated as unearned income. As a practical matter, most writers will be concerned about earned income in such areas as retirement (discussed on pages 249–51), income earned abroad (discussed on pages 252–54), and the self-employment tax, which represents Social Security contributions that must be paid by the self-employed such as free-lance writers (discussed on pages 247–49).

Basis

The cost of creating a work is called its "basis" for tax purposes. The cash basis writer, who deducts expenses currently when paid for, must remember that such expenses cannot be deducted again as the basis of the works when sold. In other words, if the writer deducts expenses currently, then the work has a zero basis and the entire amount of the proceeds from sales will be taxable. If the work is given to someone else, that person will have the same zero basis of the writer and, as mentioned earlier, realize ordinary income upon sale.

Grants

Grants to writers for scholarships or fellowships may be excluded from income only by degree candidates and only to the extent that amounts are used for tuition and course-related fees, books, supplies, and equipment at a qualified educational institution. Qualified scholarships cannot include expenses for meals, lodging, or travel. Nor can such scholarships include payments to the writer for teaching, researching, or other services performed by the writer that are required as a condition for receiving the scholarship.

A qualified educational institution is one that normally maintains a regular faculty and curriculum and has a regularly enrolled body of students in attendance at the place where the educational activities are carried on.

Nondegree candidates have no right to exclude scholarship or fellowship grants from income. More information on the taxation of grants can be obtained in IRS Publication 520, *Scholarships and Grants*.

Prizes and Awards

All prizes and awards given to writers are now included in taxable income, unless the recipient assigns the prize or award to a governmental organization or a charitable institution. This applies to all prizes and awards made after December 31, 1986. Even to be eligible to be assigned in order to avoid paying taxes, the prize or award must be for religious, charitable, scientific, educational, artistic, or civic achievement, and the writer must be selected without taking any action and without any requirement to render future services. Under the new law, the person assigning a prize or award is treated as having received no income and having made no charitable contribution. For tax purposes it is as if the prize or award were never received.

As mentioned earlier, the writer may choose to enter income from prizes and awards on Form 1040 as "Other Income" and thus avoid paying the self-employment tax on these amounts. On the other hand, if the writer is facing a home office deduction limitation or a hobby loss challenge, consideration can be given to entering such income on Schedule C to help ameliorate these problems (the home office deduction is discussed later in this chapter and the hobby loss challenge is discussed in chapter 21).

Professional Expenses

Deductible business expenses are all the ordinary and necessary expenditures the writer must make professionally. Such expenses, which are recorded on Schedule C, include, for example, writing materials and supplies, work space, office equipment, certain books and magazines, repairs, travel for business purposes, promotional expenses, telephone, postage, commissions of agents, and legal and accounting fees.

Writing Supplies and Other Deductions

Writing materials and supplies are generally current expenses, deductible in full in the year purchased. These include all items with a useful life of less than one year, such as paper, ink, pens, erasers, typewriter rentals, mailing envelopes, photocopying, file folders, stationery, paper clips, and similar items. Moreover, the sales tax on these and other business purchases is a deductible expense and can simply be included in the cost of the item. Postage is similarly deductible as soon as the expense is incurred. The cost of professional journals is deductible, as is the cost for books used in preparation for specific works. Dues for membership in the writer's professional organizations are deductible, as are fees to attend workshops sponsored by such organizations. Telephone bills and an answering service are deductible in full for a business telephone. If, however, use of the telephone is divided between personal and business calls, then records should be kept itemizing both long-distance and local message units expended for business purposes, and the cost of an answering service should also be prorated. Educational expenses are generally deductible for the writer who can establish that such expenses were incurred to maintain or improve skills required as a writer (but not to learn or qualify in a new profession). IRS Publication 508, *Tax Information on Educational Expenses*, can be consulted here.

Repairs to professional equipment are deductible in full in the year incurred. If the writer moves to a new house, the pro rata share of the moving expenses attributable to professional equipment is deductible as a business expense. More substantial deductions for reasonable moving expenses can be taken if the self-employed person's new work location is at least fifty miles further from the former residence than was the old job location and certain other requirements are met. This deduction is explained in IRS Publication 521, *Moving Expenses.*

For 1995, writers will be able to deduct 30 percent of their premiums for health insurance as an expense on Form 1040.* This deduction cannot be claimed for any month that a writer was covered by an employer's subsidized health plan, including if the coverage was under the plan of a spouse's employer. Also, the deduction must not exceed net earnings from the business paying the premiums. Any health insurance premiums that cannot be deducted on Form 1040 can be deducted on Schedule A, if deductions are itemized.

Work Space

If the writer rents work space at a location different from where he or she lives, all the rent and expenses in connection with the work space are deductible. However, the tax law places limitations on business deductions that are attributable to an office or studio at home. Such deductions will be allowed if the writer uses a part of the home exclusively, and on a regular basis, as the writer's principal place of business. Even though the writer may have another profession, if the office at home is the principal place of the business of being a writer, the business deductions may be taken. Also, the writer who maintains a separate structure used exclusively, and on a regular basis, in connection with the business of being a writer is entitled to the deductions attributable to the separate structure. Provisions less likely to apply to writers allow deductions when a portion of the home is used exclusively, and on a regular basis, as the normal place to meet with clients and customers or when the writer's business is selling at retail (perhaps of manuscripts or books) and the portion of the home, even though not used on an exclusive basis, is the sole, fixed location of that business. A sample copy of Form 8829, *Expenses for Business Use of Your Home*, appears on page 245.

For employees, the home office deduction is available only if the exclusive use is for the convenience of the employer, in addition to the criteria listed above. In a case involving employee-musicians who practiced at home, the United States Court of Appeals decided their home practice studios were the principal place of business—not the concert hall where they performed. The court wrote:

> Rather, we find this the rare situation in which an employee's principal place of business is not that of his employer. Both in time and in importance, home practice was the "focal point" of the appellant musicians' employment-related activities (*Drucker v. Commissioner*, 715 F.2d 67).

Might this discussion apply as well to writers whose home office work is crucial to their employment—for example, as teachers? Yet, in a recent case involving a self-employed anesthesiologist, the United States Supreme Court found that his office at home was not his principal place of business, despite his spending several hours each day working there and the fact that the hospitals where he worked provided no office space for him. The Court reasoned that some professionals who work in several places may have no principal place of business at all, and considered the relative importance of the work done and the amount of time spent at different locations to be crucial criteria in determining where, and if, a principal place of business existed (*Commissioner v. Soliman*, 113 S. Ct. 701). This latter decision is the target of pending legislation that would help writers by qualifying as a principal place of business any home office that is "the location where the taxpayer's essential administrative or management activities are conducted on a regular or systematic (and not incidental) basis by the taxpayer" as long as the taxpayer has no other location where these activities are performed.*

To determine what expenses are attributable to an office or studio, the writer must calculate how much of the total space in the home is used as work space or what number of rooms out of the total number of rooms are used as work space. If a fifth of the area is used as work space, 20 percent of the rent is deductible. A homeowner makes the same calculation as to the work space used. However, capital assets, those having a useful life of more than one year, must be depreciated. A house has a basis for depreciation (only the house—land is not depreciated), which is usually its cost. Depending on whether the house was acquired before the end of 1980 or after 1980, different systems are used to determine the number of years over which depreciation is taken and the percentage of basis taken each year. Thereafter, the percentage of the house used professionally is applied to the annual depreciation figure to reach the amount of the depreciation which is deductible for the current year. IRS Publication 529, *Miscellaneous Deductions*, and 534, *Depreciation*, can help in the determination of basis and the calculation of depreciation. IRS Publication 587, *Business Use of Your Home*, should be consulted regarding deductions.

The portion of expenses for utilities, insurance, and cleaning costs allocable to the work space are deductible. Repairs to maintain the house or apartment are also deductible on this pro rata basis. Property taxes and mortgage interest are deductible in full regardless of whether or not the writer's home is used for work purposes, provided the writer itemizes personal deductions on Schedule A of Form 1040. If personal deductions are not itemized on Schedule A, the portions of property taxes and mortgage interest deductible as business expenses would be entered on Schedule C.

The tax law also limits the amount of expenses which may be deducted when attributable to a home office or studio. Assuming the writer qualifies to take the deductions under one of the tests described above, the deductions for work space cannot exceed the writer's gross income from writing, reduced by expenses that are deductible without regard to business use (such as real estate taxes and mortgage interest, which can be itemized and deducted on Schedule A) and all other deductible expenses for the writing activity that are not allocable to the home office. The effect of this is to disallow any deduction to the extent that it creates or increases a net loss from the writing business. Any disallowed amount may be carried forward and deducted in future years.

For example, a writer earns income of $3,000 in a year from writing, while exclusively, and on a regular basis, using one-quarter of the writer's home as the principal place of the business of being a writer. The writer owns the home, and mortgage interest is $2,000, while real estate taxes are $1,600, for a total of $3,600 of deductions which could be taken on Schedule A, regardless of whether incurred in connection with a business. Other expenses, such as electricity, heat, cleaning, and depreciation, total $8,800. A one-quarter allocation would attribute $900 of the mortgage interest and real estate taxes and $2,200 of the other expenses to the writer's business. The writer's gross income of $3,000 is reduced by the $900 allocated to the mortgage interest and real estate taxes, leaving $2,100 as the maximum amount of expenses relating to work space which may be deducted.

Gross income	$3,000
Home office expenses allocated to the business	
Interest and property taxes	$900
Electricity, heat, cleaning, depreciation	$2,200
Total home office expenses	$3,100
Expenses of writing business excluding home	
office expenses (such as supplies, postage, etc.)	$2,400
Total expenses	$5,500

The writer must apply against gross income (1) the deductions for the writing business expenses, excluding expenses allocable to the home office, and (2) the taxes and interest allocable to the business use of the home. Since (1) $2,400 and (2) $900 total $3,300, the gross income of $3,000 would be reduced to a negative figure. A zero or negative figure means that no additional expenses may be deducted, so the other expenses allocable to the home office ($2,200) are lost for the year. However, the expenses which cannot be deducted under this test can be carried forward for use as a deduction in a future year when income is sufficient. Of course, mortgage interest and property taxes remain fully deductible on Schedule A for those who itemize deductions.

A writer who rents will make a simpler calculation, since the deduction for writing business expenses, excluding expenses attributable to the home office, will simply be subtracted from gross income from writing to determine the limitation amount.

These home office provisions work a hardship on the majority of writers who sacrifice to pursue their work despite not earning large incomes.

Professional Equipment

Traditionally, the cost of professional equipment having a useful life of more than one year could not be fully deducted in the year of purchase. It had to be depreciated. However, the constant changes in the tax laws have made an exception to this rule and changed the method by which depreciation is determined. Again, IRS Publication 534, *Depreciation*, will aid in the computation of depreciation. Form 4562, *Depreciation and Amortization*, is used for all types of depreciation discussed here. Since the method of depreciation is based on when property was placed in service, a brief overview of both current expensing and the three different time periods that are relevant follows.

1. *Current expensing.* The tax law allows a certain dollar amount of professional equipment to be deducted in full in the year of purchase. This treatment of such equipment as a current expense is limited at present (1998) to equipment with a total cost of $18,500 in any one year (may change each year). This $18,500 amount is reduced by the cost of qualified property placed in service during the tax year in excess of $200,000. If a writer chooses to treat some purchases of equipment as current expenses, an election must be made on Form 4562 for the tax year in which the equipment was acquired and the items of equipment must be specified along with the amount of the cost to be treated as a deduction for the year of purchase. Depreciation cannot be taken with respect to that part of the cost of equipment which is deducted under these provisions in the year of purchase.

2. *1987 to the present.* The Modified Accelerated Cost Recovery System (called MACRS) applies to property placed in service from 1987 to the present. MACRS depreciates property using several different depreciation methods. It places assets into different classes with different class lives. Five-year property includes cars; seven-year property includes office furniture and fixtures. Residential real property has a twenty-seven-and-one-half-year life. These classifications, and the method of depreciation, determine how quickly the cost of property can be expensed.

The tax law restricts the use of MACRS for cars (and other personal transportation vehicles), entertainment or recreational property (such as a television or record player) and computers unless these types of equipment are used more than 50 percent for business purposes. If they are used less than 50 for business purposes, special rules apply. In any case, deductions can only be taken for that portion of use which is business use, not for nonbusiness use of equipment. For the listed types of property, adequate records must be kept to document how much of the use is business use or there must be sufficient evidence to corroborate an owner's statements as to whether use is for business. This is true regardless of when the property was acquired.

Also, expensive cars used predominantly for business will nonetheless be restricted as to the amounts of the MACRS deductions which may be taken each year. A standard mileage rate may be used for cars instead of calculating depreciation and actual operating and fixed expenses for the car. Publication 534 details the interplay of these provisions, but it will often be advantageous to calculate depreciation and not use the standard mileage rate (which is adjusted periodically).

3. *1981–1986.* Almost all equipment placed in use from 1981 to 1986 must have depreciation computed under the Accelerated Cost Recovery System (called ACRS). ACRS provides different categories for depreciation which depend on the nature of the equipment acquired. Most equipment is five-year property. The basis (usually the cost of the equipment) is depreciated 15 percent in the first year, 22 percent in the second year and 21 percent in each of the third through fifth years. No determination need be made of either useful life or salvage value (since salvage value is not deducted from basis prior to application of the yearly percentages). Cars are three-year property while houses are eighteen-year property.

Instead of using the ACRS percentages, it is possible to choose an alternate ACRS method which allows basis simply to be divided out over a specified number of years. For five-year property, this recovery period could be five, twelve, or twenty-five years. If five years were chosen, 20 percent of the basis would be deducted as depreciation in each year. Again salvage value would not be relevant. This alternate ACRS allows greater flexibility in tax planning.

4. *1980 and earlier.* The computation of depreciation for equipment placed in use during 1980 or earlier tax years will be done differently from the systems just discussed for equipment placed in use after 1980. The useful life of the pre-1981 equipment has to have been determined. The useful life of such professional equip-

ment varied, but a good faith estimate based on the personal knowledge and experience of the writer (or upon the guidelines of the more complex Class Life Asset Depreciation Range System described in Publication 534) was acceptable. The salvage value of an asset (other than a house) having a useful life of three years or more could be reduced by 10 percent of the asset's original cost for depreciation calculations, and thus a salvage value of less than 10 percent did not affect the depreciation computation at all. Bonus depreciation of 20 percent of original cost could be added to the first year depreciation of an asset (other than a house) having a useful life of at least six years—as computed in Publication 534. If an asset became worthless before expiration of its estimated useful life, the remaining basis was claimed as depreciation in the year of worthlessness. Knowledge of the rule for pre-1981 acquisitions is significant, since depreciation on such equipment may be continuing now.

Travel, Transportation, and Entertainment

Travel, transportation, and entertainment expenses for business purposes are deductible, but must meet strict recordkeeping requirements. Travel expenses are the ordinary and necessary expenses, including meals, lodging, and transportation, incurred for travel overnight away from home in pursuit of professional activities. Such expenses would be deductible, for example, if the writer traveled to another city to give a lecture series and stayed several days to complete the work. If the writer is not required to sleep or rest while away from home, transportation expenses are limited to the cost of travel (but commuting expenses are not deductible as transportation expenses). Entertainment expenses, whether business luncheons or parties or similar items, are deductible within certain limits. Expenses for business meals and entertainment are now only 50 percent deductible, reflecting Congress's belief that such meals and entertainment inherently include some personal living expenses. In addition, a meal which is merely conducive to discussing business is not deductible. Nor is a meal not attended by the party taking the deduction (or an employee). To be deductible, both meals and entertainment must either be directly related to the business of being a writer or include a substantial business discussion. There are some exceptions, but these will probably not have great relevance to writers. Business gifts may be made to individuals, but no deductions will be allowed for gifts to any one individual in excess of twenty-five dollars during the tax year.

Accurate and contemporaneous records detailing business purpose (and the business relationship to any person entertained or receiving a gift), date, place, and cost are particularly important for all these deductions. The writer should also get into the habit of writing these details on copies of bills or credit card charge receipts. IRS Publication 463, *Travel, Entertainment, and Gift Expenses*, gives more details, including the current mileage charge, should the writer own and use a car. Also, self-promotional items, such as advertising, printing business cards, or sending Christmas greetings to professional associates, are deductible expenses.

Commissions, Fees, and Salaries

Commissions paid to agents and fees paid to lawyers or accountants for business purposes are tax deductible, as are the salaries paid to typists, researchers, and others. However, the writer should try to hire people as independent contractors rather than employees, in order to avoid liability for social security, disability, and withholding tax payments. The IRS applies a twenty-factor test to determine who is an employee and who is an independent contractor. Indications of independent contractor status include hiring on a job-by-job basis, with each job to be completed by a deadline, preferably at a place chosen by the person hired and with the details of the work under the hired person's control. If the writer has any concern that someone being treated as an independent contractor is really an employee, the status of that person should be checked with an accountant. Treatment of an employee as an independent contractor may result in having to pay back taxes and penalties that can be substantial.

Record-keeping expenses and taxes will be saved by using independent contractors, although Form 1099-MISC, Statement for Recipients of Miscellaneous Income, must be filed for each independent contractor paid more than $600 in one year by the writer.

Schedule C-EZ

While Schedule C is not a difficult form to complete, the IRS also makes available Schedule C-EZ. This is a simplified form which can be used if the writer meets a number of requirements: (1) there is no net business loss; (2) gross receipts are $25,000 or less; (3) business expenses are $2,000 or less; (4) there is no inventory at any time during the tax year; (5) there is only one sole proprietorship; (6) there is no home office expense; (7) there is no depreciation to be reported on Form 4562; and (8) the business has no prior year suspended passive activity losses. That's a lot of requirements, but some writers—especially those starting out—may be able to use Schedule C-EZ. A copy of Schedule C-EZ appears on page 244.

Beyond Schedule C

The completion of Schedule C—by use of the guidelines given here—finishes much, but not all, of the writer's tax preparations. The next chapter discusses other important tax provisions, not reflected on Schedule C, which can aid the writer or which the writer must observe. A sample Schedule C appears on page 242–3.

SCHEDULE C (Form 1040)	**Profit or Loss From Business** (Sole Proprietorship)	OMB No. 1545-0074
	▶ Partnerships, joint ventures, etc., must file Form 1065.	19**97**
Department of the Treasury Internal Revenue Service (O)	▶ Attach to Form 1040 or Form 1041. ▶ See Instructions for Schedule C (Form 1040).	Attachment Sequence No. **09**

Name of proprietor | Social security number (SSN)

A Principal business or profession, including product or service (see page C-1) | **B** Enter principal business code (see page C-6) ▶

C Business name. If no separate business name, leave blank. | **D** Employer ID number (EIN), if any

E Business address (including suite or room no.) ▶ ....
City, town or post office, state, and ZIP code

F Accounting method: (1) ☐ Cash   (2) ☐ Accrual   (3) ☐ Other (specify) ▶ ....
G Did you "materially participate" in the operation of this business during 1997? If "No," see page C-2 for limit on losses. ☐ Yes ☐ No
H If you started or acquired this business during 1997, check here . . . . ▶ ☐

Part I   Income

1	Gross receipts or sales. **Caution:** If this income was reported to you on Form W-2 and the "Statutory employee" box on that form was checked, see page C-2 and check here . . . . ▶ ☐	1	
2	Returns and allowances	2	
3	Subtract line 2 from line 1	3	
4	Cost of goods sold (from line 42 on page 2)	4	
5	**Gross profit.** Subtract line 4 from line 3	5	
6	Other income, including Federal and state gasoline or fuel tax credit or refund (see page C-2) . . .	6	
7	**Gross income.** Add lines 5 and 6 . . . . ▶	7	

Part II   Expenses. Enter expenses for business use of your home **only** on line 30.

8	Advertising	8		19	Pension and profit-sharing plans	19
9	Bad debts from sales or services (see page C-3) . .	9		20	Rent or lease (see page C-4):	
10	Car and truck expenses (see page C-3)	10		a	Vehicles, machinery, and equipment .	20a
11	Commissions and fees . .	11		b	Other business property . .	20b
12	Depletion	12		21	Repairs and maintenance . .	21
13	Depreciation and section 179 expense deduction (not included in Part III) (see page C-3) . .	13		22	Supplies (not included in Part III) .	22
				23	Taxes and licenses	23
				24	Travel, meals, and entertainment:	
14	Employee benefit programs (other than on line 19) . .	14		a	Travel	24a
15	Insurance (other than health) .	15		b	Meals and entertainment .	
16	Interest:			c	Enter 50% of line 24b subject to limitations (see page C-4) .	
a	Mortgage (paid to banks, etc.) .	16a				
b	Other	16b		d	Subtract line 24c from line 24b .	24d
17	Legal and professional services	17		25	Utilities	25
				26	Wages (less employment credits) .	26
18	Office expense	18		27	Other expenses (from line 48 on page 2)	27
28	**Total expenses** before expenses for business use of home. Add lines 8 through 27 in columns ▶	28				

29	Tentative profit (loss). Subtract line 28 from line 7	29	
30	Expenses for business use of your home. Attach Form 8829	30	
31	**Net profit or (loss).** Subtract line 30 from line 29.		
	• If a profit, enter on **Form 1040, line 12,** and ALSO on **Schedule SE, line 2** (statutory employees, see page C-5). Estates and trusts, enter on Form 1041, line 3.	31	
	• If a loss, you MUST go on to line 32.		
32	If you have a loss, check the box that describes your investment in this activity (see page C-5).		
	• If you checked 32a, enter the loss on **Form 1040, line 12,** and ALSO on **Schedule SE, line 2** (statutory employees, see page C-5). Estates and trusts, enter on Form 1041, line 3.	32a ☐ All investment is at risk. 32b ☐ Some investment is not at risk.	
	• If you checked 32b, you MUST attach **Form 6198.**		

For Paperwork Reduction Act Notice, see Form 1040 instructions.   Cat. No. 11334P   Schedule C (Form 1040) 1997

Schedule C (Form 1040) 1997   Page **2**

Part III **Cost of Goods Sold** (see page C-5)

33 Method(s) used to
    value closing inventory: **a** ☐ Cost   **b** ☐ Lower of cost or market   **c** ☐ Other (attach explanation)

34 Was there any change in determining quantities, costs, or valuations between opening and closing inventory? If
    "Yes," attach explanation . . . . ☐ **Yes**   ☐ **No**

35 Inventory at beginning of year. If different from last year's closing inventory, attach explanation . .	**35**	
36 Purchases less cost of items withdrawn for personal use	**36**	
37 Cost of labor. Do not include salary paid to yourself	**37**	
38 Materials and supplies	**38**	
39 Other costs	**39**	
40 Add lines 35 through 39	**40**	
41 Inventory at end of year	**41**	
42 **Cost of goods sold.** Subtract line 41 from line 40. Enter the result here and on page 1, line 4 . .	**42**	

Part IV **Information on Your Vehicle.** Complete this part **ONLY** if you are claiming car or truck expenses on
line 10 and are not required to file Form 4562 for this business. See the instructions for line 13 on page
C-3 to find out if you must file.

43 When did you place your vehicle in service for business purposes? (month, day, year) ▶ ....../....../...... .

44 Of the total number of miles you drove your vehicle during 1997, enter the number of miles you used your vehicle for:

a Business ....   **b** Commuting ....   **c** Other ....

45 Do you (or your spouse) have another vehicle available for personal use? . . . . ☐ **Yes**   ☐ **No**

46 Was your vehicle available for use during off-duty hours? . . . . ☐ **Yes**   ☐ **No**

47a Do you have evidence to support your deduction? . . . . ☐ **Yes**   ☐ **No**

  b If "Yes," is the evidence written? . . . . ☐ **Yes**   ☐ **No**

Part V **Other Expenses.** List below business expenses not included on lines 8–26 or line 30.

....		
....		
....		
....		
....		
....		
....		
....		
48 **Total other expenses.** Enter here and on page 1, line 27	**48**	

                          ♻ *Printed on recycled paper*   *U.S. Government Printing Office: 1997 - 419-557

SCHEDULE C-EZ (Form 1040) Department of the Treasury Internal Revenue Service (O)	**Net Profit From Business** (Sole Proprietorship) ▶ Partnerships, joint ventures, etc., must file Form 1065. ▶ Attach to Form 1040 or Form 1041. ▶ See instructions on back.	OMB No. 1545-0074 **1997** Attachment Sequence No. **09A**
Name of proprietor		Social security number (SSN)

Part I   General Information

You May Use This Schedule Only If You:	• Had business expenses of $2,500 or less. • Use the cash method of accounting. • Did not have an inventory at any time during the year. • Did not have a net loss from your business. • Had only one business as a sole proprietor.	And You:	• Had no employees during the year. • Are not required to file **Form 4562,** Depreciation and Amortization, for this business. See the instructions for Schedule C, line 13, on page C-3 to find out if you must file. • Do not deduct expenses for business use of your home. • Do not have prior year unallowed passive activity losses from this business.

A	Principal business or profession, including product or service		B Enter principal business code (see page C-6) ▶
C	Business name. If no separate business name, leave blank.		D Employer ID number (EIN), if any

E   Business address (including suite or room no.). Address not required if same as on Form 1040, page 1.

      City, town or post office, state, and ZIP code

Part II   Figure Your Net Profit

1	**Gross receipts. Caution:** *If this income was reported to you on Form W-2 and the "Statutory employee" box on that form was checked, see* **Statutory Employees** *in the instructions for Schedule C, line 1, on page C-2 and check here* . . . . ▶ ☐	**1**	
2	**Total expenses.** If more than $2,500, you **must** use Schedule C. See instructions	**2**	
3	**Net profit.** Subtract line 2 from line 1. If less than zero, you **must** use Schedule C. Enter on **Form 1040, line 12,** and ALSO on **Schedule SE, line 2.** (Statutory employees **do not** report this amount on Schedule SE, line 2. Estates and trusts, enter on Form 1041, line 3.)	**3**	

Part III   Information on Your Vehicle. Complete this part **ONLY** if you are claiming car or truck expenses on line 2.

4   When did you place your vehicle in service for business purposes? (month, day, year) ▶ ..... / ..... / ..... .

5   Of the total number of miles you drove your vehicle during 1997, enter the number of miles you used your vehicle for:

a   Business ....   **b** Commuting ....   **c** Other ....

6   Do you (or your spouse) have another vehicle available for personal use? . . . . ☐ Yes   ☐ No

7   Was your vehicle available for use during off-duty hours? . . . . ☐ Yes   ☐ No

8a   Do you have evidence to support your deduction? . . . . ☐ Yes   ☐ No

b   If "Yes," is the evidence written? . . . . ☐ Yes   ☐ No

For Paperwork Reduction Act Notice, see Form 1040 instructions.   Cat. No. 14374D   Schedule C-EZ (Form 1040) 1997

Form **8829**

Department of the Treasury (O)
Internal Revenue Service

Expenses for Business Use of Your Home

▶ File only with Schedule C (Form 1040). Use a separate Form 8829 for each home you used for business during the year.

▶ **See separate instructions.**

OMB No. 1545-1266

19 97

Attachment
Sequence No. **66**

Name(s) of proprietor(s)

Your social security number

Part I **Part of Your Home Used for Business**

1	Area used regularly and exclusively for business, regularly for day care, or for storage of inventory or product samples. See instructions	**1**	
2	Total area of home	**2**	
3	Divide line 1 by line 2. Enter the result as a percentage	**3**	%

- For day-care facilities not used exclusively for business, also complete lines 4–6.
- All others, skip lines 4–6 and enter the amount from line 3 on line 7.

4	Multiply days used for day care during year by hours used per day .	**4**	hr.
5	Total hours available for use during the year (365 days × 24 hours). See instructions	**5**	8,760 hr.
6	Divide line 4 by line 5. Enter the result as a decimal amount . . .	**6**	
7	Business percentage. For day-care facilities not used exclusively for business, multiply line 6 by line 3 (enter the result as a percentage). All others, enter the amount from line 3 . . . . . ▶	**7**	%

Part II **Figure Your Allowable Deduction**

8	Enter the amount from Schedule C, line 29, **plus** any net gain or (loss) derived from the business use of your home and shown on Schedule D or Form 4797. If more than one place of business, see instructions			**8**	

See instructions for columns (a) and (b) before completing lines 9–20.

			(a) Direct expenses	**(b)** Indirect expenses	
9	Casualty losses. See instructions	**9**			
10	Deductible mortgage interest. See instructions .	**10**			
11	Real estate taxes. See instructions	**11**			
12	Add lines 9, 10, and 11	**12**			
13	Multiply line 12, column (b) by line 7		**13**		
14	Add line 12, column (a) and line 13			**14**	
15	Subtract line 14 from line 8. If zero or less, enter -0- .			**15**	
16	Excess mortgage interest. See instructions . .	**16**			
17	Insurance	**17**			
18	Repairs and maintenance	**18**			
19	Utilities	**19**			
20	Other expenses. See instructions	**20**			
21	Add lines 16 through 20	**21**			
22	Multiply line 21, column (b) by line 7		**22**		
23	Carryover of operating expenses from 1996 Form 8829, line 41 . .		**23**		
24	Add line 21 in column (a), line 22, and line 23			**24**	
25	Allowable operating expenses. Enter the **smaller** of line 15 or line 24			**25**	
26	Limit on excess casualty losses and depreciation. Subtract line 25 from line 15			**26**	
27	Excess casualty losses. See instructions	**27**			
28	Depreciation of your home from Part III below	**28**			
29	Carryover of excess casualty losses and depreciation from 1996 Form 8829, line 42	**29**			
30	Add lines 27 through 29			**30**	
31	Allowable excess casualty losses and depreciation. Enter the **smaller** of line 26 or line 30 . .			**31**	
32	Add lines 14, 25, and 31			**32**	
33	Casualty loss portion, if any, from lines 14 and 31. Carry amount to **Form 4684**, Section B . .			**33**	
34	Allowable expenses for business use of your home. Subtract line 33 from line 32. Enter here and on Schedule C, line 30. If your home was used for more than one business, see instructions ▶			**34**	

Part III **Depreciation of Your Home**

35	Enter the **smaller** of your home's adjusted basis or its fair market value. See instructions . .	**35**	
36	Value of land included on line 35	**36**	
37	Basis of building. Subtract line 36 from line 35	**37**	
38	Business basis of building. Multiply line 37 by line 7	**38**	
39	Depreciation percentage. See instructions	**39**	%
40	Depreciation allowable. Multiply line 38 by line 39. Enter here and on line 28 above. See instructions	**40**	

Part IV **Carryover of Unallowed Expenses to 1998**

41	Operating expenses. Subtract line 25 from line 24. If less than zero, enter -0-	**41**	
42	Excess casualty losses and depreciation. Subtract line 31 from line 30. If less than zero, enter -0- . .	**42**	

For Paperwork Reduction Act Notice, see page 3 of separate instructions. ✪ *Printed on recycled paper* Cat. No. 13232M Form **8829** (1997)

☆ U.S. GOVERNMENT PRINTING OFFICE 1997 419-551

20 Taxes: Beyond Schedule C

$\mathcal{T}$he writer must also be aware of a number of other tax benefits and obligations in order to be able to make rational choices and to seek professional advice when necessary. These provisions, while not gathered neatly in one place like income and expenses on Schedule C, are of great significance to the writer.

Self-Employment Tax

The social security system of the United States creates numerous benefits for those who have contributed from their earnings to the federal social security system. It provides benefits for a person's family in the event of death or disablement as well as providing a pension and certain medical insurance. Writers, whether employees or self-employed, are covered by the system. Since the payments for social security are not automatically withheld for a self-employed writer, as they are for one who is an employee, the self-employed writer must file with Form 1040 a Schedule SE,

Computation of Social Security Self-Employment Tax, and pay the self-employment tax shown on the Schedule SE. Self-employment income is basically the net income of the writer reported on Schedule C, subject to certain adjustments.

If a writer and his or her spouse both earn self-employment income, each must file a separate Schedule SE. If a writer has more than one business, the combined business earnings should be totaled on Schedule SE for purposes of calculating the self-employment tax. Calculation of the self-employment tax is done by first taking all income from employers from which the social security tax has already been withheld and subtracting that from the maximum amount of income on which tax must be paid to determine how much tax must be paid on the remaining self-employment income.

Social security coverage, to gain the various benefits, is created by having a certain number of quarters for which a worker makes payments for social security. If a minimum number of years of work credit is established, the writer qualifies for benefits. The amount of benefits is based on average yearly earnings covered by social security. Therefore, the writer who pays more self-employment taxes will be eligible for larger benefits from the system.

The self-employed writer must file Schedule SE for any tax year in which net self-employment income is more than $400 (although no tax will be payable unless self-employment income exceeds $433.13 in 1995). For 1995, the writer will receive a quarter of work credit for social security benefits (up to four quarters maximum) for each $630 of income subject to social security taxes. So if 1995 self-employment income is $2,480 or more, the writer would receive four quarters of work credit.

The maximum amount of income on which tax must be paid has been increasing constantly over the years—for example, from $14,000 in 1975 to $37,800 in 1984 to $61,200 in 1995—and the rate has also increased over the years. From a tax rate of 11.3 percent in 1984 on income up to a maximum of $37,800, the rate has risen so that for 1998 it is 12.4 percent for self-employment income up to $68,400, plus an additional Medicare tax of 2.9 percent on all self-employed income (but note that self-employment income is multiplied by .9235 to reduce it before the tax calculations are made). One half of the self-employment taxes paid are a deductible expense on Form 1040.

Further information as to the computation of the self-employment tax can be found in IRS Publication 533, *Self-Employment Tax*. Additional information as to the benefits available under social security to either the writer or the writer's family is available from the local office of the Social Security Administration, including a helpful pamphlet titled "Understanding Social Security" and an information sheet titled "If You're Self-Employed." Every three years the writer should write to the Social Security Administration to be certain it has credited his or her account properly and to see what the projected benefits are based on credits earned to the date of the inquiry.

Estimated Tax

Employers withhold income and social security taxes from the wages of their employees. However, the self-employed writer must pay income and social security taxes in quarterly installments computed on Form 1040-ES, Estimated Tax for Individuals, and mailed on or before April 15, June 15, September 15, and January 15. For tax years beginning after January 1, 1998, Form 1040-ES will be required if the taxes estimated in excess of withholding exceed $1,000.

The failure to pay a sufficient amount of estimated tax subjects the writer to liability for penalties, as well as having to pay the tax deficiency. A simple way to avoid the risk of such penalties is to pay as estimated tax in the current year what the actual tax amount was in the prior year. IRS Publication 505, *Tax Withholding and Estimated Tax*, gives more detailed information regarding the estimated tax and how to avoid penalties for underpayment.

Retirement Plans

Keogh plans permit a self-employed person, such as a writer, to contribute to a retirement fund and to deduct the amount of the contribution from gross income when computing income taxes. However, the deduction is allowed in any year only if the writer places the amount to be deducted in one of the following retirement funds: a trust, annuity contracts from an insurance company, a custodial account with a bank or another person, special U.S. Government retirement bonds, or certain face-amount certificates purchased from investment companies. Even if the writer is employed by a company with a retirement program, the writer may still have a Keogh plan for self-employment income from the writing career.

There are several ways to determine the amount of contributions to be made to a Keogh plan, which are limited by certain caps. To be able to contribute this maximum amount, the writer would have to have a certain income level. If this level is not achieved, lesser contributions can be made. If a writer has employees, it is quite likely that a plan to benefit the writer will also require contributions for the benefit of the employees.

A contribution to a Keogh plan can be made before the filing date of the tax return, which is usually the following April 15, or any extensions of the filing date, as long as the Keogh plan was in existence during the tax year for which the deduction is to be taken. Because the money contributed to a Keogh plan is deductible, there are penalties for withdrawal of monies from a plan prior to age fifty-nine and a half, unless the writer becomes permanently disabled. No taxes are levied on the growth of a Keogh fund until the funds are withdrawn. Distributions are taxed when made, and must begin no later than age seventy and a half (or, in some cases, the year of retirement if the person is older than seventy and a half on retiring). The writer's tax bracket then, however, may be much lower than when the contributions were made and the funds have had tax-free growth. If a trust is created, it is possible for the writer to act as trustee and administer the investments. More information about Keogh plans can be obtained from the institutions, such as the local bank or insurance company, which administer them. Also helpful is IRS Publication 560, *Retirement Plans for the Self-Employed.*

A self-employed person may also create a SEP (Simplified Employee Pension), which is not as flexible as a Keogh plan in terms of being customized. However, SEPs need not be set up by the end of the year for which the contribution is to be made and do not have the same annual filing requirements as Keoghs (although it should be noted that one-participant Keogh plans that hold less than $100,000 are exempt from any annual filings). For writers who want to make the largest possible contributions, the Keogh is preferable to the SEP.

Separate from either a Keogh plan or a SEP, the writer may begin an IRA (Individual Retirement Account). By creation of such an account, the writer may contribute into a retirement fund up to $2,000 per year (assuming wages and professional fees amount to at least that much). A married writer with a nonworking spouse may be able to contribute $2,250 to benefit both spouses, while two working spouses could contribute $2,000 each for a maximum of $4,000 deduction. Pending legislation includes a provision allowing a $2,000 IRA contribution and deduction for a nonworking spouse, which would bring the total possible IRA deduction to $4,000.*

To qualify to make a deductible contribution to an IRA, a writer must either (1) not be covered by another retirement plan (such as a Keogh or SEP), or (2) if covered by another retirement plan, the writer must not exceed certain limits on adjusted gross income (which increase if the writer is married).

The amount of the IRA contribution is a deduction from gross income. Again, the funds contributed must be taken out of the writer's hands and placed in a trust, a custodial account with a bank or other person, annuity contracts with a life insurance company, or special U.S. Government retirement bonds. The payment, to be deductible, must be made by April 15 of the year following the tax year for which the deduction will be taken. More information may be obtained from the institutions administering Individual Retirement Accounts, as well as IRS Publication 590, *Individual Retirement Arrangements* (IRAs).

If a writer were covered by a retirement plan and could not make a deductible contribution to an IRA, it might be worthwhile to make a nondeductible contribution (subject to the current limitations on the amount of the contribution). This has the tax deferral advantage of shielding from tax the earnings on the IRA contribution. Consideration is being given to legislation that would create nondeductible IRA's. These IRA's would shield income from taxes. Withdrawals for certain purposes or at certain times would be without penalty and tax-free.

Keogh, SEP, and IRA plan contributions are claimed on Form 1040. The writer should consult with the plan administrator to determine what additional forms may have to be filed. Also, the custodial fees charged by a plan administrator may be deducted as investment expenses on Schedule A if these fees are separately billed and paid for. Commissions paid on transactions in the retirement fund do not qualify as deductible.

Child and Disabled Dependent Care

A writer's payments for child or disabled dependent care may create a tax credit. A tax credit is subtracted directly from the tax owed, so it is more beneficial than a deduction of the same amount which merely reduces income prior to application of the tax rates. The amount of the credit is 30 percent (for adjusted gross incomes up to $10,000) ranging down to 20 percent (for adjusted gross incomes over $28,000) of the employment-related expenses which a writer pays in order to be gainfully employed. Basically, this credit is available to the writer who maintains a household including either a child under age thirteen or a disabled dependent or spouse for the care of whom it is necessary to hire someone so the writer can gainfully pursue employment, self-employment, or the search for employment. The maximum credit is $2,400 per year for one qualifying dependent or $4,880 for two or more qualifying dependents. IRS Publication 503, *Child and Dependent Care Expenses*, describes in greater detail the availability of and limitations on this credit.

In addition to the credit for the care of children, proposed tax legislation would create a $500 tax credit for each child in a family as well as for certain adult family members who are mentally or physically incapacitated.*

Bad Debts

A common error is the belief that if a writer (on the cash basis) sells a work for $1,000 and the purchaser never pays, the writer can take a bad debt deduction. The writer cannot take such a deduction, since the $1,000 purchase price has never been received and included in income.

As stated in Publication 334, *Tax Guide for Small Businesses*, "Cash method taxpayers normally do not report income until they receive payment. Therefore, they cannot take a bad debt deduction for payments they have not received or cannot collect."

A cash basis taxpayer can, however, gain a tax benefit from either business or nonbusiness bad debts of the proper kind. In almost all cases, the writer's bad debts will be nonbusiness. For example, if the writer makes a loan to a friend who never repays the loan, the amount of the loan will be a nonbusiness bad debt. The loan cannot be a gift, however, and must be legally enforceable against the borrower. The nonbusiness bad debt deduction is taken in the year in which the debt becomes worthless. It is reported as a short-term capital loss on Schedule D.

Net Operating Losses

The writer who experiences a business loss, as determined on Schedule C, will carry the loss to Form 1040, where it is eventually subtracted from gross income in the calculations to reach taxable income. However, if the loss is large enough to wipe out other taxable income for the year, the excess loss can first be carried back to reduce taxable income in three prior years and then carried forward for fifteen future taxable years.* This type of loss is likely to arise when a professional writer is changing over from being employed to devoting all working time to writing. The result is that the writer will be entitled to a tax refund (if taxable income in previous years is reduced) or will save on taxes in future years. IRS Publication 536, *Net Operating Losses*, describes the net operating loss, but the writer will probably need an accountant's help for the computation of a net operating loss.

American Writers Living Abroad

American citizens, whether or not they live in the United States, are taxable by the United States government on all of their income from anywhere in the world. However, a tax benefit for many American citizens living abroad is the exclusion from American taxable income of $72,000 of earned income from foreign sources.* This exclusion can result in substantial tax benefits when the tax rates of the foreign country—such as Ireland, where a qualified writer can live tax free—are lower than the tax rates in the United States. The $72,000 exclusion can be negatively affected if a writer travels in countries restricted to United States citizens under the Trade with the Enemy Act of the International Emergency Economic Powers Act.

Publication 54, *Tax Guide for U.S. Citizens Abroad*, generally explains the guidelines for eligibility for these exclusions. The basic requirements are either a one-year residence or a physical presence in a foreign country and earned income created from work done in the foreign country. Residence is a flexible concept based on the circumstances of each individual. While the residence must be uninterrupted (for example, by owning or renting a home continually), remaining abroad for all the taxable year in question is not necessary. Brief trips to the United States do not affect the tax status as a resident abroad. However, the length of each visit and the total time spent in the United States must be watched carefully. Physical presence requires the taxpayer to be present in a foreign country or countries for at least three-hundred-and-thirty days (about eleven months) during a period of twelve consecutive months. Regardless of which test is met, the income to be excluded must be received no later than the year after the year in which the work was performed which generated the income. Certain foreign housing costs may also be excludable or deductible from income.

Assuming the writer met either the residence or physical presence test, the requirement that the income to be excluded had to be earned income often proved fatal to the writer's attempt to benefit from the exclusion. The reason for this was the definition, once found in Publication 54, of most of the income of a writer as unearned.

This unjust rule was rectified, however, in a case involving the painter, Mark Tobey, while he was a resident of Switzerland. In *Tobey v. Commissioner*, the issue before the tax court was whether Mark Tobey, all of whose "works were executed . . . without prior commission, contract, order, or any such prior arrangement," had earned income such that he could avail himself of the exclusion from United States taxable income. The court, noting that "earned" generally implies a product of one's own work, reasoned:

> The concept of the artist as not "earning" his income for the purposes of Section 911 would place him in an unfavorable light. For the most part, the present day artist is a hard-working, trained, career-oriented individual. His education, whether acquired formally or through personal practice, growth and experience, is often costly and exacting. He has keen competition from many other artists who must create and sell their works to survive. To avoid discriminatory treatment, we perceive no sound reasons for treating income earned by the personal efforts, skill and creativity of a Tobey or a Picasso any differently from the income earned by a confidence man, a brain surgeon, a movie star or, for that matter, a tax attorney (*Tobey v. Commissioner*, 60 T.C. 227).

This rationale necessarily led to the conclusion that Tobey's income was earned.

Each writer hoping to benefit from the exclusion for income earned abroad must, of course, consult with a lawyer or an accountant to determine the effect of the foregoing legal provisions on his or her unique situation. Writers already living abroad should also inquire at their American consulate to determine whether any treaty regarding taxation between the United States and the country in which they live might affect their tax status.

The writer living abroad should also consider whether any income taxes paid to a foreign government may be taken as either a deduction or a tax credit. No such credit or deduction will be allowed on foreign income taxes paid on earned income excluded from the United States taxation. IRS Publication 514, *Foreign Tax Credit for Individuals*, explains these provisions further.

Foreign Writers in the United States

Foreign writers who are residents of the United States are generally taxed in the same way as United States citizens. Foreign writers who are not residents in the United States are taxed on income from sources in the United States under special rules. A foreigner who is merely visiting or whose stay is limited by immigration laws will usually be considered a nonresident. A foreigner who intends, at least temporarily, to establish a home in the United States and has a visa permitting permanent residence will probably be considered a resident. IRS Publication 519, *United States Tax Guide for Aliens*, should be consulted by foreign writers for a more extensive discussion of their tax status.

Employee Expenses

Often writers who work as employees will find that they are required to incur expenses in the performance of their duties. The nature of the expenses is the same as the expenses which a self-employed person could deduct, such as supplies, work space, equipment, travel and so on. These expenses, if ordinary and necessary, will be deductible on Schedule A if the writer itemizes (and will only be allowed to the extent that these and certain other expenses total in excess of 2 percent of adjusted gross income). To deduct these expenses, the writer must complete Form 2106, Employee Business Expenses.

The writer who incurs expenses as an employee can consult IRS Publications 521, *Moving Expenses*, and 535, *Business Expenses*, for further information on deductibility.

Forms of Doing Business

Depending on the success of the writer, various forms of doing business might be considered. There may be both business and tax advantages to conducting the writer's business in the form of a corporation or partnership, but there may be disadvantages as well.

Generally, the nontax advantages of incorporation are limited liability for the stockholders, centralized management, access to capital, transferability of ownership, and continuity of the business. For the writer, the most important of these nontax advantages will probably be limited liability. This means that a judgement in a lawsuit will affect only the assets of the corporation, not the personal assets of the writer. The attribute of limited liability applies to all corporations—the regular corporation and the Subchapter S corporation. The tax treatment, however, differs significantly between the two types of corporations.

For regular corporations, net corporate income is taxed at 15 percent on net income up to $50,000, 25 percent from $50,000 to $75,000, 34 percent from $75,000 to $100,000, and 39 percent from $100,000 to $335,000.* Usually the tax on the corporation can be substantially avoided by the payment of a salary to the writer, which creates a deduction for the corporation. Such an arrangement can effectively average the writer's income from year to year. The Subchapter S corporation is not taxed at all, but the income is credited directly to the accounts of the stockholders and they are taxed as individuals. Both types of corporations are less likely to be audited than an individual proprietor. It may also be easier to choose a fiscal year (any tax year other than the calendar year) and, particularly in the case of a regular corporation, shift some of the writer's income into the next tax year. Some of the disadvantages of incorporation are additional record-keeping, meetings, and paper work, as well as significant expenses both for the initial incorporation and for any ultimate dissolution.

A partnership is an agreement between two or more persons to join together as co-owners of a business in pursuit of profit. Partnerships are not subject to the income tax, but the individual partners are taxable on their share of the partnership income. Partners are personally liable for obligations incurred on behalf of the partnership by any of the partners. A partnership offers to the writer an opportunity to combine with investors under an agreement in which the investors may gain tax advantages by being allocated a greater share of partnership losses. A variation of the usual partnership is the "limited partnership," in which passive investors have limited liability (but the writer, running the business actively, is still personally liable). Another variation is the "joint venture," which can be described simply as a partnership created for a single business venture.

Many states have recently legislated into existence a new form of business entity called a "limited liability company," which combines the corporate advantage of limited liability for its owners while still being taxed for federal income tax purposes as a partnership. The limited liability company offers great flexibility in terms of the mode of ownership and the capital structure of the company as well as what corporate formalities the company must observe. Its very newness suggests the need for caution when considering whether a limited liability company might be appropriate for a writer.

In general, the tax law requires that a partnership, an S corporation, or a personal service corporation (which is a corporation whose principal activity is the performance of personal services by an employee-owner) use a calendar tax year, unless there is a business purpose for using a fiscal year.

The writer contemplating doing business as a corporation, partnership, or limited liability company should consult a lawyer for advice based on the writer's unique needs.

Gifts

The writer can avoid paying income taxes by giving away his or her creations. Both manuscripts and copyrights can be transferred by gift to family members or others whom the writer may wish to benefit. The manuscript and copyright on the work can be transferred separately from one another if the writer chooses. The writer could keep the manuscript and transfer the copyright (or parts of the copyright), transfer the manuscript and keep the copyright, or transfer both the work and the copyright.

If the person who receives the gift is in a lower tax bracket than the writer, tax savings will result because income will be diverted to the person who received the gift. Gifts over certain amounts, however, are subject to the gift tax. For tax years after 1986, transfers of income-producing property from adults to children under fourteen will have a very limited tax advantage. Basically, the unearned income of the child will be taxed at the parents' top rate. Of course, the transfer of manuscripts or copyrights to the child might still be a wise decision, since these might appreciate in value without producing income until a sale at a much later date.

The making of gifts and the gift tax are discussed on pages 274–77, but careful planning is a necessity if gifts are to play an effective role in tax planning.

21 The Hobby Loss Challenge

*O*ften the writer sufficiently dedicated to pursue a writing career despite year after year of losses on Schedule C will face a curious challenge from the IRS: that the losses incurred by the writer cannot be deducted for tax purposes because the writer was only pursuing a hobby and did not have the profit motive necessary to qualify the writing career as a business or trade. A hobbyist in any field may deduct the expenses of the hobby only up to the amount of income produced by the hobby. For example, if a hobbyist makes $500 in a year on the sale of writing, only up to $500 in expenses can be deducted. On the other hand, a writer actively engaged in the business or trade of being a writer—one who pursues writing with a profit motive—may deduct all ordinary and necessary business expenses, even if such expenses far exceed income from writing activities for the year.

A Test: Three Years out of Five

But how can a writer show that the requisite profit motive is present to avoid being characterized as a hobbyist by the IRS? At the outset, there is an important threshold test in favor of the taxpayer. This test is a presumption that a writer is engaged in a business or trade—and hence is not a hobbyist—if a net profit is created by the activity in question for three of the five consecutive years ending with the taxable year at issue. Thus, many writers who have good and bad years need not fear a hobby loss challenge to a loss in one of the bad years. A writer who has not been engaged in writing for five consecutive years may elect to have the determination as to profit motive suspended until after five consecutive years have passed. The disadvantage of this, however, is that if the writer is then determined to be a hobbyist, the IRS can collect on taxes owed for each of the five years.

If a hobby loss problem is anticipated, writers on the cash basis may be able to create profitable years by regulating the time of receipt of income and payment of expenses. For example, instead of having five years of small losses, a writer is far better off having three years where a small profit is earned and two years where larger than usual losses are incurred.

Profit Motive: The Nine Factors

But even if a writer does not have three profitable years in the last five years of activity as a writer, the contention by the IRS that the writer is a hobbyist can still be overcome if the writer can show a profit motive. The regulations to the Internal Revenue Code specifically provide for an objective standard to determine profit motive based on all the facts and circumstances surrounding the activity. Therefore, statements by the writer as to profit motive are given little weight. But the chance of making a profit can be quite unlikely, as long as the writer actually intends to be profitable.

The regulations set forth nine factors used to determine profit motive. Since every writer is capable, in varying degrees, of pursuing writing in a manner which will be considered a trade or business, these factors offer an instructive model. The objective factors are considered in their totality so that all the circumstances surrounding the activity will determine the result in a given case. Although most of the factors are important, no single factor will determine the result of a case. The writer should be aware that many IRS auditors are unfamiliar with these factors both from a lack of familiarity with the regulations and because the regulations do not adequately reflect how the courts evaluate these factors with respect to writers. In particular, the auditors will often use a simplified guide titled "Tax Audit Guidelines and Techniques for Tax Technicians" which discusses the hobby loss factors only with reference to farmers. Such a guide is completely inadequate where writers are concerned. The nine factors follow:

1. Manner in which the taxpayer carries on the activity. The writer must establish effective business routines. Most importantly, there should be accurate bookkeeping procedures to record all receipts and expenses. A regularized system for correspondence, submissions, follow-ups, contracts, deadlines, and similar business matters will also be significant in showing profit motive.

2. The expertise of the taxpayer or his advisors. One important indication of expertise can be study. However, expertise can also be shown by publication credits, encouragement by agents or publishers, awards of prizes, memberships in professional organizations, recognition in critical publications, and the use of business advisors such as lawyers and accountants. Teaching, if the position is at least partially based on success as a writer, also shows expertise.

3. The time and effort expended by the taxpayer in carrying on the activity. Employment in another occupation does not mean the writer lacks a profit motive. But a reasonable amount of time—such as several hours each day—must be devoted to writing, preferably on a regular basis.

4. Expectation that assets used in activity may appreciate in value. This factor seldom has relevance to writers.

5. The success of the taxpayer in carrying on other similar or dissimilar activities. Past literary successes, either financial or critical, are relevant to present profit motive despite the fact that some period of inactivity may have occurred. This factor would not be relevant if a writer were just starting a career.

6. The taxpayer's history of income or losses with respect to the activity. Past income from writing is a very helpful factor. Also, increases in receipts from year to year would support having a profit motive. Losses may not be overly significant in showing the absence of a profit motive, unless expenses are vastly greater than receipts, income is being received from sources not related to writing, and the losses continue for a long period of time.

7. The amount of occasional profits, if any, which are earned. Here receipts are contrasted with expenses, but disproportionate expenses will be important only if the writer is wealthy enough to gain tax benefits from taking losses. If such expenses are an economic strain, such a disproportion will not have as great weight.

8. The financial status of the taxpayer. The need for additional income or the inability to support a hobby would show that the pursuit of writing had a profit motive. However, wealth or other substantial sources of income are factors which would be considered to make a profit motive less likely.

9. Elements of personal pleasure or recreation. This factor is aimed more at gentlemen farmers than writers. The writer need only be

wary of this if the writing has involved substantial travel. Otherwise writing is as difficult and demanding as any profession.

The Cases

A look at some typical hobby loss cases will illustrate the approach of the courts to these factors. While the cases may not be recent, the legal rules that are illustrated apply to current cases.

Case I: No Profit Motive. Charles Nemish began writing in high school. During college he wrote guides and articles and, after serving in the Naval Air Corps during World War II, he wrote short stories based on his wartime experiences. His gross receipts from writing in the 1940s amounted to about $2,000. In 1951 he began working as a pilot for United Air Lines, but he had sufficient free time to continue writing and had gross receipts of about $2,500 in the 1950s. From 1958 to 1965 he wrote at least fourteen short stories which were submitted—sometimes through literary agents—to the major magazine markets, but a sale in 1958 was his sole success during this period. Starting in the early 1960s, Nemish had two novels in progress—*Orion* and *Mr. Gus*.

The IRS denied him any deductions in 1964 and 1965 for his writing expenses, which had appeared as follows on the returns:

	1964	1965
Automobile expense	$972.00	$487.00
Travel expense and writing materials	840.00	980.00
Home expense	418.00	289.00
Total	$2,230.00	$1,756.00

The tax court agreed with the IRS. Although Nemish had earned about $4,500 between 1940 and 1958, he had made no sales after 1958, while deducting an average of $1,500 per year for expenses (the court assumed that expenses prior to 1958, even if not claimed on the returns, had probably averaged about $1,500 per year). Thus, over a twenty-five-year period, expenses had been greatly in excess of income. Nemish, however, explained that he believed: "sooner or later I am going to make a killing—it will be tremendous, these days a novel will go for hardly less than one hundred thousand dollars."

The court stated, "Giving consideration to petitioner's adequate income from his full-time job as a pilot, to his enthusiasm for writing evident ever since he was a child, and the lack of profits over a twenty-five-year period, we do not think he did his writing for financial gain" (*Nemish v. Semmir*, 452 F.2d 611, *aff'g per curium* 29 T.C.M. 1249).

The lack of a profit motive means that losses will be disallowed, but the court also pointed out that the automobile and travel expenses had been incurred on trips to vacation areas such as Lake Tahoe and Reno. Even if Nemish had been found to have a profit motive with respect to his writing, the court would have denied a deduction for the travel expenses since, "We do not think the record justifies a finding that the expenses of his holiday excursions were incurred for business purposes."

Case II: No Profit Motive. John Baltis graduated from college in 1948 and commenced work in the newspaper field. In 1967 and 1968 he was a copy editor for the *San Francisco Chronicle*. During the same two years, he took deductions as a free-lance writer—$1,968 in 1967 and $1,974 in 1968. Between 1948 and 1968 he had sold only three articles for a total of $550. Also, many of the claimed items of expense were for family visits. The tax court agreed with the IRS that no profit motive could be should since the trips were "undertaken primarily for personal reasons . . . whatever the free-lance writing petitioner did either on these trips or as a consequence thereof was of such relatively minor significance that it did not constitute the carrying on of a trade or business." The court also pointed out that "there was almost a complete failure to substantiate the specific items which the Commissioner disallowed" (*John R. Baltis*, 31 T.C.M. 213). Accurate record keeping is essential for the substantiation of deductions.

Case III: No Profit Motive. John Chaloner, a wealthy individual, wrote and published books over a twenty-year period. Little effort was made to sell the books and the receipts from sales were negligible. Chaloner claimed a deduction for the salaries of his secretaries, but their duties were not specified. The court concluded that no profit motive could be found and disallowed the deductions claimed for writing and publishing (*Chaloner v. Helvering*, 69 F.2d 571).

Case IV: No Profit Motive. Corliss Lamont, a philosopher who taught at Columbia University, lectured across the country on such topics as philosophy, civil liberties, and international affairs. He also wrote numerous books and pamphlets about these subjects. He had independent wealth, so he could afford the continuous losses from his writing over a thirty-year period. The court concluded, "Although continuity and efficiency of operations are criteria which would tend to support the existence of a trade or business . . . the totality of circumstances surrounding Lamont's background, his interest in the wide dissemination of his ideas, his activities and financial status justifies the conclusion of the Tax Court that a profit motive was lacking" (*Lamont v. Commissioner*, 339 F.2d 377; see to the same effect, *G. Szmak*, 376 F.2d 154).

Case V: A Profit Motive. Seymour Stern, a resident of Los Angeles, spent 335 days in New York City during 1965. He had been writing since 1926 and his credits included numerous articles and screenplays. Stern, an expert on the film director D. W. Griffith, had spent the time in New York researching D. W. Griffith's papers located at the Museum of Modern Art. The results of this work provided the basis for an issue of *Film Culture Magazine* published in 1965, and the contents of the magazine were then to be used in a hardcover book scheduled for future publication. Stern received no income from the magazine, but had a contract providing for standard author's royalties on the hardcover book.

The IRS sought to deny $6,040 of travel expenses claimed in 1965 in relation to the work done in New York City. It was argued that Stern was not in the business or trade of being a writer in 1965 and, also, that the expenses should be capitalized and recaptured. The court found in favor of Stern on both issues. Despite the lack on an immediate profit, the court concluded that Stern had "participated in that endeavor with a good faith expectation of making a profit" (*Stern v. United States*, 71-1 USTC Par. 9375 at p. 86,420). The expense, therefore, was deductible as business expense. Moreover, the court disagreed with the capitalization argument. Capitalization would have basically allowed Stern to deduct the $6,040 of expenses only when income from the books was received in the future. The court indicated capitalization might be required if the writer were a hobbyist or if the payments were for securing a copyright and plates which were to belong to the person making the payments. For Stern, however, the expenses were ordinary and necessary business expenses which could be fully deducted in 1965 when they were incurred.

Case VI: A Profit Motive. Cornelius Vanderbilt, Jr. commenced his career as a writer in 1919 and pursued it with great success for two decades. Although his wealthy family took him off his allowance early in his writing career, he persevered and published numerous books and articles in addition to founding newspapers and a new service syndicate. Motion picture producers purchased a number of his stories, and he began a successful lecturing career in 1929. During World War II, active military duty in the army interrupted Mr. Vanderbilt's civilian activities. In 1942, he inherited substantial wealth, but suffered several heart attacks which required hospitalization and, eventually, caused his discharge from the service.

He resumed his writing and lecturing career after the war. The lectures often dealt with travel and current foreign affairs topics, and much of Mr. Vanderbilt's writing—including several books—was devoted to these same topics. His business activities involved a substantial amount of travel which caused his deductions from writing to far exceed his writing income. For the six years from 1949 through 1955, his losses from writing ranged from $18,387 to $46,297 per year. Only income from trusts and dividends allowed him to continue this pattern of losses, although in 1955 he finally had a net profit of $9,277 from the writing activity.

The IRS sought to disallow the entire amount of business deductions claimed in 1951—$30,175.90—on the rationale that Mr. Vanderbilt was not in the business or trade of being a writer in that year as shown by the following factors: "(1) petitioner's large losses over a number of years with no indication from the record of a possibility of profit, (2) his background of inherited wealth as a guardian against financial disaster while engaged in his writing and lecturing activities, (3) his inattention to practical business details of his venture . . . and (4) his general propensity towards engaging in this field of endeavor whether it resulted in profit or not . . ." (*Cornelius Vanderbilt, Jr.*, 16 T.C.M. 1081).

The court disagreed with the IRS's characterization of Vanderbilt's career as bearing "a strong resemblance to that of a romanticist and adventurer." Instead, the court noted that Vanderbilt had worked with great commercial success prior to the war and continued to take his work seriously when he was able to resume working. Despite his losses after the war, the court believed Mr. Vanderbilt had a profit motive in 1951 and was engaged in the business or trade of being a writer. The court allowed all the ordinary and necessary business expenses incurred in negotiating sales, and an outlay in 1951 to pay part of a libel judgement rendered against Vanderbilt in 1924. However, the court concluded that Vanderbilt's wife lacked a bona fide business purpose in accompanying her husband abroad and her travel expenses were not deductible.

Case VII: A Profit Motive. Marian Crymes lived in Washington, D.C., in 1966 and 1967 and worked as a proofreader for the Bureau of National Affairs. Since 1960 she had been working on two booklets— "Component Good" and "Integral Spirituality"—which she wished to have reach a teen-age reading public. In 1967 she paid $1,288.97 to print one hundred copies of each of the booklets. She copyrighted the booklets and offered to sell the books to a foundation, while writing letters to others who might wish to sell the books more widely.

The court agreed with the IRS that she was not in the trade or profession of being a writer in 1967. Thus, her expenses could not be deducted as the ordinary and necessary business expenses of a writer. But the court did believe that she had a profit motive, as shown by her attempts to sell the booklets, despite her lack of success. The expenses of producing the booklets were, therefore, deductible under a section of the Internal Revenue Code permitting the deduction of ordinary and necessary expenses incurred for the production of income. The court pointed out that "the proper test is not the reasonableness of the taxpayer's belief that a profit will be realized, but whether the enterprise is entered into and carried on in good faith and for the purpose of making a profit . . ." (*Crymes v. Commissioner*, 31 T.C.M. 4).

An Overview

Writers with wealth and independent incomes, whose writing expenses are large relative to their receipts over a lengthy period, are most likely to be found to be pursuing a hobby. Writers who devote much of their time to their work, who have the expertise to receive some recognition, and for whom the expenses of writing are burdensome will probably be found to be engaged in a business or trade rather than a hobby. Especially younger writers, who are making the financial sacrifices so common to the beginning of a writing career, should be considered by the courts to have a profit motive, even if other employment is necessary for survival during this difficult early period.

Each case in which a writer is challenged as a hobbyist requires a determination on its own facts, but an awareness on the part of the writer as to what factors are relevant should aid in preventing or, if necessary, meeting such a challenge. It is advisable to have the professional assistance of an accountant or a lawyer as soon as a hobby loss issue arises on an audit. Such professional advisors can be particularly helpful in effectively presenting the factors favorable to the writer. The presence of a lawyer or accountant at the earliest conferences with the IRS can aid in bringing a hobby loss challenge to a quick and satisfactory resolution.

22 The Writer's Estate

$\mathcal{E}$ state planning should begin during the writer's lifetime with the assistance of a lawyer and, if necessary, an accountant, a life insurance agent, and an officer of a bank's trusts and estates department. Writers, like other taxpayers, seek to dispose of their assets to the people and institutions of their choice, while reducing the amount of income taxes during life and estate taxes at death. This chapter cannot substitute for consultation and careful planning with professional advisors, but it can at least alert the writer to matters of importance which will enable more effective participation in the process of planning the estate.

Written Works

Written works are unique because they are the creation of the writer and possess aesthetic qualities not found in other assets which pass through an estate. The writer may wish to exert posthumous control over a number of artistic decisions. For example, should unpublished works be published after the writer's death? If such works are published, may they be edited and, if so, by whom? If works are incomplete, can someone else finish the works so they can be published? If this is permitted, who will do the additional writing and how shall the authorship credits appear? The manner of publication—for example, hardcover or paperback—can be an issue as well. And is the writer willing to have his or her works exploited as films, on tape, records, or CDs, on computer disks, on CD-ROMs, on the Internet, or as the inspiration for novelty items? Each of these artistic decisions will also have financial implications for the writer's estate.

Related issues involve the writer's personal papers. Who will be allowed to publish letters written by the writer? In what manner must the publication be undertaken? Who will have permission to look at the writer's rough drafts, notebooks, and diaries? Who will have access to letters received by the writer? And if the writer wishes to designate an official biographer, how will this affect the estate's willingness to make information available to other researchers and the public at large?

The writer who donates manuscripts and personal papers to a university or museum may wish to know in advance the treatment which will be accorded the donated materials. For example, Frances Steloff had been active in the literary world for over fifty-five years. She accumulated letters from such writers as Ezra Pound, Gertrude Stein, Bertrand Russell, and Thornton Wilder. This collection was given to New York University with the understanding that it be kept in a James Joyce room to be created in the new library. When Miss Steloff found that no James Joyce room had been provided for by the university, she took back her collection and donated it to the Berg Collection of the New York Public Library. But what if a writer's executors are faced with a similar situation? How are they to know what the writer would have wished? If they do know, will they have the power to rectify such a breach of promise by a cultural institution? And can heirs be required to obey the writer's wishes with respect to the work?

In 1945, Eugene O'Neill entrusted the original manuscript of *Long Day's Journey into Night* to his editor, Bennett Cerf, at Random House. A written agreement between O'Neill and Random House provided that the play should only be published twenty-five years after O'Neill's death. At that time, an advance of $5,000 would be paid to his estate's executors or administrators. Within two years of O'Neill's death in 1953, however, his widow Carlotta demanded that Random House publish the play. Cerf felt honor-bound not to do so, but his desire to follow O'Neill's wishes simply resulted in Carlotta withdrawing the manuscript from Random House and having it published by the Yale University Press. She had the power to do this as executrix under O'Neill's will. O'Neill also left in his estate an unfinished manuscript of *More Stately Mansions*. He had told Carlotta shortly before his death that, "Nobody must be allowed to finish my play . . . I don't want anybody else working on my plays." On a flyleaf placed in the manuscript of *More Stately Mansions*, he had written, "Unfinished work. This script to be destroyed in case of my death!" Despite these admonitions, Carlotta permitted the work to be revised and eventually published and produced on Broadway as a new play by Eugene O'Neill. Again, as executrix, Carlotta had the power to do this.

While there are innumerable such examples, the lesson is fairly straightforward. Lifetime planning is essential for all writers who want to ensure correct posthumous treatment of works passing through their estate.

The Will

A properly drafted will is crucial to any estate plan. A will is a written document, signed and witnessed under strictly observed formalities, which provides for the disposition of the property belonging to the maker of the will upon his or her death. If the maker wishes to change the will, this can be done either by adding a codicil to the will or by drafting and signing a completely new will, both of which must also be executed under strict formalities.

If no will is made, property passes at death by the laws of intestacy. These laws vary from state to state, but generally provide for the property to pass to the writer's spouse and other relatives. An administrator, often a relative, is appointed by the court to manage the estate. A writer's failure to make a will concedes that the writer will not attempt to govern the distribution, literary standards, or financial exploitation of his or her work after death.

A will offers the opportunity to distribute property to specific persons. For literary property such as manuscripts and copyrights, this is usually done by bequest either to specific individuals or to a class. A bequest means a transfer of property under a will, while a gift is used to mean a transfer of property during the life of the person who gives the property. An example of a bequest of manuscripts (without copyrights) to a specific individual would be:

> I give and bequeath all my right, title, and interest in the following manuscripts [describe which manuscripts] to my daughter, June, if she shall survive me.

An example of a bequest to a class would be:

> I give and bequeath to my son, John, my daughter, June, and my daughter, Mary, or the survivors or survivor of them if any shall predecease me, all my manuscripts [describe which manuscripts]. If they shall be unable to agree upon a division of the said prop-

erty, my son John shall have the first choice, and my daughter June shall have the second choice, and my daughter Mary shall have the third choice, the said choices to continue in that order so long as any of them desire to make a selection.

Copyrights, of course, can also be willed. For example:

I give and bequeath all my right, title, and interest in and to my copyrights, [describe which copyrights] and any royalties there-from and the right to renewal and extension of said copyrights to my daughter, June, if she shall survive me.

The right of termination under the copyright law effective in 1978 provides that the writer's copyrights passing by his or her own will cannot be terminated. Also, the right of termination cannot be passed by will but automatically goes to the writer's surviving spouse, children, and grandchildren.

Use of a will permits: (1) the payment of estate taxes by the estate in such a way that each recipient will not have any taxes assessed against bequests received, (2) the uninterrupted maintenance of property insurance policies, and (3) the payment by the estate of storage and shipping costs so the recipient need not pay to receive bequests. The estate taxes are usually paid from the residuary of the estate, the residuary being all the property not specifically distributed elsewhere in the will.

Choosing Executors

The will allows a writer to choose the executor or executors of the estate. Since the executors must act as the alter ego of the writer and make all the decisions the writer would have made, the importance of choosing suitable executors cannot be emphasized too strongly. The executor, especially for a small estate, will often be a spouse or close relative. The writer must be certain that such a person is capable of making the necessary literary, artistic, and financial decisions for the estate. Joint executors, particularly when one is an expert with respect to writing and the other is a financial expert, would seem well suited to run the estate. When individuals serve as executors, consideration must be given to their age and health. Corporate executors offer the advantage of continuity, although their artistic insight may not satisfy the writer and the expense to the estate is usually greater.

Artistic and financial decisions are often closely intertwined. For example, the determination to sell film rights in a novel is a decision with both artistic and financial implications. The extent to which the writer may safely restrict the discretion of executors as to artistic matters may depend upon other aspects of the estate, such as whether funds are available to pay estate taxes and meet the immediate needs of the estate. If the writer absolutely bars the sale of film rights in a novel, will the funds available to the estate be sufficient? Restrictions of this kind conflict with the usually desirable practice of giving to the executor the maximum powers for management of the estate.

Each estate, whether large or small, will require a decision by the writer as to executors and executors' powers, based on the unique facts of the writer's own situation. At the least, however, clear and complete written instructions should be left for executors and heirs, detailing the treatment of work that the writer would consider ideal. Whether these instructions are in a letter or a will—and whether the instructions, if in a will, are binding or nonbinding on the executors—should depend upon decisions made by the writer after consultation with expert advisers.

Some writers divide the duties between executors, so that one executor handles general financial matters while a Literary Executor handles issues pertaining to literary works. Because financial and literary issues are likely to be woven together in a writer's estate, the duties of the Literary Executor have to be carefully delineated, along with specific provisions to resolve disputes between the Executor and the Literary Executor. Such a clause might read as follows:

> I appoint _____ to be the literary executor of my estate (hereinafter referred to as my "Literary Executor"), to have custody of, act with respect to, and be empowered to make all determinations concerning the use, disposition, retention, and control of the literary works that I have created or own, my letters, correspondence, documents, private papers, writings, manuscripts, and all other literary property of any kind created by me, whether or not any such items are unfinished or are completed but not yet divulged to the public.

Although this clause seems to give the Literary Executor absolute power over the literary work, what would happen if the literary works had to be sold in order to pay taxes? Because this is quite likely to happen, the will should indicate that the Executor's power to gather and dispose of the estate assets takes a precedence over the Literary Executor's power to decide whether to retain or dispose of the literary works.

Estate Taxes

The will also provides the opportunity to anticipate and control the amount of taxes to be levied by the state and, more importantly, federal governments. A writer who lives in more than one state may risk having a so-called double domicile and being taxed by more than one state, but careful planning can parry such a danger. The writer will also wish to benefit from a number of deductions, discussed later, which can substantially reduce the estate if planned for properly. But tax planning is especially necessary for the writer because copyrights and manuscripts are valued at fair market value in computing the value of the writer's gross estate. The valuation process creates uncertainty as to the size of the estate (because the valuation may be high or low) and raises the possibility that the estate may lack the ready cash needed to pay the estate taxes in a timely manner.

Trusts

Trusts are a valuable estate-planning device under which title to property is given to a trustee to use the property or income from the property for the benefit of certain named beneficiaries. Trusts can be created by the writer during life or, at death, by will. Trusts created during life can also be revocable, subject, that is, to dissolution by the creator of the trust, or irrevocable, in which case the creator cannot dissolve the trust. Trusts are frequently used to skip a generation of taxes, for example, by giving the income of a trust to children for their lives and having the grandchildren receive the principal. In such case the principal would not be included in the estates of the children for purposes of estate taxation. The tax law, however, severely restricts the effectiveness of generation-skipping trusts and other transfers for a similar purpose.

If the writer is concerned that the recipients, perhaps minor children, will not be in a position to make decisions regarding the literary works, trusts can be created in order to let the trustees fill this decision-making role. The writer can certainly create a trust while alive, so that the capacity of the trustees can be evaluated.

The Gross Estate

The gross estate includes the value of all the property in which the writer had an ownership interest at the time of death. Complex rules, depending on the specific circumstances of each case, cover the inclusion in the gross estate of such items as life insurance proceeds, property which the writer transferred within three years of death and in which the writer retained some interest, property over which the writer possessed a general power to appoint an owner, annuities, jointly held interests, and the value of property in certain trusts.

Valuation

The property included in the writer's gross estate is valued at fair market value as of the date of death or, if so chosen on the estate tax return, as of an alternate date which is generally six months after death. Fair market value is defined in the Regulations to the Internal Revenue Code as "the price at which the property would change hands between a willing buyer and a willing seller, neither being under any compulsion to buy or to sell and both having reasonable knowledge of relevant facts."

Expert appraisers are used to determine the fair market value of copyrights and manuscripts. But whether the estate is large or small, the opinions of experts can exhibit surprising variations. For example, Gabriel Pascal's estate included the right to produce a musical based on George Bernard Shaw's *Pygmalion*, the right to make a motion picture of the musical of *Pygmalion*, and the right to make a motion picture of *Devil's Disciple*. Shaw had refused to give his motion picture rights to anyone but Pascal, who had produced the film versions of *Major Barbara, Androcles and the Lion, Caesar & Cleopatra*, and *Pygmalion*. Shaw's estate continued this preference. However, Pascal died in 1954 without finalizing arrangements for the production of either of these works. Pascal's estate then realized great profits when *My Fair Lady* achieved a singular success as a musical and motion picture.

The issue became the fair market value of these rights as of the date of Pascal's death. In order to gain a higher basis for income tax purposes (which, as explained later in the chapter under carry-over basis, would have saved more in income taxes than it cost in estate taxes), the estate sought to value the rights in *Devil's Disciple* at $153,400 and the rights in *Pygmalion* at $1,140,000. The IRS contended that the fair market value of the rights was $30,000 for *Devil's Disciple* and $200,000 for *Pygmalion*. The tax court pointed out that, upon Pascal's death, no start had been made toward exploiting these rights. The experts who based their opinion on the success of *My Fair Lady* had not fairly valued the work based on reasonable expectations as of the date of death. Accordingly, the court concluded the correct fair market value was that contended for by the IRS (*Estate of Gabriel Pascal*, 22 T.C.M. 1766).

More commonly the estate will seek a lower valuation to save estate taxes. The sculptor, David Smith, left four-hundred-and-twenty-five works of substantial size and weight. His executors estimated the retail price of each piece if sold individually at the date of death. This totaled $4,284,000, which the executors discounted by 75 percent because any sale made immediately would have to be at a substantial discount. The IRS stayed with the original figure of $4,284,000, since the higher amount would yield the most in estate taxes. The court, in a

"Solomon-like" decision, concluded the fair market value of the works to be $2,700,000. Even so, Smith's estate lacked the cash to make an immediate payment of the taxes (*Estate of David Smith*, 57 T.C. 650).

Fair market value is not only important for determining the value of an estate, but also for determining the value of gifts and contributions. Prior to the Tax Reform Act of 1969, writers could donate copyrights or manuscripts to universities or museums and take a charitable deduction for income tax purposes based on fair market value. Since 1969, such a donation by the writer creating the work (or a donee of the writer) would create a charitable deduction based only on the cost of the materials in the work—a negligible amount. It should be noted, however, that anyone who inherits the work from the writer's estate can make a charitable deduction at fair market value.

In 1967 and 1968, when fair market value was still the relevant test for life-time charitable gifts by writers, the well-known composer Maurice Jarre was requested to and did donate music manuscripts and related materials to the University of Southern California. Jarre had won Academy Awards for his musical scores for the films *Lawrence of Arabia* and *Dr. Zhivago*. His donated manuscripts comprised over four thousand pages, including the scores for such films as *Dr. Zhivago*, *Grand Prix*, *Night of the Generals*, *Behold a Pale Horse*, *Is Paris Burning?*, and *Gambit*. Jarre retained the copyrights on the donated manuscripts.

One appraiser for Jarre found the fair market value of the donated materials to be $54,200 in 1967 and $61,900 in 1968, and this income tax deduction was claimed. At the trial another appraiser testified for him that the fair market value for the donations was $61,996 in 1967 and $35,918 in 1968. But the appraiser for the IRS believed the materials donated in 1967 had a value of $7,615, while the materials donated in 1968 had a value of $4,915. The tax court gave an excellent summary of the factors to be considered in determining the fair market value of manuscripts:

> . . . the composer's standing in his field and popularity of his works in general; the critical acclaim and popular appeal of the particular works contributed; the relative place and importance of the contributed works in the composer's career; the condition and content of the contributed works; whether the contributed works are originals, fair copies, or photo copies, are written in the composer's own hand, are signed, or are in ink, pencil, or typed; the length of the individual contributed works and the sizes of the pages containing them; whether the mental processes of the composer are shown (i.e., working versus souvenir or finished manuscripts), including annotations; the demand in the market-place

for the type of works contributed and for the particular works contributed; the associative character of the contributed works (such as the film, its actors and actresses, its director, or its subject); the quantity, or conversely the rarity, of the contributed material (including whether the composer is dead or alive); and the length of time necessary to sell the contributed works (*Jarre v. Commissioner*, 64 T.C. 183, 188).

The court concluded that the fair market value of the donations was $45,000 for 1967 and $31,000 for 1968—another compromise between conflicting appraisals. It was favorable to Jarre, because the court appeared impressed with the expertise of his appraisers.

These cases dealing with fair market value illustrate how extreme the variations in appraisals can be. Especially when estate taxes are concerned, the writer must prepare for variations in the valuation of the gross estate by attempting to gauge and prepare for the payment of estate taxes.

Taxable Estate

The gross estate is reduced by a number of important deductions to reach the taxable estate. The deductions include funeral expenses, certain administration expenses, casualty or theft losses during administration, debts and enforceable claims against the estate, mortgages and liens, the value of property passing to a surviving spouse subject to certain limitations, and the value of property qualifying for a charitable deduction because of the nature of the institution to which the property is given.

The marital deduction provides an important tax advantage. The deduction equals the value of property left to the surviving spouse (provided that the value of the property has also been included in the gross estate). A spouse is entitled in any case to a share of the deceased spouse's estate by law in most states. In New York, for example, a surviving spouse has a right to one-half of the deceased spouse's estate, but the right is reduced to one-third if there are also surviving children. The value of property used for the marital deduction must basically pass in such a way that it will eventually be taxable in the estate of the surviving spouse. The marital deduction thus postpones estate taxes, but does not completely avoid them.

The charitable deduction is of particular interest to the writer, since this provides the opportunity to give copyrights and manuscripts to institutions such as universities or museums which the writer may wish to benefit. The fair market value of such donated works is deducted from the writer's gross estate. A will clause is used stating that if the institution is not of the type to which a bequest qualifying for a charitable deduction can be made, the bequest will be made to a suitable institution at the choice of the executor.

The tax effect of willing a work to a charity is similar to the writer's destroying the work prior to death. If the work is willed to a charity, fair market value is included in the gross estate, but the same fair market value is then subtracted as a charitable deduction in determining the taxable estate. But even if the estate tax rate were as high as 55 percent, keeping the work would still pass 45 percent of the value to the recipient under the will.

However, if the estate does not have cash available to pay the estate taxes, charitable bequests may be an excellent way to reduce the amount of the estate taxes. Also, the intangible benefits, including perpetuating the writer's reputation, may well outweigh considerations of the precise saving or loss resulting from such bequests.

Once the gross estate has been reduced by the deductions discussed above, what is left is the taxable estate.

Unified Estate and Gift Tax

A progressive federal tax applies to the writer's cumulated total of taxable gifts and taxable estate. The progressive rates rise from 18 percent if the cumulated total of taxable gifts and taxable estate is under $10,000, to 55 percent if the cumulated total is over $3,000,000. The amount of tax on the cumulated total of the taxable gifts and the taxable estate is reduced by a tax credit of $192,800. The tax credit means that an estate will only pay a federal tax if the cumulated total of taxable gifts and the taxable estate is greater than $600,000. Pending legislation may increase this $600,000 to $750,000.* Some states also have death taxes.

A single writer who made taxable gifts of $70,000 and left an estate of $80,000 would owe, according to the rate schedule, a unified gift and estate tax of $38,800. The $192,800 tax credit would cause no federal tax to be payable. If the writer made taxable gifts of $475,000 and left a taxable estate of $525,000, the unified tax would be $345,800. This would be reduced by the credit of $192,800, so that the tax payable would be $153,000. It should be noted that the federal estate tax is reduced by either a state death tax credit or the actual state death tax, whichever is less.

Liquidity

Estate taxes owed must normally be paid within nine months of death at the time the estate tax return is filed. For the estate unable to make full payment immediately, it may be possible to spread payment out over a number of years. One of the best ways to have the cash available to pay estate taxes is insurance policies on the life of the writer. The proceeds of life insurance payable to the estate are included in the gross estate. So are the proceeds of policies payable, for example, to a spouse or children if the insured writer keeps any ownership or control over the policies. But policies payable to a spouse or children and not owned or controlled by the writer will not be included in the writer's gross estate. If a spouse or children are the beneficiaries under both insurance policies and the will, they will naturally want to provide funds to the estate to pay estate taxes so that the assets of the estate do not have to be sold immediately at lower prices. Such policies should probably be whole life insurance, rather than the less expensive term insurance which may be nonrenewable after a certain age or under certain health conditions. Also, such life insurance may sometimes best be maintained in a life insurance trust, especially when a trustee may have greater ability than the beneficiaries to manage the proceeds. This stage of estate planning requires consultation with the writer's insurance agent and attorney to determine the most advisable course with regard to maintaining such life insurance.

Another method for easing estate liquidity problems may be available to a writer's estate. Upon a showing of reasonable cause, the district director of the Internal Revenue Service may extend the time for payment up to ten years. The interest on such unpaid taxes is adjusted to reflect the current prime interest rate.

Tax deferral might also be achieved under a different tax provision. If more than 35 percent of the adjusted gross estate consists of an interest in a closely held business (such as being the sole proprietor engaged in the business of writing), the tax can be paid in ten equal yearly installments. And, if the executor so elects, the first installment need not be paid for five years. Interest payable on the estate tax attributable to the value of the business property (up to $1,000,000) receives a special rate of 4 percent.

Gifts

After seeing the tax computation, the writer may decide that it would be advisable to own fewer copyrights or manuscripts at death. If the writer makes gifts of copyrights, manuscripts, or other assets while alive, the value of the gross estate at death could be reduced. The incentive for making gifts is a yearly exclusion of $10,000 applicable to each gift recipient. If an unmarried writer in one year gave copyrights with a fair market value of $11,000 each to three children and two friends, there would be total gifts of $55,000. The gift to each person, however, would be subject to a $10,000 exclusion applied each year to each person to whom a gift is given—one person or a hundred. Thus, the $11,000 gifts to each person would be taxable only to the extent of $1,000. The total taxable amount would, therefore, be $5,000. The writer who can afford gifts should usually take advantage of the yearly exclusions.

If the writer were married rather than single, the writer and spouse could elect to treat all gifts as being made one-half from each. This has the effect of increasing to $20,000 the yearly exclusion for each gift recipient. Also, a writer may generally make unlimited gifts to a spouse without payment of any gift tax.

Gifts must be complete and irrevocable transfers, including transfers in trust, for the benefit of another person or group. The entire copyright need not be transferred—for example, a valid gift can be made of the right of exploitation in one medium—but a mere gift of income must be avoided since such income will still be taxable to the writer. Every effort must be made to show a gift has truly been given. This can be done by delivery of the gift, execution of a deed of gift, notification of the publisher, and, if necessary, filing of a gift tax return. After the gift, the writer must completely cease to exercise control over it. If the writer retains powers, there will not be a valid gift for tax purposes. In that case the income generated by the gift can be taxed to the writer instead of the donee, and the value of the gift will be included in the writer's gross estate. Also, the writer should not serve as custodian of gifts given to minor children, since such custodianship will again cause the value of the gift property to be included in the writer's gross estate. The complexity of this area makes legal advice necessary if the writer is to ensure that gifts will be effective. Gift tax returns must be filed on an annual basis. The failure to file a gift tax return can result in assessments of interest, penalties and, in some cases, even criminal charges.

The writer can also make gifts to charities without having to pay a gift tax. But charitable gifts have no advantage over charitable bequests under the will in terms of saving estate taxes. After the gift of a work, the writer of course would not own the work at death and its value could not be included in the gross estate. While the value of the same work would be part of the gross estate if owned at death, a charitable bequest would reduce the gross estate by the value of the work. The taxable estate is the same in either case. If the writer's estate is in a low estate tax bracket, or if it will pass free of estate tax to the writer's spouse, the best plan may be to keep the work in the writer's estate so that the spouse or other beneficiary can give the work to the charity and take an income tax deduction for its fair market value. After 1981, both a manuscript and its copyright are considered separate properties for estate charitable deductions. So, under certain circumstances, a charitable deduction would be allowed for valuable manuscripts bequeathed to a charity even if the copyright was not also transferred to the charity. There is no similar provision in the gift tax.

Basis

The recipient of a copyright as a gift holds the copyright as ordinary income property and takes the basis of the writer who gave the gift. But a beneficiary who receives a copyright under a will holds the copyright as a capital asset with a stepped-up basis of the copyright's fair market value as included in the gross estate. For example, a writer in 1995 created a literary work with a zero basis. If the copyright were given to a daughter, the daughter would have a zero basis and receive ordinary income when she sold it. If the sale price were $5,000, she would receive $5,000 of ordinary income. On the other hand, if the artist died in 1998 and the copyright were valued in the estate at $5,000, the daughter who received the copyright under the will would have a basis of $5,000. So if she sold it for $5,000, she would not have to pay any tax at all. If she sold it for $7,500, the tax would be on $2,500 and at the favorable capital gains rates. This difference in treatment may be an important factor in determining whether to make gifts or bequests.

The Estate Plan

The planning of a writer's estate is a complex task often requiring the expertise of accountants, insurance agents, and bank officers, as well as that of a trusts and estates lawyer. But an informed writer can be a valuable initiator and contributor in creating a plan which meets both the artistic and financial estate-planning needs of the writer.

23 Grants and Public Support for Writers

*T*he important role of the writer in society raises the issue of what assistance society should appropriately offer to the writer, especially to the creative writer. The dramatic reduction in funding for the National Endowment for the Arts makes this issue all the more significant for those who believe that writers are deserving of governmental support.

Earning a living has often been difficult for the novelist, the playwright, and the poet. Second careers are frequently a necessity. T. S. Eliot, for example, took employment in the foreign department of Lloyds Bank in London from 1917 through 1925, after which he worked for the rest of his life with the publishing house of Faber and Gwyer (later Faber and Faber). The horror with which some of Eliot's contemporaries viewed the full devotion of Eliot's working days to the bank was reflected in Ezra Pound's Bel Esprit scheme. Pound proposed to raise enough funds from those interested in the arts to permit Eliot to devote all his time to writing, but the plan never reached fruition. Thousands of writers less famous than Eliot struggle to create while maintaining other sources of livelihood, such as teaching careers. Few creative writers in the United States can live from the income generated by their books. And, as corporate conglomerates control more and more publishing houses, profit margins take precedence over any obligation to publish quality literature. This has led to fears that the younger, serious writers will find publication ever more difficult.

The National Endowment for the Arts

The legislation creating the National Endowment of the Arts (the "NEA") in 1965 stated:

> [T]hat the encouragement and support of national progress and scholarship in the humanities and the arts, while primarily a matter for private and local initiative, is also an appropriate matter of concern for the Federal Government . . . [and] that the practice of art and the study of the humanities requires constant dedication and devotion and that, while no government can call a great artist or scholar into existence, it is necessary and appropriate for the Federal Government to help create and sustain not only a climate encouraging freedom of thought, imagination, and inquiry, but also the material conditions facilitating the release of this creative talent.

Whether the NEA has created such material conditions remains a matter of debate, since most supporters of the arts contend that far more should be done to aid writers and other artists than the NEA has achieved. It is ironic, therefore, that the funds for the NEA are being cut back in the current political climate and the very existence of the NEA brought into question.

NEA Funding

The budget for the NEA in 1966, the first year of operation, was $2,500,000. This budget increased to $174,459,000 by 1993, then decreased to $170,000,000 for the 1994 fiscal year. For 1995, the original budget was $167,400,000, but was subsequently reduced to $162,000,000. For 1996, the projected budget is $99,500,000. This budget, however, has to be allocated among all the arts. Also, the amount allocated to written work does not simply go to individual writers. Grants are available to individuals, but much of the funding goes to the official arts agencies of the states and territories, to tax-exempt, nonprofit organizations, university residence programs, small presses, literary magazines, and national service organizations.

For example, the amount allocated to the Literature Program

($4,400,120 for 1994 and projected to be $4,797,000 for 1995) includes support given to such organizations as P.E.N. American Center ($108,800 in 1994), Academy of American Poets ($30,400 in 1994), Teachers and Writers Collaborative ($53,950 in 1994), and Poets and Writers, Inc. ($101,500 in 1994), as well as several other such organizations which together provide a broad spectrum of assistance for writers. The Literature Program provided seventy-eight $20,000 grants to individual creative writers in 1994 for a total of $1,680,000.

> The Literature Program supports the many voices of America's literary present by bringing to audiences all across the country the best contemporary writing and writers. The program fosters the highest literary standards, encourages a range of contemporary writing that reflects the diversity of the American experience, and promotes projects that bring together authors and audiences. It assists individual writers of excellence or promise, encourages wider audiences for contemporary literature, and helps support nonprofit organizations that foster literature as a professional pursuit (National Endowment for the Arts, *1994 Annual Report*).

Funds from the NEA also aid writers in programs such as Artists-in-Schools and Developmental Theater—New Plays, New Playwrights, New Forms. Starting in 1995, NEA funding underwent restructuring. In the future, according to the NEA, though grants to writers will still be available, there is unlikely to be separate funding specifically allocated to the Literature Program. Funding for research and writing projects in the area of the humanities, as distinguished from the arts, may be available to writers through the National Endowment for Humanities, 806 15th Street, N.W., Washington, D.C. 20506.

State Support

The first state arts council was created in 1902, but by 1960 only six such councils were in being. However, the period since 1960, when the New York State Council on the Arts was created, has seen the creation of an arts council in every state and territory.

According to the National Assembly of State Arts Agencies, the total state arts council appropriation for fiscal 1994 is $246,710,469. And, according to the National Assembly for Local Arts Agencies, there are approximately 3,800 local arts agencies. Their grants total an estimated $600,000,000, spread across all the arts. While the latter figure is an approximation due to the difficulty of gathering data on the local level, it emphasizes the magnitude of local arts support. It should also be noted that most local support goes to organizations or to individuals working with organizations.

The Writer in the Great Depression

One model for public support of writers was created in the 1930s, when the Great Depression made the precarious profession of the writer even more untenable. The federal government, as part of the overall effort to create work, developed the Works Progress Administration's Federal Writers' Project. The project began in 1935 and lasted until 1943. To be employed by the project (at wages varying from $50.00 to $103.50 per month, the variance due to geographic adjustments), an individual had to meet a strict relief test. This made many talented writers ineligible, while the eligible people often had a very limited background in writing. The writer's specialty made no difference, so novelists, poets, advertising copywriters, newspaper reporters, and all other conceivable types of writers (including occasional and would-be writers) were joined together in the project. With rare exceptions, the projects did not permit creative writing, but instead employed the writers on such efforts as state guidebooks; research on the arts, history, and localities; preparation of special studies on topics in economics, sociology, the arts, and similar areas; preparation of a guide to governmental functions and publications; and information on the project itself. Also, the geographic distribution of jobs under the project had little bearing on where writers lived, causing unfortunate misallocations.

By 1942 the project had created over one thousand books, pamphlets, and leaflets which covered a vast range of subject matter drawn from the American experience. The employment peak came in April 1936 when the project had a work force of 6,686 men and women (women comprised about 40 percent of the employees). Included among those employed were many who later gained prominence, such as Nelson Algren, Saul Bellow, John Cheever, Loren Eiseley, Ralph Ellison, and Richard Wright. By 1939 the number of employees had been cut to 3,500 and by 1943 the project had been terminated. The total cost of the project was $27,000,000, a different magnitude of support for writers than the NEA can generate today. But the project suffered from political turmoil, mainly accusations of Communist influence, which caused some to doubt its accomplishments and significance.

The need for a model—perhaps a modified version of the Federal Writers' Project as it existed in the 1930s—suggests the value of looking abroad to where other countries have created their own systems to support and encourage writers and the arts. Two of these countries—Japan and Ireland—are presented as examples.

Ireland

In 1969 the government of Ireland enacted an unprecedented law designed to give tax relief to writers, artists, and composers within the boundaries of Ireland. The minister of finance, in presenting the legislation to the Dail Eireann, stated:

> The purpose of this relief is . . . to help create a sympathetic environment here in which the arts can flourish by encouraging artists and writers to live and work in this country. This is something completely new in this country and, indeed, so far as I am aware, in the world . . . I am convinced that we are right in making this attempt to improve our cultural and artistic environment and I am encouraged by the welcome given from all sides both at home and abroad to the principle of the scheme. I am hopeful that it will achieve its purpose.

The legislation completely frees the writer, regardless of nationality, from any tax obligation to Ireland with respect to income derived from writing. The main requirement for application is that the writer be resident of Ireland for tax purposes. Simply explained, this requires the writer to rent or purchase a home in Ireland and work at that home during a substantial part of the year. However, while the residence must be uninterrupted, a writer does not necessarily have to be in Ireland for the entire year. Brief trips back to the United States, for example, would not affect a writer's tax status as a resident of Ireland. Every United States writer should remember, however, that the United States reserves the right to tax its citizens anywhere in the world. Pages 252–4 should be consulted for the United States tax law applicable to writers who live abroad.

Either a resident or a non-resident writer may apply for exemption on the grounds that he or she has produced "original and creative work(s) having cultural or artistic merit." The determination of "cultural or artistic merit" is made by the Irish Revenue Commissioners after consultation, if necessary, with experts in the field. Once a writer qualifies, all future works by the writer in the same category will be exempt from Irish tax. The application forms can be obtained from the Office of the Revenue Commissioners, Secretary Taxes Branch, Cross Blocks 8-10, Dublin Castle, Dublin 2, Ireland. For the writer exempt from Irish tax, the sole Irish tax requirement is that a tax return showing no tax due be prepared and filed with the Revenue Commissioners in Dublin.

By early 1994, however, only 2,055 people had qualified to live tax-free in Ireland (including artists and composers as well as writers). This was true despite the ease of application, absence of excessive tax paper work, and high percentage of applicants approved by the Revenue Commissioners (approximately 50 percent are approved). The assistance to the individual writer who comes to Ireland is certainly valuable, but Ireland's hope to create a new Byzantium has yet to be realized.

Japan

Japan has a unique approach whereby an organization or an individual can be registered as a "Living National Treasure." Legislation in 1955 created the National Commission for Protection of Cultural Properties, which can designate people and organizations as living national treasures for their role in aiding and continuing the culture and arts of Japan. Fields where living national treasures have been designated include ceramic art, dyeing and weaving, lacquered ware, metalwork, special dolls, Noh and Kabuki acting, Banraku puppets, music, dance, singing, and so on. The living national treasures receive a stipend in order to be able to improve their special artistic talent while training students to perpetuate their art form. If the United States were to adopt analogous legislation, poets, novelists, and playwrights might well be designated living national treasures for our country.

Grants

For the writer who considers seeking a grant there are several funding sources: The National Endowment for the Arts, individual state agencies, private foundations, and prizes and awards.

The NEA, as previously described, funds a variety of disciplines, each with program guidelines which can be obtained from the National Endowment for the Arts, The Nancy Hanks Center, 1100 Pennsylvania Avenue, N.W., Washington, D.C. 20506-0001. The telephone number for the NEA is (202) 682-5400.

All fifty states, as well as the District of Columbia, Puerto Rico, and the Virgin Islands, have agencies for the arts. The programs and application procedures differ from state to state. Since many state agencies give most of their grants to organizations, individuals seeking grants often must be affiliated with an eligible organization. The addresses for the state arts councils can be obtained from the National Endowment for the Arts in the *State Arts Agency List,* which is also available in most libraries.

Of the thirty-four-thousand private foundations, a relatively small number currently offer support to individual projects. Application procedures vary with each foundation or grant-giving agency. It is important that applicants pinpoint the organization best matched to their qualifications, so careful preliminary research is necessary.

An excellent source of reference for grant seekers is The Foundation Center Network, an independent national service organization which provides authoritative sources of information on private philanthropy. The Foundation Center has its main office at 79 Fifth Avenue, New York, New York 10003. Branch offices are located at 1001 Connecticut Avenue, N.W., Washington, D.C. 20036; 1422 Euclid, Cleveland, OH 44115; and 312 Sutter Street, San Francisco, CA 94108. There are also one hundred cooperating library collections, which can be located by calling the following toll-free information number: 1-800-424-9836.

The Foundation Center publishes a number of invaluable books, including *The Foundation Directory* and *Supplement* which contains over six-thousand-seven-hundred listings of grantmakers giving interests, addresses, telephone numbers, financial data, grant amounts, gifts received, plus full application information. *Foundation Grants to Individuals* is the only publication devoted entirely to foundation grant opportunities for individual applicants. The listings include over two-thousand-two-hundred-and-fifty independent and corporate foundations.

Awards, Honors, and Prizes (published by Gale Research Company in Detroit) is a two-volume directory of awards for many disciplines, including writing. It describes many programs that include trophies, medals, scrolls, and monetary awards. It is updated every two years.

Another organization that provides information concerning grants and fellowships is the Grantsmanship Center, P.O. Box 17220, Los Angeles, CA 90017. The Center conducts proposal-writing workshops and publishes a quarterly newsletter for public and private nonprofit organizations. The Center's services, and benefits programs, are designed for organizations, not for individual writers who are working independently.

An excellent resource for writers is *Grants and Awards Available to American Writers*, which is sold to the public for $10 by P.E.N. (see page 13).

24 How to Avoid or Resolve Disputes

W̶e would all love to live in a world where we could fully trust our publishers, agents, collaborators, and other business associates. Unfortunately, in many cases such trust will lead to frustrating misunderstandings, painful disagreements, and costly litigation. The best advice is to require a signed contract in every case, even when dealing with family members or close personal friends. There's nothing like a well-drafted contract to preempt potentially complex disputes and foster relationships that will be ongoing, mutually satisfying, and profitable.

The next line of defense is to learn to recognize the warning signs that a dispute may be imminent. Writers who become aware of the warning signs discussed in this chapter can begin to take the necessary steps to avoid or resolve disputes. Much like early treatment of a disease, such steps can help rein in the dispute, prevent its escalation into full-blown litigation, and preserve the relationship.

In case the relationship does break down, which can happen even when the proper precautions are taken, this chapter will also investigate mediation, arbitration, small claims court, and how to find a lawyer.

Warning Signs

Editors who express serious uncertainties about whether or not they are interested in a project, due to internal politics within the client corporation or fears that their own careers will suffer if the article or book is not successful, should be avoided. An editor who is uncertain of the project at the outset is unlikely to be of much help if difficulties arise down the line.

A writer may also want to avoid an editor who doesn't have at least some experience in the relevant field. Such an editor may make unreasonable demands because of a lack of understanding of what a satisfactory manuscript of this type looks like. Also, the editor's lack of concrete experience may result in an inability to help the writer complete a manuscript that is objectively satisfactory.

The publisher whose budget is unrealistically low, who makes other unreasonable demands such as setting deadlines that can never be met, or whose contract is blatantly one-sided, should cause the writer to question the project.

Finally, the agent who says he or she will try some small number of publishers and no more, who doesn't seem to understand the work, or who is difficult to reach, should send up the warning flag.

Certainly, anyone—whether it be an editor, publisher, agent, coauthor, or packager—who is reluctant to sign a written contract to ensure that the writer's interests are protected should, in almost every case, be avoided.

The editor, publisher, or agent with a big ego and no apparent literary sensibility is likely to be beyond educating. One sign of an enlarged ego is the inability to listen. If the other person is too busy massaging his or her ego to hear what the writer has to say, trouble is likely to be close by.

A related problem is someone who has a low regard for writers, perhaps because he or she has failed as a writer. Within almost every editor and publisher is a frustrated writer struggling to get out. If such people enjoy abusing power, the writer may be treated like a lowly factotum and disputes are likely to occur.

In the obvious category of risks are all clients who tell of the tortuous law suit still in progress with another writer. In fact, if they mention litigation with anyone, beware. Everyone, except the lawyers, loses in a lawsuit—if not on the merits, at least in time and legal fees. All litigants, except those that are totally immoral, sound as if they were wronged and that justice will be served by their winning the lawsuit.

If the writer has any doubt at all, he or she should not sympathize but simply walk away.

Mediation and Arbitration

Of course, even after reading this chapter, it may not be possible to avoid litigation-causing situations. When those situations arise, the writer should understand that there are several steps short of a lawsuit that can be taken.

The American Arbitration Association is well known for providing arbitration. If the writer prefers, he or she should simply choose a trustworthy acquaintance or colleague to act as arbitrator. In cases where it seems clear from their prior contacts that both parties are amicable, want a speedy resolution, and are simply looking for help in finding a fair solution, mediation is the way to go. On the other hand, if there is animosity, or a substantial amount of money involved, arbitration is the better course of action.

Of course, not every dispute can be resolved so nicely. What if a party is unwilling to settle and does not want either mediation or arbitration?

Forcing Arbitration

No organization, except a court, has the right to force mediation or arbitration on unwilling parties. However, the parties themselves often agree by contract that they will mediate or arbitrate in the event of a dispute. For example, a contract might include the following provision:

> All disputes arising under this agreement shall be submitted to binding arbitration before _____ in the following location _____ and shall be settle in accordance with the rules of the American Arbitration Association. Judgement upon the arbitration award may be entered in any court having jurisdiction thereof. Notwithstanding the foregoing, either party may refuse to arbitrate when the dispute is for a sum of less than $_____.

This contractual provision forces both parties to submit to arbitration if either party demands it. In the absence of a provision such as this, arbitration will only be possible with the agreement of both parties. The financially superior party may choose to go to court instead and hope to wear down the other party.

A writer in the New York City area might choose a place in New York as the arbitration site while a writer in California might want to specify the San Francisco or Santa Monica Arts Arbitration and Mediation

Services of the California Lawyers for the Arts. Use of the last sentence of the arbitration provision should be decided on a case-by-case basis. If the small claims court in the artist's area is quick and inexpensive, it may be preferable to sue there for amounts less than the maximum amount for which suit can be brought in small claims court.

Another approach might be to require mediation before arbitration, but this may only prolong the procedure. Among the advantages of both mediation and arbitration are the speed of resolution and the lower expenses than would be incurred in court.

The savings on legal fees can be enormous. For amounts above the small claims court limit and less than five-thousand dollars, it is very difficult to bring a lawsuit because of the likelihood that lawyer's fees will devour any damages that are recovered (or devour the litigant's savings if the case is lost). An agreement to arbitrate ensures that justice can be had in disputes involving amounts within this problematic range.

Nor must any party fear that they will face a hostile arbitration panel. Most arbitration procedures allow for a method by which both sides can avoid or remove arbitrators who they feel might be biased in any way.

Writers outside of areas which have mediation or arbitration facilities can sometimes have disputes handled by a mediator or arbitrator who deals with each party through the mail or who conducts a conference call.

To obtain additional information about mediation and arbitration, writers should contact the American Arbitration Association, the nearest volunteer lawyers for the arts group, or an organization for writers.

Small Claims Court

Publishers and agents generally pay writers what they owe. When they do not, however, the writer should first determine whether this may have been due to a legitimate deduction. If the writer determines that the deduction is not proper, the writer should attempt to collect the money owed through persuasion and persistence. Suing will involve time, energy, and expense on the writer's part, not to mention the almost certain outcome that the writer will never be able to deal with the publisher or agent again. The writer should always assume that errors were no more than innocent mistakes which a brief phone call can clear up. If it becomes clear that no payment will be forthcoming without pressure, that writer should start off with a systematic barrage of letters, phone calls, faxes, registered letters, and finally a threat to report the publisher or agent to the Authors Guild, the Association of Authors' Representatives, the Better Business Bureau, or similar groups. Only after this process should a writer consider litigation.

In many cases, however, turning to a lawyer may not be cost-effective and the writer may choose to sue in small claims court. Such courts provide an avenue for the inexpensive resolution of disputes, especially when the writer is only seeking to collect amounts up to several thousand dollars. The small claims limit varies between jurisdictions but is usually in the area of $1,500 to $5,000. A call to the local bar association or courthouse will provide the relevant information as to the location of the small claims court, which in turn can advise as to local procedures.

Retaining a Lawyer

If the writer decides to retain a lawyer to handle the case, pages 13–14 may be consulted with respect to finding an attorney who will be familiar with the issues that writers are likely to face.

Selected Bibliography

Balkin, Richard. *A Writer's Guide to Book Publishing.* New York: Plume, 1994.

Brinson, J. Diane (and Mark F. Radcliffe). *Multimedia Law Handbook.* Menlo Park, CA: Ladera Press, 1994.

Bunnin, Brad (and Peter Beren). *The Writer's Legal Companion.* Reading, MA: Addison-Wesley Publishing, 1993.

Crawford, Tad. *Business and Legal Forms for Authors & Self-Publishers.* New York: Allworth Press, 1990.

Curtis, Richard. *Beyond the Bestseller: A Literary Agent Takes You Inside the Book Business.* New York: Plume, 1990.

Doyle, Robert P. *Banned Books.* Chicago: American Library Association, 1995.

DuBoff, Leonard. *The Law (in Plain English) for Writers*. New York: John Wiley & Sons, Inc., 1992.

Goldfarb, Ronald (and Gail E. Ross). *The Writer's Lawyer*. New York: Times Books, 1989.

Kirsch, Jonathan. *Kirsch's Handbook of Publishing Law*. Los Angeles: Acrobat Books, 1995.

Levoy, Gregg. *This Business of Writing*. Cincinnati: Writer's Digest Books, 1992.

Litwak, Mark. *Dealmaking in the Film and Television Industry*. Los Angeles: Silman-James Press, 1993.

Litwak, Mark. *Contracts for the Film and Television Industry*. Los Angeles: Silman-James Press, 1994.

Norwick, Kenneth (and Jerry Simon Chasen). *The Rights of Authors, Artists, and Other Creative People*. Carbondale, IL: Southern Illinois University Press, 1992.

Perle, E. Gabriel (and John Taylor Williams). *The Publishing Law Handbook*. New York: Prentice Hall Law and Business, annual supplements.

Pinkerton, Linda F. *The Writer's Law Primer*. New York: Lyons & Burford Publishers, 1990.

Ross, Tom & Marilyn. *The Complete Guide to Self-Publishing*. Cincinnati: Writer's Digest Books, 1994.

Scott, Michael. *Multimedia Law and Practice*. Englewood Cliffs, NJ: Prentice Hall Law and Business, 1993.

Multimedia and the Law. New York: Practising Law Institute, 1994.

Watkins, John J. *The Mass Media and the Law*. Englewood Cliffs, NJ: Prentice Hall, 1989.

Index

Other Books by Tad Crawford

AIGA Professional Practices in Graphic Design
The American Institute of Graphic Arts

*The Artist-Gallery Partnership: A Practical Guide to
Consigning Art,* Revised Edition

Legal Guide for the Visual Artist, Third Edition

*The Secret Life of Money: How Money Can Be
Food for the Soul*

Business and Legal Forms for Photographers,
Revised Edition

Business and Legal Forms for Crafts

Business and Legal Forms for Graphic Designers

Books from Allworth Press

Business and Legal Forms for Authors and Self-Publishers, Revised Edition *by Tad Crawford* (softcover, 8½ × 11, 192 pages, $19.95)

The Secret Life of Money *by Tad Crawford* (softcover, 5½ × 8½, 256 pages, $14.95)

Mastering the Business of Writing: A Leading Literary Agent Reveals the Secrets of Success *by Richard Curtis* (softcover, 6 × 9, 272 pages, $18.95)

The Writer's and Photographer's Guide to Global Markets *by Michael Sedge* (softcover, 6 × 9, 288 pages, $19.95)

How to Write Books that Sell, Second Edition *by L. Perry Wilbur and Jon Samsel* (hardcover, 6 × 9, 224 pages, $19.95)

Writing for Interactive Media *by Jon Samsel and Darryl Wimberley* (hardcover, 6 × 9, 320 pages, $19.95)

The Writer's Internet Handbook *by Timothy K. Maloy* (softcover, 6 × 9, 192 pages, $18.95)

The Writer's Resource Handbook *by Daniel Grant* (softcover, 6 × 9, 272 pages, $19.95)

The Writer's Guide to Corporate Communications *by Mary Moreno* (softcover, 6 × 9, 192 pages, $18.95)

Photography for Writers: Using Photography to Increase Your Writing Income *by Michael Havelin* (softcover, 6 × 9, 224 pages, $18.95)

The Copyright Guide: A Friendly Guide for Protecting and Profiting from Copyrights *by Lee Wilson* (softcover, 6 × 9, 192 pages, $18.95)

Writing Scripts Hollywood Will Love: An Insider's Guide to Film and Television Scripts That Sell *by Katherine Atwell Herbert* (softcover, 6 × 9, 160 pages, $12.95)

The Internet Research Guide *by Timothy K. Maloy* (softcover, 6 × 9, 208 pages, $18.95)

Please write to request our free catalog. To order by credit card, call 1-800-491-2808 or send a check or money order to Allworth Press, 10 East 23rd Street, Suite 210, New York, NY 10010. Include $5 for shipping and handling for the first book ordered and $1 for each additional book. Ten dollars plus $1 for each additional book if ordering from Canada. New York state residents must add sales tax.

If you would like to see our complete catalog on the World Wide Web, you can find us at ***www.allworth.com***.